Daily Bread

Art and Work in the Reign of Quantity

Brian Keeble

Daily Bread

*Art and Work
in the Reign of Quantity*

Edited and introduced by
Andrew Frisardi

Cover lettering by Tom Perkins
Back cover design by Michael Schrauzer

CONTENTS

Things made by art answer to human needs, or else are luxuries. Human needs are the needs of the whole man, who does not live by bread alone. This means that to tolerate insignificant, i.e. meaningless conveniences, however convenient they may be, is beneath our natural dignity; the whole man needs things well made to serve at one and the same time needs of the active and contemplative life. On the other hand, pleasure taken in things well and truly made is not a need in us, independent of our need for the things themselves, but a part of our very nature; pleasure perfects the operation, but is not its end; the purposes of art are wholly utilitarian, in the full sense of the word as it applies to the whole man. We cannot give the name of art to anything irrational.

ANANDA K. COOMARASWAMY

Introduction

I FIRST CAME across Brian Keeble's essays while I was browsing one day at Foyles in London, and spotted a yellow-orange paperback spine with the title *Art: For Whom and for What?* I had recently read a review of that essay collection, Keeble's first, and the questions its title posed were on my mind, so I purchased a copy.

At that time, the late 1990s, my wife was a painting student in our home state, at Massachusetts College of Art. One of the students' projects there was a series of prints of his own anus. A few years earlier, in the U.K., Damien Hirst had notoriously displayed a shark, immersed in a tank of formaldehyde. Tracey Emin was about to exhibit her unmade bed with some used condoms, bloody underpants, and other personal objects scattered around it—an "installation" that sold for £2.2 million in 2014. When Emin was asked in an interview what makes a messy bed art, she responded that it was art because she said it was. In such a context, the title-questions of Brian Keeble's book—and, as I went on to discover, the ideas within it—were a welcome alternative indeed. As Keeble notes in chapter 2 of the present volume, it is perversely ironic that, in recent years,

> an arrangement of builder's bricks on the floor of an art gallery is somehow art in a way the same bricks, arranged, in all innocence and as a game perhaps, by the builder's child in the builder's yard, is not art. Even worse, by the terms of this exclusive group of art-things, the man who made the bricks . . . is not entitled to consider himself an artist even though the making of bricks requires knowledge and practiced skill.

Criticism of the contradictions and pretenses in post-modern art is not uncommon. A number of contemporary Anglo-American critics have written cogently about what and whom the arts are for, and how their raison d'être is inseparable from fundamental, perennial human values that tend to get lost in the culture of "originality" and shock-value novelty. It is rare, however, to encounter essays on

i

art, such as Keeble's, which penetrate to underlying principles that explain and eradicate the confusion so succinctly illustrated by Emin's interview statement.

According to Brian Keeble and his Perennialist or Traditionalist mentors, the confusion about values having to do with art and work is fundamentally a symptom of *metaphysical* disorientation.[1] In Scholastic thought—articulated for example by Jacques Maritain—art is a virtue of the practical intellect. As Keeble writes, it is "a type of rational wisdom that imitates, ultimately, a divine prototype";[2] the intellectual disposition to make and shape things well: baked goods and furniture no less than paintings and poems. The virtue of art involves knowing how to shape a preconceived form in material—otherwise known as mastery of a craft. In this view, then, intellect rather than sentiment is essential to art. The artist has to be both a good contemplative and a good maker, since only through contemplation can the artist's mind apprehend the Form to be embodied in the making. Such pre-modern, traditional insights offer, not only tools for seeing beyond blind spots in the contemporary mentality, but suggestions on how to effect micro-changes in our approach to art and work.

It is important to note that although traditional metaphysical thought is prominent in Brian Keeble's writing, this hardly means that his insights are merely theoretical. Rather, his wider, more incisive view of modern culture also includes livelihood—what people do for a living—and the practical, physical aspects of daily life, even economics and ecology. How many of our art and literary critics can be said to do the same? Among recent U.S. writers only Wendell Berry (whose ideas are the subject of chapter 8) and Gary Snyder come to mind. No doubt I am forgetting or not aware of other

---

1. *Perennialists* and *Traditionalists* are names applied to the association of writers and visionaries led by René Guénon, Ananda K. Coomaraswamy, Frithjof Schuon, Titus Burckhardt, Seyyed Hossein Nasr, and others dedicated to the *philosophia perennis* and the interpretation-critique of the modern world in light of it. I will explain what the "tradition" in *Traditionalists* means later in this introduction.

2. Unless otherwise stated, all quotations from Brian Keeble come from the present volume.

important exceptions, but I do know that such holistic scope is a rare commodity.

This is not surprising, since most contemporary thought is still conditioned by the so-called ontological inversion, a form of meta-physical amnesia that goes back to the early Renaissance.[3] It was a momentous change in western thought, when reason took on a life of its own and the spiritual intellect (which, as I will explain below, is quite different from what modern usage intends by *intellect*) faded from view. Individuals then were left with logical reasoning, personal emotion, sensation, and memory, with no conscious faculty directly associated with the transcendent. The result was a split in our minds and hearts, between outer and inner, active and contemplative, secular and sacred. From Petrarch to Voltaire was a long but inexorable step, until eighteenth-century Deism placed the Creator outside His creation like an operator of a machine. The machine analogy is pertinent, to say the least, to what Brian Keeble observes about the state of modern work and art. One constant in his essays is the idea that the traditional view of art would have it that art remains *inside* the artist; that it is a habit of mind to "pursue a true course of action in making something." What the modern world calls art is actually, in this view, a work *of* art; one does not "make art," one makes *with* it. As Keeble and his sources often emphasize, modern industrial, machine-based methods entirely subvert these dynamics, with the result that our work is robbed of its art. Much of Keeble's writing on art and work, consequently, includes a critique of the negative effects of the modern scientific mentality on human life and creativity.

Keeble is aware of course that he is writing against the common current, and that no amount of argument is going to suddenly dispel the hold that modern applied science has on the collective mind. As he writes: "On the face of it nothing could be more futile than to bring into question both the direction and the apparently unstoppable impetus of our modern technological society. It is, after all, this

---

3. I take the phrase *ontological inversion* from the English theologian Joseph Milne; see for example, "The Forgotten Metaphysics," in *The Mystical Cosmos* (2013), pp. 9–24.

by now global process that has delivered a great many material rewards to a significant proportion of the world's population." For instance, no one can deny the success of the human genome project—the results of which promise, researchers say, cures for such devastating diseases as diabetes and multiple sclerosis. How can we criticize a system that holds the potential for such liberating break-throughs? Keeble answers that, while human beings are better at surviving than we used to be, the price for this seems to be that we are a lot worse at knowing *who* we are who have mastered survival—an oversight which in fact (and ironically) threatens our very existence.

> Nothing is easier than to point to the many ways in which life has been made easier by the machine. But are these benefits such that we may have full confidence in the direction and final goal towards which the machine blindly forces us? There is little point in arguing that life is now more comfortable and convenient for the mass of men and women (which is far from being incontrovertible in any case) than it has ever been before if we do not consider at the same time the ultimate price of this achievement.

In other words, even as we use and enjoy our labor-saving devices we should also consider how their effects on our daily existence are leading us into places where we (or our descendants) might regret going and be unable to leave. There is the danger, for instance, that they remove much of our *experience* of being alive, since, as Keeble emphasizes, work is so foundational to truly human life. But technological advances create the impression that machines will progress eventually to the point where there is no further need for human physical labor. Related to this, an entire "leisure industry" exists whose role it is to foster the fantasy that life will finally be perfected as soon as we have absolutely nothing left to do:

> The so-called "leisure" of our consumer society is a parody of that spiritual condition of true inactivity, the contemplative interiority of a state of being in which we must finally acknowledge that we are only truly "free" when we are released from the necessity to re-act to the demands of the external world.
> The idleness that characterizes the leisure society (where no one has time to do nothing) is a condition of sloth in which the will to

act to some meaningful end is, as it were, suspended in a state of restless neutrality.

As Keeble further argues, the progressive, positivist view of human history is blind to its own absurd implications. If modern science is the apotheosis of human knowledge, making all earlier ways of knowing obsolete, "we have no choice but to conclude that our ancestors were, to say the least, immoderately deceived." If modern empirical science is superior in every way to the knowledge offered by the great saints, mystics, and poets of the past, then we might expect "the culture that surrounds us and which is the expression in its own sphere, of that secular, scientific mentality" to have many instances of art and thought that surpass, in depth and magnificence and beauty, the greatest works of the past. And yet clearly this is not so.

One purpose of our work and art is to situate us within a cosmological frame of reference that takes account of our ultimate destiny. Man's actions and creativity are answerable to a supernal order; human beings, paradoxically, are not fully human until we, as Keeble writes, "transcend our humanity. . . . Only by relating everything to the deepest interior principle of our subjective being can we become 'objectively' what we truly are." Obviously, this is a central teaching in the world's great wisdom traditions. In an essay on Eric Gill that is not included in the present volume, Keeble explains that Gill used the conceptual framework of Aristotle's doctrine of the four causes—formal, material, efficient, and final—to put human activity in perspective, since this doctrine "situates the uncreated at the beginning and at the end of all created reality."[4] This demonstrates that it is man's nature to be a "being beyond doing." It follows from this that culture and daily work cannot truly sustain and nourish us—cannot actually be substantial and real—unless they have a metaphysical ("uncreated") reference point, the "unmoved mover" (to continue with the Aristotelian language) of all our activity. Thus, Keeble criticizes the unchecked scientism that

---

4. Brian Keeble, "Eric Gill's Radical Critique of Industry," in *Art: For Whom and for What?* p. 102. Brian Keeble's books and other works are listed in the bibliography at the end of this volume, where publication details can be found.

conditions nearly all aspects of contemporary life, and its effects on areas of activity and experience that it cannot account for or adequately guide:

> The modern mind is above all characterized by its undeniable tendency to value quantitative over qualitative thought. So much so that it regards metaphysical and spiritual intuition as, at worst, inadmissible and at best an abstraction.... This tendency lends it what seems the natural bias of naive materialism, ascribing a higher ontological status to the perceptions of external phenomena, with its counter-tendency to devalue intuitive and imaginative modes of apprehension. In the fields of the arts this has led to a far higher status being placed on aesthetic sensations than on cognitive value.

The emphasis on aesthetic sensation in the "fine arts," says Keeble, has its negative complement in the brute artlessness of modern industry. What the modern world calls art and work are opposites that compensate for and consequently diminish each other. In his critique of modern work practices, Keeble is a descendant of an Anglo-American school of radical thought that has questioned the basis of industrial society—writers and artists, some of them the subjects of essays in this volume, such as William Blake, William Cobbett, Thomas Carlyle, William Morris, Gill, David Jones, H.J. Massingham, and, in the United States, Wendell Berry. (See chapter 10, "Eric Gill and a Holy Tradition of Working," for this book's most detailed discussion of this important background.) One point that Keeble emphasizes—surely a self-evident, if often forgotten one—is that the "ultimate value of work is as much related to the needs of the soul as to the needs of the body." But in a society such as ours, whose ruling principle denies the inner human being, "the inspired moment [of making something well is] comprehensively betrayed by the industrial process whose sole concern is for the economic advantage of the final product *regardless of the means employed.*" This "means" is what Keeble focuses on; in our industrial and post-industrial society, he says (echoing his mentor, the great scholar-metaphysician-critic Ananda K. Coomaraswamy), we tend to be interested in what we *get from* work, rather than what we get *by* working. Eric Gill complained that the process of machine manufacture hampers intellectual responsibility for what the worker makes, because there is a fundamental difference between making things with a tool and making them with a machine: the latter "reproduces in a predetermined way"; the worker is denied the right of making conceptual and executive judgments in his or her work. "The tool-user or craftsman works according to occasion and convention to re-create after a *type*, whereas the machinist attends a process that re-produces a duplicate. The distinction is one of kind and not of degree."[5] As René Guénon, another key source for Keeble, writes, the machine is not simply an elaborated tool. Modern machines differ *essentially* from traditional tools, in that the tool is actually an *extension* of the human body, "whereas the machine reduces the man to being no more than its servant. . . . The instinctive reactions of the artisans against the first machines thus explain themselves."[6]

Keeble's critique of the industrial system, then, unlike most radical critiques, focuses less on the injustices done to people by people, and more on "the system's injustice to man *as* man." Or, as Keeble says about David Jones: "Jones saw that we must begin to find answers [to our social and environmental crisis] by starting, not from *where* we are, but from *what* we are." The divine revelations on which the world's great spiritual traditions are based are unanimous about what we are: we are a being made in God's image. Needless to say, this is a view that finds little acceptance—or indeed comprehension—in contemporary culture. A widespread, if unspoken contemporary view, even among many who self-identify as religious, is that religion is only an opinion, something superimposed upon or added to the otherwise neutral human mind—like consumer preference or like being a fan of a particular football team. But the truth of the matter is that the sacred is simply what things truly are, and spirituality is as close to us as our own breath, or Blake's "throb of an artery." Only a superficial, even puerile view of spirituality and religion could come up with the scientistic apologetics that get such

5. Ibid., p. 103.
6. René Guénon, *The Reign of Quantity and the Signs of the Times* (1972), p. 341, n.31.

airtime in our society—such as, for example, those of Richard Dawkins. Yet clerics and religious authorities offer little to the faithful in the way of the mental tools necessary for seeing through these challenges; religion consequently either gets reduced to quasi-secular ethics and morality, or it overcompensates with fanatical, all-too-often violent, dogmatism.

In any case, as Keeble points out, if human beings do not actually have a soul or a spiritual dimension, why, in a place and time that offer more for our bodily appetites than ever before, are we still so lacking in contentment and peace of mind? Every wisdom tradition agrees with Jesus' answer to this question: "Man does not live by bread alone, but by every word that comes from the mouth of God."[7] Most of us do not have the option or even the desire to live the contemplative life of the monk. At the same time, in our day-to-day activities we have to obtain nourishment not only for the body but for the soul and spirit. In this regard, Keeble often refers to the traditional notion of man as *homo faber,* man the maker. As Coomaraswamy wrote many times, the sharp divide between the "fine arts" and the "crafts" is a modern invention. The traditional understanding of human making or the "active life" does much to render art, not merely relevant, but essential—not only to the individual but to the human social enterprise: "The artist . . . as [David] Jones [understands him] is not a self-sufficient 'genius intent upon upsetting accepted values and conditions on the basis of personal innovation,' but one whose 'self-possession' is the unifying principle in the integration of not only his own individuality but also the collective body politic."

Our society, says Keeble, tends to teach most of us to dread work as a time in which we are engaged in activity that corresponds to nothing within us—so we are offered the promise of "leisure" or passive inactivity. And this split is manifest in all we produce: "In the industrial society we have an art that is a formalism of shapes, textures, and colors that offers aesthetic stimulation for its own sake, standing in opposition to sub-human standards of manufacture applied to technical contrivances from which our spiritual

7. Matthew 4:4.

needs have been expressly eliminated." We are demoralized, in other words, by the chasm in our daily lives between art and ordinary work. And yet, in the words of another important mentor of Keeble, Frithjof Schuon, "art is [simply] the perfection of work." As Keeble comments in the afterword to his essay collection *God and Work*, this statement is deceptively simple. To understand it, as to comprehend much of the content of the essays in the current volume, we must acclimate ourselves to a way of thinking—to an "excluded knowledge," in Kathleen Raine's phrase—which the modern world has to deny or denigrate simply to maintain its own mode of existence.

One of the most trenchant, comprehensive critiques of the modern world in these terms is to be found in the writings of Guénon, in particular his *Crisis of the Modern World* (originally published in 1927) and *Reign of Quantity and the Signs of the Times* (1945). Fundamental to Guénon's thesis—and pervading Keeble's thought—is the notion that we are living in a late phase of the so-called Kali Yuga (which means the "Age of Kali"), the Hindu equivalent of the Iron Age (which comes after the Gold, Silver, and Bronze Ages) in western tradition—narrated, perhaps most famously, at the beginning of Ovid's *Metamorphoses*. In this view of the four ages, the primordial Age of Gold is by far the longest, while each subsequent age is shorter and ever more decadent and disoriented. Obviously this is a concept to which many in our time would respond with the familiar objection that all ages consider earlier ones to have been the golden (or silver or bronze) age. Such objections inevitably include the comment, which in fact is irrefutable, that life in every age has always seemed worse than life in some idealized past. Yet, the Hindu theory provides cause for reflection when one notes that it posits the beginning of the Kali Yuga as *six thousand* years ago. What is at stake is the integrity of the primordial tradition, which is the timeless covenant between heaven and earth—the epoch of primordial man, for whom Adam in the Genesis story is a figure. More will be said about this below. In any case, it is worth considering this claim about the late Kali Yuga if for no other reason than that certain unprecedented catastrophes—the environmental crisis being the most obvious—*are* in fact underway in our era. In addition, and more fundamentally, is there any doubt that our age excels at grasping and controlling the external world, in direct proportion to our ignorance, in comparison to previous ages, about the worlds of soul and spirit? The result is the "dissociation of sensibility" referred to by T.S. Eliot, a radical split between thinking and feeling, head and heart—and importantly for the theory of art, between beauty and utility. These notions are scattered throughout the present volume, and are especially focused upon in chapter 3, "A Time of Darkness."

The symptoms of decline are less important, ultimately, than the reasons for them. Guénon elaborates that the late phase of Kali Yuga or the Iron Age is characterized by maximum dispersal and distance from the Divine Principle, so it is also an age of maximum forgetfulness of that Source. This is why, Guénon says, the denial of principial knowledge—of "gnosis" in the etymological sense[8]—is characteristic of modern thought, whereas traditional cultures assume its existence and base their customs and practices upon it. It is also why profane science (the one science acknowledged as such in our time) only takes into consideration the realities of the senses and of reason, claiming to reduce *all* realities to them. So, the mind is seen as a secondary by-product of matter—the exact opposite or inversion of the traditionally universal view that mind or spirit ("the Divine") is the principle of all things. Scholastic philosophy refers to the power of matter to divide and limit as the principle of individuation, which is associated with the individualizing tendency we find in the Judeo-Christian story of the Fall from original unity. So, the reduction of the mind to materialistic thought *must* manifest as a fixation on quantity as opposed to quality. As Plato puts it in *Parmenides*, when the One is denied, the shadows, which are attributed with a greater intrinsic reality than is their due, multiply exponentially. When there is no unifying transcendent principle, a "reign of quantity"— of multiplicity divorced from the One—necessarily will usurp its place. This, Guénon argues, is the root cause of the interchangeableness of identical units in mass society. We see this effect, for example, in the way that contemporary biotechnology treats genetic units as interchangeable or at least potentially so; and, most tangibly, in the

8. That is, not in the sense of the "Gnostic" sects early in the Christian era.

massive quantity of identical products that emerge from our factories, each of which could be identically produced regardless of which interchangeable factory worker was operating the machine that made it. In this scenario, *uniformity* replaces unity—a uniformity of individualism expressed in the ever-new objects of appetite created by consumer culture, where each has his or her "I"-device with its infinitesimally differentiated personalized ("My") settings. This state of affairs may be convenient and diverting, but it also extends to a previously inconceivable degree an image of reality based on the self-delusions of the ego. Again, this is the inversion of the traditional view—that the task of the ego is to surrender to and serve the higher Principle, which alone is truly Real.

Clearly, as Keeble writes, if "work is the imposition of order on matter, matter transformed by human intention and will," the ontological inversion depicted by Guénon would also cut the interior, essential dimension of work off at its roots. If mind is merely an epiphenomenon of matter, how could matter ever be transformed by human intention, by *art*? Rather, it is far more likely that the mind will capitulate before the materials it would stamp with its informing principle. In such a state of spiritual paralysis, it is only to be expected that an individual may claim that an unmade bed is art, and be taken seriously merely because art is what people who call themselves artists call art. How different this is from the view of art and work elucidated in Keeble's essays, wherein *intelligibility* is the very essence of any work of art. And the rejection or indifference to intelligibility is inseparable from the rejection or indifference to Beauty. Keeble is fond of quoting Thomas Aquinas on the association of beauty and cognition or knowledge: "The Being of all things derives from the Divine Beauty"[9]—the very Being that is Intellect itself. So, as Keeble writes, "if Beauty has its formal cause in knowledge, then the beauty of art[works] must be incompatible with that which is without intelligible form";[10] vagueness and "chance" in art

---

9. From Aquinas's commentary on Pseudo-Dionysius's *De divinis nominibus* (On the Divine Names); quoted in Brian Keeble, "William Blake: Art as Divine Vision," in *God and Work*, p. 95.

10. Keeble, "William Blake: Art as Divine Vision," p. 95.

are defects by definition. Dante Alighieri, for one, would entirely agree with these statements.[11]

As we have seen, the notion of art and work based on metaphysical principles actually ends up being quite *practical*, since it aims for a marriage of matter and spirit.

> None of this is in any way meant to deny that our acting upon a material substance is conditioned by that substance proceeding through our senses. But at the very core of the act the senses are not consciously involved and there is an immediate and unconditioned intuition in the soul of the timeless source of action.... And no degree of perfection in work is attained that does not touch upon this stasis of Perfection itself. That is the spiritual function of skill.

Art, then, is work spiritualized, or in the traditional formulation, making arising from contemplation. This is what Schuon was referring to in the quotation given earlier, that "art is the perfection of work." That the art-work is "spiritualized" means that it is informed by intellect; the idea in the intellect is the work's Form—that form of a thing which Boethius said is like a light by which the thing is known.[12] This is what is implied when Keeble and his sources state that art is a habit of mind, a "discernment that remains in the artist"; it is what *informs* the material that is worked upon. It is this *active* role of the artist that imitates God in the creation of things. The work, then, is created, like the human soul, in the image of its Creator. *This* is the sense in which "art imitates nature in its manner of operation," as Thomas Aquinas famously put it.[13] The creative act of work that is art takes place always in the timeless moment of Genesis.

The "unconditioned intuition" mentioned in the above passage is also known as the spiritual intellect, or (in Plato, for instance)

---

11. "It would be shameful for one who wrote poetry dressed up with figures or [rhetoric] not to know how to strip his words of such dress, upon being asked to do so, showing their true sense. My best friend and I are only too well acquainted with poets who write in such a stupid manner" (*Vita Nova* 16.10 [xxv.10]); translation from my annotated edition of the *Vita Nova* (2012).

12. Quoted by Keeble in "William Blake: Art as Divine Vision," p. 89.

13. *Summa theologica* I, q. 117, a. 1; in this, Aquinas follows Aristotle, *Physics* II.2, 194a.20: "hē technē mimeitai tēn physin," art imitates nature.

Reason, or simply as Intellect—obviously, quite different from what *intellect* means in ordinary contemporary speech. Since this notion, as well as the special sense of the word *tradition*, referred to earlier, are pivotal to understanding the view of art and work presented in these pages, a brief explanation of them might be useful.

Tradition in this context refers to traditional wisdom, that which St. Augustine described as "uncreated Wisdom, the same now, as before, and the same to be for evermore."[14] This is the sense in which the primordial tradition, mentioned earlier, is primordial. Timeless, principial Truth is also known, in the Christian tradition, as the Logos, by which, according to the Nicene Creed, all things are made. We should note here that "all things" implicitly includes things made by human art and skill. This is the same Logos who states, "Before Abraham was, I am"; and this principle is given voice in other traditions as well, for example, when Krishna explains to Arjuna in the Bhagavad Gita that he formerly imparted the same teachings to the sun god.[15] Primordial tradition, then, is synonymous with the "perennial philosophy"; it is perpetual renewal from a sacred source, the transmission of the living knowledge of the nature of reality. Because human beings are not, to put it mildly, entirely lucid, but rather see reality through a glass, darkly, we need prophets and seers—and the divine revelation they express and serve—to guide us in the right direction toward renewal of this knowledge.

It is important to note, too, what tradition is *not* in this usage. It cannot be equated with any one historically conditioned form, and it is not merely temporal continuity of custom, as many conservatives use the term, even if custom and specific forms are essential for its practical transmission. (For this reason, teacher-guides such as Schuon are adamantly against the sort of syncretistic homemade religion common in our time.) It is not, then, an accumulation of human endeavor: tradition has a supernatural (divine) origin. In a "normal" civilization, the arts, sciences, and other activities are formal embodiments of tradition. It is in this sense that modern civilization—the "reign of quantity" outlined above—is *not* nor-

14. *Confessions* IX.X.24.
15. John 8:58; Bhagavad Gita 4:1.

mal, but rather, is an anomaly. This abnormal state is most tangible, perhaps, in the ever-increasing rate of change we witness all around us. Because it reduces man to reasoned sensation, the reign of quantity is *essentially* anti-traditional; this explains the obsession with innovation, even though, in the traditional view, "there is nothing new under the sun." As the painter Cecil Collins, a friend of Keeble and a frequent subject of his publications, put it, we are spiritual barbarians; despite our great technological sophistication, "we are absolute amateurs in the spiritual life—which to the great civilizations was a technical affair."[16]

If tradition is another word for traditional wisdom, the spiritual or intuitive intellect is the agent of its living transmission. Meister Eckhart famously wrote, in words that echo those of Augustine on traditional wisdom: "There is something in the soul that is uncreated and uncreatable . . . the intellect"[17]—in Greek, *nous*, the highest faculty in man, which, when it is purified (like a polished mirror), enables us to know the inner essences of things, directly and without mediation. Reason or *dianoia* formulates representations of things, and bases its deductions on those representations or concepts. But the "simple cognition" of intellect (as St. Isaac the Syrian called it), the eye of the heart or *oculus cordis*, knows directly, because its *knowing* is *being*. Such knowledge involves an identification between the knower and the known—hence its central role, described in the earlier quote from Keeble, as that which informs the creative act. As Keeble writes: "The intuitive intellect is the ultimate agent of the present moment in which life is lived, . . . the true subject, the timeless witness" outside the flux of time. The Hesychast tradition in Greek Orthodox Christianity is particularly rich with commentary on the spiritual intellect, as even a casual perusal of one of its key guides to the spiritual life, *The Philokalia*, reveals. I am focusing on instances of this in the Christian tradition, since

16. Cecil Collins, "Why Does Art Today Lack Inspiration?" in Keeble, ed., *Every Man an Artist*, p. 203.

17. Quoted often by writers drawn to the *philosophia perennis*, for example, by Thomas Merton in "Ascetical and Mystical Theology," in *An Introduction to Christian Mysticism* (2008), p. 191.

that is my main background, but the same notion occurs repeatedly in Sufi and Vedantic writings, as well as in other traditions.

And these testimonies only scratch the surface of the voluminous, universal, written and symbolic references to this transcendent principle. How curious, then, that our own time generally views this concept as mere "opinion," or worse, "superstition," as though such a great number of brilliant, serious minds had no idea what they were talking about or were outright lying. It seems to me far more likely that if this faculty has been attested to by many thousands of sages and saints since time immemorial, something more substantial than opinion must be at stake. And yet, the denial of the spiritual intellect, which to traditional thought is the human faculty par excellence, is endemic to modernity. Religion becomes just a matter of "belief," which is interpreted to mean a more or less blind, sentimental adherence to a religious doctrine. Knowledge or gnosis (the sapiential core of religion) is pushed to the margin or left out of the picture altogether. This, says Guénon, is an inversion of spirituality, another manifestation of the reign of quantity. In this way, religion itself is reduced to the ego's dimensions. The denial of the spiritual intellect results also in reason being left to its own devices—hence "rationalism," which is the denial of a principle of knowing that is superior to reason. The result is that "modern man, instead of attempting to raise himself to the truth, seeks to drag truth down to his own level."[18]

Admittedly, religious fundamentalism the world over shows us how dangerous it can be simply to reject modernism—as though there is any plain choice in the matter. We may very well be living in the final phase of the Kali Yuga, but it also happens to be the only *yuga* we've got. All the artists and writers who are the subjects for the essays in Part II of this book are aware of this. As David Jones wrote, referring to his search for the "sleeping Lord" in the current age, "it is easy to miss Him at the turn of a civilisation."[19] Brian Keeble approaches this dilemma without compromise but also without ever

18. Guénon, *Crisis of the Modern World* (2001), p. 66.
19. From Jones's poem "A, a, a, Domine Deus," in the collection *The Sleeping Lord and Other Fragments* (1974).

being deluded about the possibility of a "restoration," and certainly without recommending an antiquarian "revival" of the arts. Rather, first, he acknowledges that we are living at the end of a major cycle, the dissolution of a civilization, and that this process is actually irreversible. He applies traditional wisdom to come to terms with the impoverishment of culture, an impoverishment that "is nothing less than a depletion of the proper content and practice of life."[20] And he affirms that the principles gleaned from that wisdom, applied in whatever way possible to daily practice, work, and thought, at the very least keep a flame alive for those who come after us.

Keeble realizes, because he has experienced it in his own work and life, that those who attempt to practice art and work in the traditional sense described in this book do so in an incoherent, fragmented, and dissipated setting. As he writes in his introduction to an anthology of essays which he edited, *Every Man an Artist,* all such artists and writers "express a sense of having to work against the grain, of struggling with a lack of coherence, of a certain impoverishment of context, when it comes to making effective the full practice their art requires." This statement applies to its author with the full weight of its burden. A reader who is not familiar with Keeble's work might assume that he comes from a privileged, affluent background. How else could he find the freedom necessary for challenging the very means of earning a livelihood which our society offers? And yet this is very far from the case. The author himself would never raise this point; like Plotinus, who refused that a portrait be done of him because he saw no use in making a "copy of a copy," Keeble leaves his personal life out of his work. I, however, feel it is important to mention something of what he has done and the circumstances in which he has done it, since it is a testimony to the arguments and claims of this book.

As a young man, Keeble found himself in a working-class family environment that offered every opposition and discouragement to his interest in poetry and the arts (he originally wanted to be a painter). Opportunities for economic advancement or relief were nil; and marriage and children at a young age, along with relatively

---

20. Preface to *God and Work,* xiii.

limited work options, created a tension between creative aspiration-inspiration and physical need. Because Keeble has lived these conflicts directly, his thoughts on the matter are that much more focused and urgent:

> We have set in place a society where the artist in us is free to work for the good of his feelings provided he does not expect, in so doing, the right to earn a livelihood. At the same time the workman in us is free to work for the good that is material necessity provided he does not thereby expect the right to an inherent satisfaction from the work he must do to secure a livelihood. . . . Work is not something we must be freed from—indeed cannot be freed from unless we are freed entirely from action—but something we must engage in in such a way and at such a level that it is revealing of our deepest nature. It must contribute to our spiritual life while serving our bodily needs.

As a result of these circumstances, "art appreciation" in our society becomes a sort of bonbon (often not a very tasty bonbon at that!) we can pop in our mouths during work breaks. As Keeble adds: "Can we really believe that a visit to an art gallery, in our 'spare' time, is sufficient to compensate us for the meaninglessness of a humdrum experience of work unrelieved by any personal satisfaction?" He voices here what many have felt, stuck in jobs that nourish nothing but physical exigencies—assuming that even *that* need is met sufficiently. How far this state of affairs is from the traditional exhortation *ora et labora,* pray and work, in harmonious God-centered balance.

Encouragement and guidance did come to Keeble, starting in his early twenties, through contact with some remarkable creative people: the poets Peter Russell and Kathleen Raine, the painter Cecil Collins, the architect Keith Critchlow, the translator-writer-theologian Philip Sherrard, and others. Kathleen Raine would prove to be an especially decisive source and mentor. In the early 1980s, with Raine, Sherrard, and Critchlow, Keeble founded the journal *Temenos,* whose editorial policy was to publish work that represented, sustained, and nurtured "the arts of imagination." In thirteen more or less annual issues, *Temenos* published some of that period's most acute writing on the arts and culture.

Several years before *Temenos* started, Keeble founded his own publishing venture, Golgonooza Press. He did so while precariously supporting his family through full-time employment and after only one year of college education. (A letter of reference from Kathleen Raine did enable Keeble to study for a year at Newbattle Abbey College for adult working people, near Edinburgh, where the poet Edwin Muir had been warden in the 1950s.) Golgonooza books, which Keeble produced for thirty years, not only always had important content—by Perennialist authors such as Coomaraswamy and Seyyed Hossein Nasr, and poets and artists such as Cecil Collins and Vernon Watkins—but they were always beautifully made. Keeble himself was the designer of all the books. His profound knowledge and love for lettering and calligraphy is illustrated in the current volume in the chapter on the father of modern British calligraphy, Edward Johnston. And Keeble has put his theories on art and work into practice by commissioning master artists for his books' production. The English lettercutter Tom Perkins (whose letters adorn the cover of the present book) and the calligrapher Gaynor Goffe, for instance, have executed the lettering for the covers of several Golgonooza books. Keeble's craftsmanship and standards as editor and designer were recognized many times by the British Printing Industry Federation, which exhibited every year the hundred finest-made books in Britain, including, frequently, those of Golgonooza. *Temenos Academy Review*, also designed by Keeble, won an award for design as well.

Since the publication of *Art: For Whom and for What?* Keeble has produced numerous books—I provide a bibliography with details at the end of this volume. The integrity and consistency of his vision, going back to the mid-1970s, is such that one is struck by the force of what can only be called a vocation, in the traditional sense of that word. The essays in *Daily Bread* are chosen to represent the author's scope and abiding themes. Part I presents some of Keeble's theoretical pieces, essays that explain his views on art and work; Part II consists of pieces on individual artists and writers. The one exception to this organization is the Wendell Berry piece, which I placed in Part I because it is more about Berry the farmer-ecologist than Berry the writer, and it nicely represents Keeble's own practical bent. In Part II, each study of an artist or poet becomes an occasion to meditate upon the holistic principles explored in the theoretical pieces of Part I. For example, the essay on the potter Michael Cardew explores the mysterious relationship between potter and clay, effected, as we have seen, by the art within the artist:

> By developing the habit of prolonged concentration upon his repetitive tasks the potter induces in himself a state of physical and mental integration, a state of receptivity whereby the conscious effort of actually forming his material becomes effortless and unconscious. This state permits his inspiration to flow unheeded and for the resulting work to embody those hidden possibilities of formal beauty that reside, as it were, objectively in the clay.

And in the essay on Cecil Collins, the non-dualistic notions of Hindu Vedanta and esoteric Islam, which occur often in the writings of Keeble's sources, find expression in the artist's representation of the unity of intellectual image and natural phenomena.

The final three chapters in this volume are about poets—Vernon Watkins, David Gascoyne, and Kathleen Raine. All three of these poets placed metaphysical contemplation at the center of their work, dressed in archetypal symbolism—often imagery from nature, in the cases of Watkins and Raine; liturgical-Biblical in Gascoyne's poem-sequence that is the subject of chapter 17. It is clear that Keeble has lovingly studied his poet-mentors for years, since his own poetry speaks in a similar vein. In an essay on Edwin Muir published in *Agenda* in 1975, Keeble made the following statement, which could be a manifesto for his own writing: "By an irony that escapes too many today it is the contrived and the novel that most immediately bears witness to artistic success, whereas that which is anonymous and traditional—furthest removed from the invention and exploration of 'subjectivism', is that by which art remains ultimately accessible; in the profoundest sense *intelligible*."[21] The currently widespread view of poetry as self-expression and an occasion to (as the MFA programs put it) "write what you know" is very different from the intensely inward vision of poetry articulated in this

---

21. "Edwin Muir: Our Contemporary and Mentor," 81 (italics in original).

book. Keeble dismisses the modern obsession with artists' lives and the cult of personality. Rather, the poetry that Keeble writes and admires is, like in Eliot's famous formulation, an *escape* from personality—it arises from the longing to be liberated from oneself. In the same spirit, Keeble's dedication to *Art: For Whom and for What?* reads: "To the anonymous craftsman."

This notion of the anonymity of men and women in the interiorized moment of crafting something, also accounts for the phrase *Daily Bread* in the present volume's title. The Lord's Prayer is not only a miracle of linguistic economy; it is an expression of the perfect economy of life, describing a cycle of continual movement between the above and the below. Spoken in the voice of anonymous-man-as-such (the third-person-plural "Our"), it opens with the Principle, the highest ("Father"), whose name must be "hallowed," kept holy, as a precondition for all that follows. This is the first of the seven petitions that Christian tradition identifies in this foundational prayer and meditation. The final petition, "deliver us from evil," refers to the lowest ontological level, the world of appearances or Plato's shadows, where we are in a state of confusion because we are most remote from the Divine Principle. In the pivotal center is "our daily bread," which, as everyone is quite aware, we have to earn, but which the prayer asks that God "give us." This bread, then, is both the corporeal bread we work for and the manna-grace given to us as part and parcel of what we give of ourselves to our work, perfected into art. Heaven and earth meet in this act, as Brian Keeble has been tireless in reminding us.

ANDREW FRISARDI
February 7, 2015

PART I

Art and Work
in the Reign of Quantity

1

Introductory Remarks

It is only possible to answer for the final truth of principles, not for the direct success of plans.

JOHN RUSKIN

ON THE FACE OF IT nothing could be more futile than to bring into question both the direction and apparently unstoppable impetus of our modern technological society. It is, after all, this by now global process that has delivered a great many material rewards to a significant proportion of the world's population. But to sound a note of misgiving about the final outcome of this process is no longer novel. The dissection and analysis of why and where modern, secular man's dream of an earthly paradise of material prosperity has gone wrong is by now part and parcel of the very industry of inquiry on which that dream proceeds. Today, there is hardly any area of human thought and conduct that is not subjected on a daily basis to the most rigorous and painstaking analysis, an analysis that all too often ends by sounding alarm bells of misgiving as to the wisdom of the whole enterprise.

Indeed, slowly but surely the idea that the whole process is itself a means of instituting a fundamentally anti-human, even diabolic, form of life and imposing it upon whole masses of the earth's population seeps into the consciousness of an ever greater number of people from all walks of life. Ought we to be surprised by this? When we are faced on all fronts by examples of the willful pollution and destruction of our natural environment, of vast currents of human injustice suffered for the supposed necessity of economic survival, of the ineptitudes of political gesturing that mask the far greater powers of social manipulation of capitalist enterprise—not to mention the sub-human banality of much in our midst that

1

passes for culture—we are surely entitled to pause and ask ourselves what has gone wrong.

We know, if we care to give the matter any thought, that the world was once otherwise, and in ways that allowed man the opportunity (even at its most constrained) to live his life in a habitat both natural and man-made, for which he is fitted by his physical aptitudes, his psychological constitution, and his spiritual destiny. What for millennia have been considered the innate features of his earthly existence are more and more seen to be displaced in the contemporary environment that is the post-industrial world. In the pressured and artificial urban habitat that is characteristic of modern cities, and which is gradually becoming the inevitable destination of populations world-wide, man's physical aptitudes are less and less given their natural expression, his psychological constitution shows every sign of breaking down faced with the imposed strain, and his spiritual destiny is simply abolished by a conspiracy of silence. Which is nothing less than to say that man himself—for whom this state of affairs has been pursued—seems likely to be obliterated by the very process set in train for his benefit.

The studies presented here are intended as a modest contribution to a task we ignore at our future peril: to inquire into why and how this state of affairs has come about. They do not present the systematic exposition of a thesis meant to arrest the progressive decline of all that has been meant, for virtually the whole of human history by, for instance, such terms as *God, spirit, soul, art, work,* even the notion of "the human self-image," and the realities that correspond to them. But if not systematically, then I must hope that the reader finds these studies cumulatively to contain a thesis capable of penetrating issues that persist in the face of conditions that, were those issues not founded upon perennial truths, would long ago have ceased to be of interest to anybody. The justification for the use made here of the *philosophia perennis*—that body of wisdom and sapiential doctrine that underpins these studies—resides in the power of its truth to summon in the human heart and mind those resonances of affinity and significance that link men and women of all ages and differing climes and to bring them to a common recognition of their unchanging, spiritual destiny. In so far as these studies appeal to this *sophia* they do so not arbitrarily, as one might choose one philosophical system in preference to another and work within its terms, but because, as Ananda K. Coomaraswamy once observed, writing to Aldous Huxley, the "self-authenticating intelligibility" of the *philosophia perennis* "explains more things than are explained elsewhere." It remains the case, doubtless all the more "awkward" for modern man for being so evident, that there has always been an incomparably greater degree of unanimity as to ultimate values in the revealed traditions than has ever been the case with modern philosophy and science. Given the nature of the issues involved it could never have been otherwise.

If the vast array of theories and conjectures that represents the imposing edifice of modern scientific knowledge can be taken to indicate the final triumph of human knowledge, a final scaling of the heights of true wisdom, then we have no choice but to conclude that our ancestors were, to say the least, immoderately deceived. We are forced to accept by sheer weight of evidence that all the great saints, mystics, philosophers, poets, and artists, in the unanimity of their acceptance of the divine origin of things, of seeing man as made in the divine image and as having by his very nature a spiritual destiny, were quite simply wrong. And so any talk of spiritual attainment, any proposition of an analogous nature that supposes there is a correspondence between heavenly and earthly levels of reality is sheer poppycock, and the departments of the humanities in our universities should have as their primary concern the task of dismantling this insubstantial and fraudulent construction of misbelief in order to offer us something better.

If all this was in fact true then what might we expect to find in the culture that surrounds us and which is the expression, in its own sphere, of that secular, scientific mentality. Surely we might expect to find, to give just a few examples more or less at random, students in the departments of philosophy at our universities having put aside the *Summa theologica* (once a student textbook) because, having mastered it, they had passed on to something superior and more all-encompassing. We would expect to see our leading architects building structures to equal in beauty and magnificence the Gothic cathedrals, the Alhambra, cities like Siena and Isphahan. We might expect to be reading poets on a par with Homer, Rumi, Dante, and Shakespeare in the depth and breadth of their understanding of the whole human predicament.

It should be all too evident that the time has not yet come for us to reject the spirituality and culture of the past as being a misguided enterprise based on inadequate modes of intelligence. In the absence of a metaphysic that conclusively demonstrates the inadequacy of a Shankara, an Ibn 'Arabī, a Meister Eckhart, perhaps we might be forgiven for concluding that in modern man the human race has not finally reached its full stature by the attainment of a wisdom superior to that of his ancestors. Indeed, given the multidimensional crisis that confronts him at every turn, there is ample evidence that modern man has regressed into a gradually narrowing articulation of reality that causes even his best endeavors to pale into insignificance when compared to the cultural riches of the past. We have to recognize that in these "monuments of unaging intellect" (as W.B. Yeats called the greatest artistic achievements of the past) we are summoned to a final term whose attainment effectively means—supreme paradox!—our humanity is only properly fulfilled in being transcended. If we will not live by that perennial truth which has always served to direct man to his ultimate goal then we must suffer the lingering death of a thousand transient falsehoods of our own fabrication. These studies are meant to challenge some of these falsehoods as they have been applied to the sphere of human making.

The ancient and widespread tradition of the handicrafts as instruments of livelihood and devotion, conceived and elevated to the level of a spiritual discipline, allowed man to live for millennia in harmony with himself in harmony with his fellow men and in harmony with nature. The industrial system, on the contrary, after only two centuries, has been seen to set man against himself, man against man, and man against nature. It threatens crisis in all directions. So much so that it is surely worth reminding ourselves that the whole history of the human race has taken place, that is to say has been *lived*, according to meanings and values which by their very nature make human life precisely what it is (and to which any given level of technological innovation neither adds nor subtracts), without the machine that will be invented tomorrow: the machine that tomorrow we will be persuaded is of vital necessity for our future survival and well-being.

All human existence has to address the central questions that surround man's brief existence on an earth that manifestly is not the ultimate term of his destiny—an experience of life that unceasingly confronts us with innumerable paradoxes and poses an unending stream of questions that demand answers. The fact that there are powerful economic and social forces of persuasion—forces to which we need not grant a deterministic inevitability—should not lead us to believe that these paradoxes and questions can only be resolved by our acquiescence to each and every next stage of development of the technological juggernaut.

The signs are that we should no longer delude ourselves that the momentum of progress such a development harbors takes us one step nearer the moment of our necessary self-enlightenment. It is time to renounce the futile task of trying to identify life itself with that dynamic sequence of events that is history. It is time to seek our rightful place in the order and stability of the Real by means of an interior cognizance that takes account of the timeless and eternal roots of temporal, external levels of reality. These studies are meant to serve this radical call for a change in the use of the mind. There is nothing new in this. Blake, Ruskin, Morris, Gill and many others have responded to the call. G. K. Chesterton in *The Outline of Sanity* wrote:

> Before we begin any talk of the practical problem of machinery, it is necessary to leave off thinking like machines. It is necessary to begin at the beginning and consider the end. Now we do not necessarily wish to destroy every sort of machinery. But we do desire to destroy a certain sort of mentality. And that is precisely the sort of mentality that begins by telling us that nobody can destroy

machinery. Those who begin by saying that we cannot abolish the machine, that we must use the machine, are themselves refusing to use the mind.

Shifting the weight of emphasis away from the outward rewards of human labor, and toward the wellsprings of human motivation, these studies, each from its different angle of approach to its subject, ask what it is a man and a woman may get *by* working rather than what they might get *from* working. This approach becomes necessary once we ask the question, what is the benefit of any outward effort once we stop confusing its value with the price it will fetch in the marketplace? To challenge the industrial conception of labor in this way is all the more necessary if we are to loosen the stranglehold of that type of mentality which presupposes that the manipulation of matter for productive ends is a right that takes precedence over man's being as such. In the eyes of such a bias, as its advocates would claim, the right to be productive is called for for the sake of human survival. It must be admitted that there is a degree of logic to this bias which, in theory, lends it a certain truth. But in practice it is the law of the brute, a law that effectively denies the deepest dimension of our being. And if such a right is practiced in isolation from, and to the exclusion of all other values then, as the modern world looks set to prove, that right becomes a tyranny that will, in the end, hardly permit the survival it was meant for.

Seeing that man is a creature who at all times and in all places has to confront the same primordial question, "Who am I?" (a question that inescapably poses two others, "From whence did I come?" and "Whither am I bound?"), the only fitting counter-proposal with which to challenge the notion of laissez-faire expansionism—for that is what it amounts to—must be, "Seek ye first the Kingdom of Heaven and all these things shall be added unto you."

Clearly this injunction calls for an act of internalization seeing that the "Kingdom of Heaven is within." So the question of what possible role the "outwardness" and "materiality" of productive effort should play in our fitting survival becomes one of asking, "the survival of whom?" Work is a mode of objectivizing the soul whereby man—who as a "fallen" being is not yet a perfectly integrated being—may conform the world of his outward action to the inner state of his being. In this connection there is a certain appropriateness to calling the domain of work the "theater of redemption" for *homo faber*. A man is only able to know who he is to the degree he knows how to be what he does. The perfect identity of thought and action (in the sphere of outward action this is analogous to the union of the knower and the known in the sphere of inner contemplation) takes place where the subject is objectivized in a form that perfectly realizes the subject's unity of being. We all desire the "heaven" of the perfectly accomplished piece of work, the perfectly coordinated action in which an "unseen hand" seems to lift us to a level beyond our customary, average, achievement. It is this inspired moment that underpins the whole question of the possible spiritual content of work, a moment comprehensively betrayed by the industrial process whose sole concern is for the economic advantage of the final product regardless of the means employed. The raison d'être of mechanization is to displace the workman precisely because it envisages the worker as a creature who has nothing to lose by being freed from the exertions of labor. In a machine milieu the only human "content" of work is the expenditure of effort. Toward the end of his life Eric Gill concluded that it was not on the grounds of its general "beastliness, vulgarity, inefficiency, anti-socialness [and] ugliness," that the industrial commercial world should be denounced but because of its fundamental "*unholiness*"!

Much of the underlying cause of our present predicament is due to habits of thought that tend to isolate from one another the spiritual and material, a distinction that isolates the mental (or psychological) and the physical. As a further consequence of the unnatural separation we think of art and work as serving two different human needs. This being so, we can no more look to the world of art in any hope of finding things freer from the dichotomies that undermine the world of work and industry, the causes and conditions of which these studies are meant to address.

Any modern artist or craftsman who, by whatever path, comes to the realization that there is a necessary affinity between work, art, and spirituality is immediately confronted by two problems—the one entailed by the other. The realization of such an affinity will lead on to an instinctive sense that certain creative possibilities are likely to be beneficial to spiritual development while others are likely to be detrimental. In other words, he will feel an instinctive need for some guidance in negotiating the difficult territory over which is discovered how the aesthetic and spiritual are bound together in such a way as to give a natural expression to their mutuality. But in the modern world such guidance is absent owing to the almost complete lack of unanimity of values on all levels; spiritual, social, psychological, cultural, and aesthetic.

This first "external" problem leads on to a second "internal" problem; that one has no option but to seek a resolution of the first problem on an individual basis—as a matter of personal choice. And so the whole situation is compounded.

Strictly speaking it is not possible for the modern artist or craftsman to function as a traditional artist—that is one whose livelihood at the practical level gives a natural expression to and is the integral application of truths and principles of a divine origin. For that, ultimately, is what the affinity between work, art, and spirituality is. But the absence of unanimous values and the subsequent resort to matters of personal taste inevitably introduces a note of personal identity that is foreign to the sacred milieu of tradition. If we examine the widest range of representative examples of traditional artefacts, from cities and architecture to the most common everyday objects, we cannot fail to notice the complete absence of that artistic individualism that is the hallmark of their modern counterparts. The individual identity of the artist in the traditional context is a factor of negligible importance in the production of works of art. Even further, our understanding of the traditional cultures leads us to acknowledge that they exist primarily as a means to align the soul of man to the cosmic scale of his destiny. Their function is to orientate his earthly existence to values and meanings that validate his identity with the supra-human rather than with the accidents of his empirical personality.

To this end the traditional artist is provided with ample guidance and precept both spiritually and artistically. Compared with the modern artist, who has to "go it alone," the traditional artist refers to established precedent at every step of the way in matters theoretic and practical. Whether written or orally transmitted he inherits a virtual manual to guide his every movement according to conventions that free him from the impulses of a nebulous spontaneity that urges him to do something new, to accomplish something uncalled-for in order to make his mark in society. In a sense the modern artist is also given a "manual," even if by default, but it is marked "do your own thing." The modern artist is on his own when it comes to discovering what psychological and practical possibilities he might implement in seeking a closer alliance of art with the sacred.

Part I of the following studies attempts to chart the causes and weight and prevailing conditions of this situation. Part II attempts to understand the way in which individual figures have come to terms with the inevitable rupture of art from the sacred in the present state of things. Given the complexity of our predicament with respect to all the issues involved there can be no question here of offering a formula for resolving the perplexities we are faced with. Nor is it within the bounds of possibility that an individual artist could transform a situation that goes beyond the sphere of art itself. In the sphere of art there are no absolutes. No society has ever been, or is ever likely to be, in whatever measure, "saved" by art. We should emphatically reject such a thesis whenever it is explicitly or implicitly present in much contemporary cultural analysis and debate. Similarly, there can be no question of "going back." Any supposed "golden age" of our history is as irrecoverable as any part of our past lives.

The term *tradition*, as it is used throughout this book, refers to that body of truths, both principial and doctrinal, that are ultimately of divine origin and which are mediated to man through the revealed religions, their avatars, prophets, and spiritual masters. It has been the vocation of certain authors to demonstrate the universality of this body of knowledge as the primordial means by which the immutable, sacred nature of the True and the Real is disclosed to man. It should be beyond dispute that there has never been a true civilization or culture which has not been, in a manner appropriate to the portion of humanity to which it is addressed, the extension and application of the sacred knowledge that is tradition. This knowledge, in accordance with its very nature, binds man to God through its transcendent mode and to the essential in its immanent mode in a manner that validates the ultimate meaning and value of his existence on earth. For these studies it is axiomatic that there is no such thing as a secular culture. Deviation and impoverishment must ever fail to supply the terms of positive achievement, as the new barbarism makes plain.

This admission calls for a further note of clarification: for if the sacred is here ranged against the secular no less is it that qualitative understanding is ranged against quantitative knowledge; precisely the polemical component of these studies.

In these pages reference is made, whether directly or indirectly, to the "modern mind." The reader should understand by this term the pre-disposition of contemporary thought toward quantity and its external, manifold character as opposed to quality with its internalizing, unitive function. The modern mind is above all characterized by its undeniable tendencies in this direction. So much so that it regards metaphysical and spiritual intuition as, at worst, inadmissible and at best an abstraction (not much more than a symptom of thought) and favors empirical demonstration as "concrete" evidence in its attempt to discover the real. This tendency lends it what seems the natural bias of naive materialism; ascribing a higher ontological status to the perceptions of external phenomena, with its counter-tendency to devalue intuitive and imaginative modes of apprehension. In the field of the arts this has led to a far higher status being placed on aesthetic sensations than on cognitive value. These studies are in part meant to challenge this bias and its consequent direction.

In the final analysis there is only Truth and our deviation from it. It is a matter of seeking to recover something of the spiritual anthropology of the sacred traditions, of recognizing the greater inclusiveness of their visions of the totality of the Real. One way of doing this is to determine what has been lost to us by a process of historical development that has brought man to countenance, on a global scale, social and economic agendas that now threaten his very survival. The question that overwhelmingly presents itself is whether and to what degree we are prepared to return to the full amplitude of our proper nature, rather than to the impoverishments of the reductive logic of the modern mentality. The schizomorphic tendency of the modern mind seeks to accommodate man to the dimension of a reality that must, in due course, lose him altogether in the flux of history—among the detritus of his own productions. Let it be recognized that man is more than he makes, more than a brief epiphenomenon on the surface of history, followed by an inglorious oblivion.

2

Notes on *Art* and *Imagination*

AT THE OUTSET the word *Temenos* may well have come as a surprise to some readers of this review.[1] Yet by now what it denotes should have become more familiar: it is the sacred space, the holy ground or place given over to the enactment of the sacred. What the adoption of this title presupposed was that the significance and meaning of our contributors' work was, in whatever measure, orientated toward the sacred.

Now that *Temenos* has reached its sixth issue it may be worthwhile examining more closely the two words that figure most prominently in its sub-title, *art* and *imagination,* and to consider aspects of their meaning in the context of what *Temenos* stands for. That these considerations have a bearing on our understanding of the nature of work and employment, at a time when there is much discussion as to their nature and value to society, should become evident.

The real tragedy of our predicament in this field is perhaps its double nature; which is that those who have no work must suffer as well the deprivation of losing a major opportunity to exercise their humanity. This is widely, even if not in every quarter, acknowledged. But what of the second dimension of the tragedy: that those who do have employment do not have work in any real sense. All too often, and increasingly so, those who do have employment are obliged to perform tasks that do not call for the exercise of any quality that is essential to their humanity. Doubtless such a dilemma has been, for all sorts of obscure reasons, a long time in

---

1. [This essay first appeared in 1985 as the editorial to the sixth issue of the journal *Temenos,* whose cover identified the journal's devotion "to the arts of the imagination." Hence the topic of this editorial.—Ed.]

the making; but that it is a form of spiritual sickness and issues in a pervasive social malaise can no longer be denied. The promised paradise of Leisure State consumerism has become the hell of a corrosive apathy that threatens to engulf us all when the wellsprings of life are stifled by mere comfortable convenience. But what has all this to do with "art" and "imagination"?

The word *art* and what we understand by that term has in the last two or three centuries in the West undergone a shift of emphasis to the detriment of our understanding of its primary meaning. By gradual stages *art* has come to refer almost exclusively to the actual product of art and the way we value, in personal and social terms, that product rather than, as it should, to the way such products are made. We ought more properly to refer to "works of art" since the word *art* connotes human skill, method, contrivance, with a particular emphasis on the fact of its being a human attribute, since art results from a knowledge and practice such as only men and women possess and of which they are the only agents. Instead, and in short, we have allowed art to acquire a certain snob value. The word *art* has come to refer to an exclusive group of things which are somehow set apart from the wider category of things made whether by hand or machine. (In passing we might note that the word *manufacture*, which originally meant "made-by-hand," has come to assume the quantitative and derogatory sense of production *by machine!*) This wider category mysteriously, if only by implication, then comes to be thought of as non-art. In belonging to this exclusive group art-things puzzlingly acquire a certain mystique, a certain status not possessed by non-art things. For instance, an arrangement of builder's bricks on the floor of an art gallery is somehow art in a way the same bricks, arranged, in all innocence and as a game perhaps, by the builder's child in the builder's yard, is not art. Even worse, by the terms of this exclusive group of art-things, the man who made the bricks, given that they were manufactured, is not entitled to consider himself an artist even though the making of bricks requires knowledge and practiced skill. (Surely Marcel Duchamp's "Readymades" long ago called such deceitfulness and confusion into question?) For all sorts of reasons it has become desirable, even at times imperative, to be seen to be doing art-things and not non-art things. The result has been, firstly, confusion as to what art is, followed by over-valuation of the artist himself and, finally, an inevitable devaluation of the workman and what it is he makes.

This change of emphasis in the way we understand art has run concurrently with, as we might expect, a complementary change in the way we understand work. Indeed, it has partly come about as a result of the displacement of the crafts as the true basis of human culture. This displacement, effected by the industrial revolution, has reduced that class of men and women who once possessed and exercised a special skill or art, and which, in whatever measure, bore something of the mark of its maker, to a proletariat whose only purpose is to consume the non-art products of the machines they have to mind. An instinctive recognition of the impoverishment that this process entails has of course led to an attempt to rehabilitate the hand crafts in our society. And this is all to the good. But here again we need to be on our guard, for much of the ideological impetus behind the revival of the crafts is itself bedeviled by the same confusion and double standards we find in the "art-market." That is to say, the modern craftsman all too often demonstrates a willingness to embrace the spurious values of the art-market—an over-inflated sense of the maker's individuality, the desire for personal status via exhibition, the self-expression of idiosyncratic styles, and the like. We have all seen examples—if only in glossy magazines designed for the purpose—of pottery, jewelry, weaving, and so on, that could only be valid within the closed context of the exhibition gallery in which the gulf between work and life is made to seem a positive necessity. In all this we have, as it were, the two sides of a self-mutilation: on the one hand the artist has been relieved of the necessity for doing anything useful, while the workman is only of use so long as he undertakes tasks that seem to deny the exercise of any inner faculty that he can recognize as giving meaning to his humanity.

All this flies in the face of reason and common sense. The word *art* was and is a perfectly adequate word to signify *how* a thing is made by human thought and skill. What we need to do is to make every effort to put art back *inside* the artist. Art is not a special property miraculously given to the few to the exclusion of all others. It makes no sort of sense, beyond acknowledging a difference of degree rather than of kind, to refer to the art of the poet while at the same time denying that the carpenter or the gardener possesses also the art of making something well, of shaping, of fitting to purpose, of cultivation. If we would only return to the primary meaning of the word *art* we would see that there is no reason to make this arbitrary division of things into the categories of art and non-art. If we could only recover the habit of understanding art as that skill, that propensity for conceiving, for making and doing well, which is characteristic of all human work, we would see that all men (and women—think of that currently undervalued skill, among others, which is the art of motherhood!) are indeed artists. We need not pretend that this would cure all the ills of our society at a stroke, but it would be an essential step toward a more general recognition that we owe it to our humanity to make "work" and "art" reflect our essentially spiritual nature.

Let us now turn to the word *imagination*. To imagine something is to conceive the image of a likeness, to make a mental image of something. This presents no problems when what is pictured in the mind is the likeness of an object first perceived by the senses. But again, it flies in the face of reason as well as our actual experience to limit artificially the function of imagining to that of picturing in the mind only likenesses of sensible things. Almost coincidental in time with the complementary shift of meaning in the word *art* and the change in the way we view work has been the philosophical questioning of the ontological status of mental images. As the province of the artist has become more removed from the reality of daily life, as the difference between life and work widened, work approximating more readily to the condition of physical labor and art becoming more abstract, its hold on reality consequently more attenuated and over-refined, so it became a matter of importance to locate and define the real source of the artist's creative and imaginative life. This "fantasy" or "fancy versus reality" debate in which the notion of creative imagination was considered to be the central value, began in the eighteenth century with philosophers such as Locke and Hobbes. It gave shape and substance to the Romantic movement throughout Europe—in England, for instance, the notion of the creative imagination was obviously of fundamental importance. All this raised questions as to the ontological status of the imaginative function that are hardly resolved yet. Indeed, the attempt by the French scholar Henry Corbin to reinstate the traditional metaphysical value of imagination as an active spiritual function has once more called into question the very premises of the debate. But why was the debate necessary? The full ramifications of this question cannot be dealt with here. Let it suffice that we offer the following contribution toward a fuller answer.

As "reality" has come to be attributed to the external, the quantifiable, so the internal, non-quantifiable has come to seem somewhat "unreal." By way of compensation for this usurping impoverishment of human experience several things have come about. Most important, art has come to be thought of almost exclusively as the expression of non-quantifiable feelings and emotions. That is not to say that works of art did not previously express feeling and emotion; they did so less personally, less as something to be valued privately, and more as existing on the periphery of states of being validated, as it were, by a more objective and pervasive collective wisdom. Moreover, individual feelings and emotions have been over-emphasized in modern "art" at the expense of the contemplative dimension that is possible in the many acts of doing and making that are not necessarily or primarily meant to evoke or embody purely subjective emotions. And so the workman—the artisan—and the artist are forced into separate categories of activity with the result that rather more human value is accorded the artist's ever more attenuated individuality than is accorded to the increasingly depersonalized workman. It is as if we turn a blind eye to the fact that both belong first of all to the category *homo faber* and thus of necessity draw upon much the same resources to achieve their respective ends: concentration, effort, method, and skill in handling materials as well as having in the mind's eye—in imagination—a prior image of what it is they intend to make. What is in the imagination is the motivating raison d'être, is indeed the formal cause of every act of human making.

Yet just as we may have the image of a single, sensible thing in our mind, so we may equally well have an image, more complex and less distinct perhaps, of the pattern of our possible life, an image of the shape of our particular destiny, the pattern it has to follow. There is abundant reason to think that when such a pattern is missing men are somehow less than themselves. Or that when what the pattern follows is obscured from view or is, for whatever reason, beyond our grasp, then the full potentiality of life goes unrealized and that life is lived with an awareness that it is in some sense at a sub-human level. And this awareness of an insufficiency implies something very important. It points to the central function of the imagination—as indeed of art—which is to hold up before us some image, some re-presentation of the nature and terms of our existence. By means of imagination in this, its most universal sense, man is able to shape and make his life after the pattern of what is truly higher and greater than the accumulation of worldly experience. There is nothing in mere worldly experience to prepare us fully and adequately for the transcendent value of those monuments of past civilizations, from temples and cathedrals, manuscripts and sculptures, down to the innumerable objects of everyday use that the various crafts have sought to supply and that are so admired both in and out of museums throughout the world. Who, seeing such things, has not been touched by an intimation of a vision of some higher reality that at all times and places impinges upon our thoughts and acts? What is more, our own experience confirms that it does not make consistent sense to suppose that such shaping and making of our lives after the impulse of some intangible reality affects only some parts of our being and not others. We make ourselves whole or we do not make ourselves at all. A thing unfinished is a thing unmade. When it comes to the making of things we work in co-operation with, seeking a degree of mastery over, some specific material, tangible or otherwise. But in the making of ourselves we have to wrestle with that intractable substance life itself: and that is the hardest work of all.

But perhaps the most profound link between art and imagination can be traced through the etymological connotations of the word *art*. Here we note that art is a Middle English inflexion of AM, which, like *is* and *are*, comes from the Indo-European root *es*—to exist. From *es* we derive *esse*: "essence," that is, actual as opposed to potential being. Hence, ultimately, *art* expresses that which exists; that which is true. Thus art, in the fullest potentiality of its meaning, is an affirmation of being. So we may point to the fact that a thing wrought to the perfection of its being is an affirmation of the unity and wholeness of Being itself. For, by implication, when a thing is well and truly made some reverberation of that thing's archetypal perfection has taken place and thus some sanctity has been brought down into human life. No perfection of work is achieved without some degree of self-mastery—some transcendence over the more fugitive and ephemeral aspects of our selves. In every degree of such mastery some sanctity is present.

In so far as man has at his disposal whatever faculties and potentialities are his he has no choice but to know and to act. And in so far as he recognizes his knowing and doing are open to sanctification by virtue of their relation to the affirmation of Being, so he has no choice but to accept the sacred as the measure of his humanity. Thus the ultimate goal of his knowing and his acting is to trace all things back to their roots in the archetypal forces that shape his being. This all men may do in all they do in the utmost exercise of what it is their nature to be. "The Whole Business of Man Is The Arts & All Things Common," wrote Blake. In that work which it is ours to do we re-imagine the world after the manner of its original Imaginer. For if He did not imagine the world and all things in it after His own image it could never be known. Through the perfection of their art every human being can know something of the sanctity of life. Modern man, artist and workman, has lost the art of sanctifying things at hand. To the recovery of this lost art the pages of *Temenos* would hope to contribute.

3

A Time of Darkness

Nothing but truth itself can be the exact measure of truth.
NICHOLAS OF CUSA

IN RECENT CENTURIES it has been the norm for critical philosophy to turn its back on the doctrines of metaphysics, assuming, quite rightly, that they have little or nothing to offer a dialectic more or less entrenched in its materialist assumptions. But in recent years it has become apparent to a generation impatient with the sterility and impotence of academic philosophy that there is much in the sacred traditions of both the West and the East that might offer a way out of the impasse that modern philosophical thought seems to have created.

The disparity between modern philosophy and the metaphysical doctrines of the sacred traditions follows on from what the Renaissance instituted, namely, a gradual isolation of knowledge from the spiritual. As a result we have what amounts to an abandonment of those criteria which safeguard against the dangers of developing human knowledge in isolation from metaphysical truth. The ontological status of knowledge has been impoverished so as to preclude, in the act of knowing, the spiritual regeneration of the knower. In this—in effect the indissoluble duality of knower and known—the problem of the ultimate nature of intellect is expressly shelved.

That philosophy in the West has considered the discourse of metaphysics as meaningless, is only the logical outcome of attempting to build a philosophy of being, not on the first principles of metaphysical certainty, but on the partiality and findings of the empirical, quantitative sciences. To this extent critical philosophy has proven itself largely unable to avoid the pitfall of all relativism—

19

that of positing as an "absolute" truth that nothing but the relatively true exists.

All this points to the need to reaffirm the true nature of the metaphysical since, as René Guénon has pointed out, there is nothing from which the metaphysical dimension is absent and only by recourse to its permanent principles can contingent and relative domains of thought find their orientation in relation to truth. Certainly we cannot afford to confuse metaphysics as understood by modern critical philosophy with the metaphysic that is the subject of the metaphysical traditions of the East and of the Scholastic West.[1] An examination of the concept "metaphysics" and its relation to the decline of western culture may not then be untimely.

> Metaphysic is the knowledge of the universal principles on which all things necessarily depend, directly or indirectly; in the absence of metaphysic, any other knowledge, of whatever order it may be, is literally lacking in principle, and if by that it gains a little in independence (not as a right, but as a matter of fact), it loses much more in import and depth. That is why western science is, as it were, all on the surface. While scattering its energies among countless fragments of knowledge, and losing its way among the innumerable details of fact, it learns nothing about the true nature of things, which it declares to be inaccessible in order to justify its powerlessness in this respect.[2]

Here Guénon pinpoints the paradox of the materialist mentality which is largely responsible for the present character of western culture and civilization. While by its methods it must declare truth to be unknowable, intelligence must nonetheless proceed on the assumption that truth is the logical and ultimate end of all its operations. In consequence, no answers are forthcoming that entirely satisfy the need for an ultimate knowledge as to the nature of the Real, of man and of human destiny. Such questions remain seem-

---

1. For an exposition of the meaning of metaphysics from a universal perspective see René Guénon, "Oriental Metaphysics," in *The Sword of Gnosis*, edited by Jacob Needleman (1974), pp. 40–56. In this essay Guénon gives his reasons for the use of the singular *metaphysic*. The present chapter is indebted to Guénon's exposition.
2. René Guénon, *East and West*, translated by William Massey (1941), pp. 57–58.

ingly insoluble, or, when posed, elicit only superficial and incomplete answers in the rationalist context from which they arise. The prodigious efforts of virtuosity that comprise the intellectual history of the West during the last five centuries are surely indicative of an anguished desire for certitude on the part of man, an inquiry which is symptomatic of his dispossession as the central intelligence in the order of created beings.

If the scientist feels some justification in upbraiding the metaphysician for his lack of "proof" he nevertheless has to admit that his own speculations are founded upon assumptions that cannot be verified absolutely. That man's intelligence is never satisfied with less than truth suggests that intelligence itself has essentially something in common with the Absolute. If there is no certainty in knowledge, why think; if there is certainty in knowledge that is proof that intelligence has something in common with Truth—the absolute identity of knowing and Being. At its ontological and intuitive roots, the function of intelligence is to distinguish between the Real and the illusory, the permanent and impermanent, and this is not possible so long as human knowledge is developed in isolation from the sapiential doctrines of a tradition. Every tradition stems from a revelation and is, as Seyyed Hossein Nasr has stated, both *the* religion and *a* religion. That is to say it possesses, inherently, the Truth and the means of attaining the Truth. This integral spirituality of a tradition will emphasize a particular perspective of Truth according to the spiritual and psychological needs of the section of humanity whose destiny it shapes. But in so far as a tradition contains the objective manifestations of the Spirit it offers the possibility of an adequate representation of the Absolute, so that we are justified in considering its metaphysical principles as the ultimate referent of all spiritual and intellectual experience. The essential identity between the Absolute and intelligence provides not only the principial orientation for all modes of intellection but also the objective criteria for the contingent truths of discursive thought. For the intelligence to fully understand one thing it must needs have some grasp of the intelligible itself: that is intellectual intuition, which implies the comprehension of Being in itself as well as in connection with things.

> Like a container, like content, and vice versa: in nature a container is made for a corresponding content and proves the reality of the latter, indicating that such proof, though not necessary to every understanding, has its secondary and provisional utility. A human womb proves the existence of the human seed ... similarly, human intellect proves its essential and total content, namely absolute and therefore transcendent Reality and, together therewith, the reverberations of the Absolute in the contingent.[3]

The part cannot be fully understood without the whole, for any part involves the whole. The very "act" of intuition participates in the intelligible *form* of the totality of possibilities—the *form* of all things conformable. Truth is inconceivably yet paradoxically conceived in every conception. Intuition is not an object of knowledge open to the scrutiny of the rational mind, but is the ground upon which any necessity to give an intellectual account of things must proceed. In the unmanifest essence of intuition inheres every ultimate criteria and value of human knowledge. From this essence all modes of knowledge derive their reality.

As to the term *metaphysics* it is of the utmost importance that we do not have in mind here the metaphysics of such philosophers as Descartes, Spinoza, Kant, or any modern philosophical system. For these, metaphysics constitutes an attempt at a systematic explanation of all that lies beyond facts—in other words it attempts by discursive means to encompass that which makes rational thought possible. Thus for the rationalist philosopher metaphysics, rather than being any particular field of thought, is a wisdom about thinking, "an analysis of what it means to think, and an inquiry as to what may be the ultimate reference of thought." Being rational in its operation, it can never transcend "thinking" as such. Moreover, this philosophic metaphysics,

> or human wisdom about things known or knowable, must be systematic, since it is required by hypothesis that its perfection will consist in an accounting for everything, in a perfect fitting together of all the parts of the puzzle to make one logical whole;

---

3. See Frithjof Schuon, "Man and Certainty," in *Logic and Transcendence*, translated by Peter N. Townsend (1975), chapter 19.

and the system must be a closed system, one namely limited to the field of time and space, cause and effect, for it is by hypothesis about knowable and determinate things, all of which are presented to the cognitive faculty in the guise of effects, for which causes are sought.[4]

It would also be a mistake to think of metaphysics as the principle of knowledge, for it is not that all knowledge is deduced analytically from it but rather that it is the apprehension of a reality prior to thoughts or even "thinking." Just as the eye cannot see sight so we cannot attempt an explanation of vision by means of the objects we see. Any attempt to yoke metaphysics to philosophy in a systematic, discursive manner cannot escape the fundamental error of deducing Being from thought itself. To annex the transcendent truths of metaphysics proper to philosophical thinking is to substitute a theory of knowledge for knowledge itself.

The word itself gives the clue to its meaning, which is the knowledge of what is "beyond" (*meta*) "nature" (*physis*)—that is, the intuited essence of experience itself before we ascertain the nature of what is experienced. Being essentially constituted by that which is "beyond physics," the metaphysical is limitless and universal, and is by that fact properly speaking incommunicable except by means of the analogical discourse of myth, symbol, and ritual. Accordingly every other point of view other than the metaphysical is more or less partial and specialized and therefore subject to certain limitations. This is true of theology as well as of science and philosophy. Even during the Scholastic Middle Ages, metaphysics came to be treated as being dependent upon theology. The primary function of Scholasticism was to combat error rather than provide a means of contemplation and realization. Although metaphysics must at all times presuppose the essential unity and oneness of Being, nonetheless,

> pure being is neither the first nor the most universal principle, for it is already a determination. It is thus necessary to go beyond being, and it is this that is of the greatest significance. That is why in all true metaphysical conceptions it is necessary to take into

4. Ananda K. Coomaraswamy, "On the Pertinence of Philosophy," in *What Is Civilisation?* (1989), p. 15.

account the inexpressible; just as everything that can be expressed is literally nothing in comparison with that which surpasses expression, so the finite, whatever its magnitude, is nothing when faced with the Infinite. One can hint at much more than can be experienced, and this is the part played by exterior forms. All forms, whether it is a matter of words or symbols, act only as a support, a fulcrum for rising to possibilities of conception that far outstrip them.[5]

That the empirical sciences cannot provide such "possibilities of conception" should be obvious. Whenever the modern rationalist mentality, operating more often than not on the basis of its empirical knowledge, wishes to establish first principles, it is forced to do so in terms of conceptions of reality and truth already colored by its own mental products. This characteristic of the modern mind has dogged the West ever since Descartes envisaged Universal Being in terms of a private awareness of one's own separate existence. Here, the appeal to "truth" becomes, in effect, an appeal to the objectivity of the subjective experience of phenomena. This fails to see that the experience of phenomenal knowledge is a form of mentation that takes for granted its own indefinable and non-discursive essence,

> the reality of which has been consistently denied by modern philosophy, which has failed to grasp its real nature whenever it has not preferred simply to ignore it; this faculty can also be called the pure intellect, following the practice of Aristotle and his Scholastic successors, for to them the intellect was in fact that faculty which possessed a direct knowledge of principles. Aristotle expressly declares [*Posterior Analytics*, book II] that "the intellect is truer than science," which amounts to saying that it is more true than the reason which constructs that science; he also says that "nothing is more true than the intellect," for it is necessarily infallible from the fact that its operation is immediate and because, not being really distinct from its object, it is identified with the truth itself.[6]

A culture whose tacit conception of being derives from the forms

---

5. Guénon, "Oriental Metaphysics," p. 44.

6. René Guénon, *Introduction to the Study of the Hindu Doctrines*, translated by Marco Pallis (1945), p. 117.

and modes of reflexive knowledge and which denies the immediate and intellectual nature of the metaphysical, will in practice insist that art is the object of the secondary faculties of "emotion" and "feeling." Ours is perhaps the first culture to value independently and for their own sake the incidental aesthetic, emotional qualities of the auditory, tactile, and visual elements that are properly the *means* of art. In so doing, we appear to have relinquished the right to enquire of a work of art whether it is good or bad without first knowing "about" or "of" what it may be good or bad. In such a context, the idea that the various arts can be conceived as an analogical discourse in which Truth is embodied and reflected according to the nature of the activity of art itself must seem, to say the least, far-fetched. But only by such means can human creativity have an effective and living relationship to Truth. In any culture based upon the meaning and value of the sacred, through a qualitative cosmology, the contingencies of human existence are at all times orientated toward assimilation of the sacred as the ultimate reference of any human activity or aspiration. This being so, at any point in time or space an individual's existence can be symbolically related to two presiding ideas: that of its sacred center and that of its spiritual origin.

This, the metaphysical view as one might call it, acknowledges that, as the *disposition* by which we make things by the aid of a true rule (Aristotle),[7] art in all its modes of making and doing, is the application and extension of principles which must be subject to the criteria of the intellect. This implies that, for the artist, immersion in the purely personal and individual for its own sake is meaningless when the subjective as such cannot be situated within a context relating it to the destiny of the whole man—body, soul, and spirit. For the artist so situated, art is the making manifest of that which is at once "hidden" and "revealed" in the cosmos—it is to render the events of this human life after the "model" of an archetypal world of the Spirit. That is, for traditional man "neither the objects of the external world nor human acts, properly speaking, have any autonomous intrinsic value. Objects or acts acquire a

---

7. Aristotle's is only one such formulation; the Scholastic definition of art as a "virtue of the practical intelligence" would do equally as well.

value, and in so doing become real, because they participate after one fashion or another, in a reality that transcends them."[8]

The analogical cosmologies that are the qualitative discourse of the sacred traditions are the only properly comprehensive re-presentation of the sacred since, in the integrality of the tradition in question, they are rooted in the Divine Principle itself. Functioning within the spiritual context of such a traditional cosmology intelligence participates in the essential reality of the Cosmos. In this way, what man is and does is experienced in a paradigmatic fashion that contributes to the regeneration of the primordial Unity of all things. By disregarding metaphysical intuition, modern man's thought is cut off from the modes of reality by which it could attain to an apprehension of the Creation and man's place in it as the interplay of theophanic energies. That is to say, of experiencing the Creation, in all its variegated wonders as the expression of a redemptive cosmic environment. It is further to say that modern man lacks any guide that would lead him to a point from which time and space can be seen to be metaphysically "unreal" when experienced as anything other than the projection of a timeless Now without extension and duration.

Such a moment, paradoxical to common experience, can be known by means of the mediating symbol—whether in the formal symbol itself, in ritual—that is "symbol in action"—or in the "crystalized" archetypal experience of mythical structures. The analogical language of these symbolic perspectives prepares us for the regenerative experience of the sacred. Traditionally, man, created in the divine image, does not identify himself with his psycho-physical being. For him, as Mircea Eliade has written,

> an object or an act becomes real only in so far in so far as it imitates or repeats an archetype. Thus, reality is acquired solely through repetition or participation; everything which lacks an exemplary model is "meaningless," i.e., it lacks reality. Men would thus have a tendency to become archetypal and paradigmatic. This tendency may well appear paradoxical, in the sense that the man of a traditional culture sees himself as real only to the extent that

8. Mircea Eliade, *The Myth of the Eternal Return*, translated by William R. Trask (1954), pp. 3–4.

he ceases to be himself (for a modern observer) and is satisfied with imitating and repeating the gestures of another. In other words, he sees himself as real, i.e., as "truly himself," only, and precisely, insofar as he ceases to be so.[9]

In contrast, modern man, in as much as he is the embodiment of his own theoretical construct of himself, can only postulate his "self" by means of the interaction of his bodily experience with his psychological personality. But at any given moment his personality, as a postulation, is no more than a sequence of observed behaviors linked to form a continuum that he thinks of as "himself." But in such a continuum he is always becoming something else and so his identity, *who* he is, has no permanence, except in a very conditional sense. Only in the non-discursive essence of intellect can man be said to participate in what is immutably real, and therefore unconditionally true—a truth that is both metaphysically and logically the prior reality and ground of everything that "was" or "is to come." We recall Aristotle: "Nothing is more true than the intellect." Eternity is more true than time since time is a projection or moving image of the Eternity from which it derives its reality. Time can only proceed on the basis of a stasis that alone could give meaning to the notion of a "beginning of Time"—a presence altogether beyond even an indefinite extension of duration. Intuition itself shares in this relationship in that, being infallibly and immediately identifiable with Truth—the eternal moment that is *Now*—it forms of necessity the absolute stasis on which the contingent existence of the knowing subject is projected. Thus the conditional reality of the psycho-physical self can be likened to a shadow that, because it has a discernible presence, thinks of itself as an autonomous agent.

The close alliance of sapiential doctrine with human knowledge throughout the Middle Ages in Europe characterizes those centuries as Europe's most metaphysical age. Yet even during this time the language of metaphysics and the language of theology were not clearly differentiated. Even here intellect was conceived in the mode of rational thought. The idea of intuition was colored by the forms of empirical knowledge. In time this in itself permitted the emer-

9. Ibid., p. 34.

gence of the characteristically modern, humanist, and materialist view of the Creation,[10] a shift of perspective that eventually led to the supremacy of those modes of knowledge for which psycho-physical experience is the model. The collapse of Scholastic doctrine in the fourteenth century lent strength to the polarization of thought toward human, as distinct from sapiential knowledge, eventually leading to the eclipse of the metaphysical perspective as the primary orientation of intelligence.

Although Scholasticism was directed toward the sapiential and metaphysical essence of man, its rationalist bias, by marginalizing the intuitive "ground" of knowledge, eventually neglected, as it were, to acknowledge its own non-discursive essence. This prepared the way for the assimilation of the spiritual discourse of theology to philosophical metaphysics. What the dissolution of the medieval cosmology permitted was

> the destruction of the idea of a qualitatively and ontologically dif-ferentiated world, and its replacement by that of an open, indefi-nite and even [quasi-] infinite universe, united and governed by the same [general] laws; a universe which, in contradiction to the traditional conception with its distinction . . . of the two worlds of Heaven and Earth, all things are on the same level of Being. . . . The Laws of Heaven and the laws of Earth are merged together. . . . And this implied the disappearance from the scientific outlook of all considerations based on value, on perfection, on harmony, on meaning and on purpose.[11]

10. One should add that the modern age is no longer "humanist" in the Renais-sance sense but continues to show every sign of an increasing dehumanization—the logical end of the humanist view?

11. Alexandre Koyre, *Metaphysics and Measurement* (1968), p. 20. It is necessary to change "universal" to "general" in this passage since what the author has in mind is a knowledge accessible to the discursive faculty which itself is closed to all that is truly universal. Such "laws" pertain to the individual order of manifestation. As Guénon has pointed out, it is important to distinguish the universal from the gen-eral, thereby saving endless confusion, seeing that the terms have become inter-changeable in modern speech. The "universal" is not a summation or collectivity of all particular things, any more than the infinite is an indefinite summation of the finite, or eternity the indefinite extension of time. And this accounts also for the addition of *quasi*.

Thus theology, philosophy, art, the sciences, gradually shorn of their qualitative and unifying cosmology, gained in independence and increasingly aligned themselves with a model of knowledge derived from empirical experience.

Thus, immediate "reality" rather than the ultimately Real, by subtle degrees became the arbiter of artistic value, whether as the direct perception of phenomena in the visual arts, or as "feeling" response in the auditory arts. Individual experience was to be the basis of all thought and action. Art was directed toward personal emotion. Henceforth, only the faculties of the psycho-physical self were to be called upon for their subjective response. Meaning, in the arts, began its descent toward gradually accepting only a psychic or phenomenal source as the causal "energy" of all creating and perceiving.

This capitulation to a psycho-physical order of things eventually replaced the medieval conception of intellect as something divine that underwrites the arts by means of which man creates according to the laws of a paradigmatic model of supra-human inspiration. The divine nature of the intellect as knowing subject was essential to all medieval thought, which never forgot man's immortal destiny. St. Bonaventure, with an eye fixed on the ultimate goal of man, speaks of a divine rather than a "psychic" faculty when he comments, in *Retracing the Arts to Theology,* that the purpose of the artificer is to make visible in his works that which is eternal and invisible so that all men might be lead through such creations to the Creator. He continues: "If we consider the *effect* [of the artefact] we shall see therein the *pattern of human life* for every artificer, indeed, aims to produce work that is beautiful, useful, and enduring, and only when it possesses these three qualities is the work highly valued and acceptable."[12]

For all that, medieval man still did not "know" God except as a final cause. He was the supreme principle of a metaphysics that crystalized its approach to the Infinite in a logic that was refractory to its real mystery. Between the medieval, Christian view of God as

---

12. The translation of Bonaventure, *De reductione artium ad theologiam*, is that of Sister Emma Therese Healy (1955). With the Renaissance the beautiful and the useful are seldom thereafter to form a unity in the West.

the Creator of the world *ex nihilo*, and the eighteenth-century view of Him as some huge mechanical inventor, a power appealed to to account for the creation of atoms there was no middle ground. The real spiritual need of man, how an understanding of God—the assimilation of the Divine—can lead to a discernment of the Real and the illusory and an attachment to the Real, is side-tracked into the problem of how the intelligence can rationally account for the reality we call "God." Nonetheless the medieval view was able to acknowledge a divine cause and a spiritual end for the contingencies of human thought and action. And it did permit a symbolic and contemplative view of nature interpreted in terms of substance, essence, matter, form, quality, and quantity, and not, as with the rationalist science of the seventeenth century, in terms of space, mass, energy, and the like. As Seyyed Hossein Nasr has observed:

> The Middle Ages thus drew to a close in a climate in which the symbolic and contemplative view of nature had been for the most part replaced by a rationalistic view, and this in turn through the criticism of nominalist theologians had led to philosophical scepticism. Meanwhile, with the destruction of the gnostic and metaphysical elements within Christianity the cosmological sciences became opaque and incomprehensible and the cosmos itself was gradually secularized.[13]

The Renaissance began a development that subtly changed the symbolic and mythical expressions of metaphysical truth. If the Middle Ages accepted these modes of analogical discourse as the outward, tangible expression of a hidden, intangible reality, then the Renaissance reversed the process and instituted the study of myths, concentrating upon the problem of whether or not myths are objective, historical facts, and, if not, what their "inventors" intended by them.

When we consider the thought and art of the new secularism, we discover in them an over-riding concern for "self"-expression and "self"-analysis. We witness the beginnings of the artist as a "personality"—the historical perspective gains increasing validity. After the

---

13. Seyyed Hossein Nasr, *The Encounter of Man and Nature* (1969), pp. 63–64.

Divine Comedy the question of whether it is valid for a life or a work of art to represent an eternally present heavenly model or prototype was pushed to the margins of thought and artistic experience. Increasingly the artist strives to place his art in the context of profane history and secular values. And this characteristic becomes increasingly important for a viewpoint which, lacking a cosmology that validates the passage of time in terms of sacred history, is increasingly weighed down by the cumulative content of an ever-evolving existential duration. Hence an escape from this burden is sought in elaborations of retrospective thought or abstract idealism. It is here that we find the nineteenth-century hypostatization of history prefigured. In the centuries before Dante a metaphysical viewpoint made of this life a preparation for the life beyond. A need to escape into the past would only have been conceivable in terms of a return to the paradigmatic "Golden Age." Although the thought and art of the two centuries that followed Dante did not see man as a completely autonomous being or deny the gift of Grace there is little doubt that it was the sensational nature of the individual human spirit that was its central motif.[14]

The Renaissance was the beginning of the discovery that the world need not be considered a mirror of a celestial reality, and that man might be considered in existential isolation from the Divine. And since this entails the beginning of the abolition of even human values, God in turns becomes merely a principle of a theoretical metaphysics—as He is in Descartes where, once he is "proven," He

---

14. "Sensation is very frequently identified so closely with Self that it is held to be the deepest level of man's being. In the western world it so happens that feeling is more usually identified with the Self than any other faculty, for which cause the feeling element in religion—moral value, ecstasy, consolation—is apt to be regarded, not as analogy of the ultimate Reality, but as its very essence. This predominance of what Guénon terms the 'sentimental' element in religion gives the modern Christian a standpoint from which metaphysics seems cold, amoral, and impersonal, if not absolutely meaningless." Alan W. Watts, *The Supreme Identity* (1950), p. 73.

is best forgotten. But more than anything else is incurred the loss within every intellectual discipline, of that sapiential dimension upon which all knowledge depends, and by means of which the mind has its hold upon the qualitative essences of things. In myth, symbol, and in art generally, metaphysical truths become opaque to the intelligence. The great delight of the Renaissance intellectuals was to study the ancients as *allegory*. The studies of Gombrich, Wind, Panovsky, and Seznec demonstrate that, because of the increasing validity of the historical perspective, the Renaissance artists and poets looked back to the Greek and Roman mysteries to allegorize them into morality figures. Thus the symbolism of the Middle Ages, having lost its contemplative basis, begun to veil rather than *reveal*.

In as much as modern man is heir to the Renaissance, so he is the victim of these metaphysical transpositions effected during the all-important years between 1400 and 1600. It may be that philosophy in the West is still prepared to postulate to the rational intelligence that there remains a portion of man's being that transcends both time and space; but that man is made *in the image of God*, in the milieu of the arts, is now a proposition rarely defended. The sapiential doctrines of the sacred traditions nonetheless are founded upon just this principle: that there is in man an immortal Spirit and a mortal soul and the immortal Spirit is the *essence* of every being as well as its ultimate end. The Renaissance and every humanist development since have seen to it that man remains subject both to a nature opaque to his thought and to truths contingent upon merely personal experience. It is more than possible to argue that thought and art since the beginning of the Renaissance have "descended" through the hierarchy of the faculties so that today all they demand is a mere passive ideation or *sens*ation. The loss of objective criteria implicit in such a descent limits the intelligence to merely subjective truth or falsity, seeing that it is the hopeless prisoner of a "self"-willed autonomy. In this measure the modern mind can be likened to a man of partial sight staring into a shattered mirror.

4

Art: For Whom and for What?

The father that dwelleth in me, he doeth the works, . . . believe me
for the very work's sake.

JOHN 14:10–11

One whose understanding is deluded by egotism thinks: "I am the
doer."

BHAGAVAD GITA 3:27

NOTHING engages us with such seeming ease and naturalness as the
feeling that we *are*, in some interior sense, and that we are called
upon in life to take action in a world external to us. The reality of
both the subjective "I" we suppose and the objective world we act
upon is something we seldom stop to question. The potter who
makes a pot could hardly doubt that he is a "someone" who manip-
ulates a substance called clay that is "other" than who he is. That the
effect of his taking certain actions results in an object that has been
caused by those actions. The potter's sense of the reality of this situation is fundamental to all acts of making and doing. After all, to
make anything is to see an object take shape under our very eyes as
the result of actions we have taken, whether by deliberate intention or
intuitively as we say when we are unable to rationalize or recall the
mental processes that guide us toward certain choices and not others
in order to effect the outcome of those actions. That much is obvious.

Or is it? Will the truth of this situation bear scrutiny? Or might
we conclude, on closer examination, that what has so far been
assumed owes more to unthinking habits of thought and reaction
than to the underlying reality of the process? And if we should be so
persuaded, what implications follow from our unmasking a state of
affairs that seems so incontrovertibly true from repeated experience? It is the purpose of this chapter to explore what underlies
these habits of perception.

There are some things we do not see. Not because they are immersed in a darkness we cannot penetrate but because they are possessed of a blinding brightness that obscures their presence. Such things escape our perception because they are too close to us. If you look straight into a light, before long you see only darkness. Metaphysical truths blind us precisely because they form the pre-conscious condition of all our thinking. The superabundant illumination of the spirit makes possible every mode and manner by which we attempt to define and objectivize our identity and our destiny. Metaphysical truth orientates us in this way for the very reason that we are its *place* of manifestation. "If the doors of perception were cleansed everything would appear to man as it is, infinite," said Blake.

In living a life, even in its most simple and unregarded actions, we respond to certain positive and negative possibilities. Sometimes with careful deliberation, sometimes with an instinctive impulse, we choose one path of action against another. While it is certainly true that some of what contributes to such actions will be responses acquired as a result of our experience of sensory data, nonetheless our responses can also include a sensitivity to and an appreciation of such things as love, justice, and beauty that in themselves transcend our mundane life as such. Indeed, it is doubtful whether we could lead any sort of life worthy of the name without the intervention of these things.

All this would seem to indicate that, even in what might be our most unregarded actions, we have already presupposed a potential if not actual pattern that life might take, a path to be followed that we in part create rather than simply accept as inevitably laid down for us. And such a pattern, at some deep level, might hold the key to the implied principle life should conform to if it is to be more than just the continuum and accumulation of events and actions that, in flowing through it, make up our everyday experience. Might we not go so far as to say that we only truly act when we fully realize just such a pattern—when it is a life-informing reality for us—since anything less must be a *reaction* to some circumstance imposed upon us; an imperative for which we are the passive agent?

Can we not go one step further and acknowledge that it is in the nature of this pattern that it should enable us to recognize that our lives are somehow inadequate, somehow fail to realize their full potential, if we ignore the validity of this pattern to shape our experience in accordance with its ultimate significance—the cardinal end of life itself? For the ephemeral and fleeting strands of experience that are woven into the fabric of our everyday life, as we all recognize, inescapably involve some sort of evaluation. And this in turn, if we are not to be condemned to invincible ignorance, implies that we already possess within ourselves some adequate principle from which to derive the ultimate meaning of life itself—some fundamental precept that is "other than" our reactions to the shifting panoply of appearances and substances that confront us on a daily basis. And can we not say that, as a result of our possession of such a principle, one that is "other than" the constant interplay of subjective reactions to objective events, all things point to something beyond themselves? Proof enough of this possibility is the fact that we are able to pose the question "From whence?" and its corollary, "To what end?" In other words to pose such questions in itself indicates that there is something of our being capable of recognizing the diminishment implied by the absence of any answers to such questions—a recognition of some principle not derived from but possessing, as it were, an adequacy not found in the life of external experience.

And, to take one further step in this line of argument, given our possession of the faculty of objectivity (for that is what it amounts to, and without which we would not even conceive of a subject) we must conclude that the totality of our experience is not confined exclusively to a self-contained prison of phenomenal appearances and chronological events. That man himself contains an organ of knowledge that possesses of its nature the unity of wholeness we recognize must underwrite the diversity and multiplicity of the world of empirical experience.

If this puts what seems like too heavy an emphasis on the internality of experience, at the expense of the world of external objects we find ourselves obliged to acknowledge and deal with, then perhaps we ought to recall how little effect, in recent centuries, so-called progress, civilization, and the trappings of culture have had on ridding man of his imperfections and his inadequacies. These are the very things that are founded upon his false identification with that subject or ego that precludes him from attaining those qualities of his being he might judge to be his proper nature rather than his attendant failings.

The ego, or empirical self, is that which, assuming the identity of an agent, ascribes to itself the reality that is the generality of psycho-physical activity. But the fact that the ego can never objectivize itself, can never purify itself of that to which it is a response, is sufficient indication that it cannot be the ultimate agent of action. What the ego knows is in truth a series of interactions or *re*-actions in the sphere of empirical existence from which it is never free, by reason of the fact that, as René Guénon reminds us, "action cannot have the effect of liberating from actions." And, as Ibn ʿArabī observes, "outward existence can perform no act of itself" since it depends upon an agent or principle that is free and objective in relation to the aggregate of existential experience. It follows that, not only is the ultimate agent of action located beyond the sphere of psycho-physical experience, but that, as Ibn ʿArabī goes on to point out, this very "outward existence is passive, and action cannot be attributed to it."

The implication for the artist of this metaphysical view of things is, to say the least, far-reaching. Nothing less than to see that the truest action of the artist—the maker—is not so much the effort of a subject to shape an objective substance that is *other* than himself but a response to circumstances which in the fullness of their denotative compass seek to locate and celebrate the ultimate nature of the "doer." In the light of a metaphysics that does full justice to the amplitude of our perception of what distinguishes the Real from the illusory, art ought not to be the demonstration of those feelings and responses we ascribe to the personal ego, but an effort to realize the intrinsic coherence of things as we participate in it and as it comprises the essential order of being. Plato's banishment of the artist from his ideal Republic was precisely on the grounds that the expression of ego—the art of false ascription—disrupts the harmony that is the universal order that coheres in all things. This makes perfect sense of those traditional texts that speak of the artist (artisan) as one who upholds the order of the universe, as well as those texts that speak of the disequilibrium that follows from the production of things for personal aggrandizement: "Destruction of the natural integrity of things, in order to produce articles of various kinds, this is the fault of the artisan" (Chuang-tzu [Zhuangzi], 9).

It is now widely admitted that the crisis which confronts the westernized world stems directly from the reluctance of the modern mentality to admit that a worldview, conceived after the model of phenomenal reality and articulated in a rationalist science of materiality, is unable to reveal the source of those meanings and values by which life is ultimately lived. That is to say, the modern scientific worldview quite simply excludes an adequate principle for the raison d'être of human existence. This is nothing more than to acknowledge that modern man, for some four centuries, has been heir to a culture that has attempted to function in denial of the metaphysical dimension of things. To all intents and purposes, and in every quarter, the unmanifest, supra-empirical perspective of unity, oneness, coherence, and ultimate permanence—always the implied context of meaning—that underwrites all possible reality is glossed over. Instead of seeing this hidden—better say veiled—context as the timeless source and final term of all human endeavor, this eternal perspective is simply set aside and considered as an irrelevance when it is not denied outright. In thrall to the materialist model, so far as westernized consciousness is concerned, the natural world has to be understood on its own terms and without reference to any principle or criteria that is beyond or outside it, an experience of life circumscribed on the one hand by ego-bound consciousness and on the other by sensory data or its mathematical surrogate.

Given the all-pervasive sense of relativity and impermanence that characterizes the consciousness of those incapable of surmounting this state of affairs, to insist on an immutable, eternal core at the heart of human experience must seem at best a case of special pleading, at worst an act of perversity. However, it is not a matter of supposing that such an immutable core, were it real and effectively present in things, would be immediately apparent and discernible without the least effort or preparation on the part of anyone who wishes to know something of it, any more than it is a question that, because of our existential condition, we are of necessity forced to accept the world's insufficiencies as the sole claimants to our attention. In any case, against *what* are such insufficiencies to be demonstrated? No. It is more a question of real needs and what it means to satisfy a real need.

In this respect the secular man of westernized consciousness is like one who comes to a feast at which every conceivable luxury is laid out before him. But he arrives without even a conception of what it means to have a real taste, a real appetite. (Eric Gill once remarked, "a real taste is a mortified taste.") The situation in which modern man finds himself, the feast to which he is bidden, is one in which he supposes that he has access to the whole history of man's cultural heritage. In books, films, recordings, libraries, exhibitions, archives, museums, computer files, and the like, from the most profound masterworks of spiritual enlightenment down to the humblest tribal artifact, the entire sum of man's cultural endeavor seems to be his for the asking. Yet there is a price to pay.

The configuration of historical events that permits such a feast to be arranged is the very same one that grants man the illusion that he does actually have access to the inner riches of this heritage. This illusion, nothing less than the fact of his secularized consciousness, is the very same illusion that obscures that amplitude of his being that he must actualize within himself if he is to join with the *meaning* and *purpose* of all but a fraction of man's past spiritual attainment. For this dimension of his being, were it fully effective, would take him out of historical time—that "funeral cortège" of chronological events, as Henry Corbin called it—and situate his consciousness within the eternal perspective of the Sacred that is integral to a real attachment to the Divine: the same attachment, let it be admitted, which was the very occasion of that past cultural effort modern man is at such pains to amass, record, catalog, celebrate, explain, and promote. Except for the period of the classical decadence and the secular centuries of the post-Renaissance—from the elaborate geometry of the Gothic cathedrals to the most delicate tracings of the North American Indian sand painting, from the simplest steps of a peasant dance to the over-arching vision of the *Divine Comedy*—it has always been the purpose of art to situate man within a cosmological frame of reference that takes account of his ultimate destiny; to form the connecting link between his earthly experience and the light of the Divine Reality.

Like it or not, the eclipse in his being of that which actualizes his affinity with the Divine is the very same eclipse that allows secular modern man to become what he has become, a cultural polymath who consumes the spiritual culture of others because he cannot create his own, one who is dispossessed of the archetypal vision that alone gives access to the meaning of his spiritual heritage—the vision that alone validates a true culture. The real and urgent need of westernized consciousness is to be able to see beyond the ephemerality that now mesmerizes it to the point of obscuring its accordance with the Divine, in order to plunge the roots of its transient existence into that eternal principle which does not yield to the flux of a world that is ever-changing into something else, created and annihilated at every moment.

The advent of a purely empirico-historical view of the world has been largely responsible, not only for the impoverishment of art itself (an art for the most part content merely to record the passing show mirrored in the most fugitive of emotions), but also for a way of looking at works of art that tends to exclude the atemporal, supra-sensual origins of creative motivation. This way of looking at art also tends to obscure the fact that art is only partially explained by being studied in the historical context of its time. To study art as being of its time is to approach it from the point of view of an abstract time that is lived by no one.

No man is wholly *of* his time, for man is joined to "his times," as Goethe noted, by his weaknesses. At the heart of his being he is his own time in a spiritual way analogous to that of the experience we each have of being at the center of physical space. Such is this "blinding" evidence that it is all too easily overlooked that only on the premise of a timeless dimension to subjective experience—the transcendent and supra-conscious witness to the fugitive reality of sensory data—can the cognitive polarity of consciousness function. Only on the basis of this inscrutable intuition can consciousness form that polarity without which there could be no conception of a subject facing or acting upon an object: the primary datum of all making and doing.

The difference in orientation is vital to an understanding of the studies in this book. For they all imply that the ultimate value of a work of art is not fully explained in any appreciation of how it is *of* its historical time, or even in the internal consistency of its making, but that the value of a work of imaginative vision (and all works of making must in some degree proceed qualitatively from imaginative vision) is integrally *of* the presence of its creator as he is located and identified with the timeless source of his inspiration.

Furthermore, these studies are meant to imply that we are able to grasp the value of works of art only to the extent that we have developed the capacity to be effectively present as a witness at the same source of inspiration. (Dante said the purpose of his masterwork was "to remove those who are living in his life from the state of wretchedness to the state of blessedness.") A work of art can only have a real and intelligible meaning, can only *signify* something above and beyond the complex of operative and aesthetic procedures that have permitted it to find its manifest form, in the effective presence of just such a witnessing subject. Now what is entailed by this?

Facts are *known* by, events *happen* to, circumstances are *part* of a subject without which these same terms would be meaningless. No man lives in future time, which is not yet, as no man lives in past time, which is no more. Yet, however closely we narrow the gap between them there still remains a dimensionless gulf that will not let future time be joined to past time. The very terms *future* and *past* imply a moment that is *now*. And all things live *now*, or they are not yet, or have been. Without a *now* past and future could have no reality since it is *from* this transtemporal moment we project a future, and *to* this same moment we recall a past. And it is *in* this moment that all human knowledge, in so far as it is present in consciousness, is present as living, coherent experience. Even the memory of past things and the forecast of future things takes place in the present moment. And what threads the warp and the woof of things and events to produce this coherence is the cognitive polarity of subjective and objective consciousness that is the *modus operandi* of the intuitive intellect. This intuitive intellect is the ultimate agent of the present moment in which all life is lived, the term to which all experience is brought. This is the true subject, the timeless witness to the fact that future time ceaselessly flows into past time yet, as witness, is never part of that past or that future.

Here we have to invert the all-too-prevalent habit of secular consciousness of seeing what a work of art implies by what can be deduced from it. We have to see what the undisclosed intuitive intellect itself implies—all those meanings that have their reality in virtue of the presence of this sapiential intuition and what it is its nature to mediate.

It has been the perennial purpose of works of imaginative vision, whether in symbolic forms, iconic images, mythical narratives, ritual enactment, as well as contemplative modes of experience, to highlight, to separate out from the attributes that comprise the jigsaw pattern of temporal causality, to affirm this permanent, metahistorical level of reference. The thesis of most of human culture, as the works of Ananda K. Coomaraswamy and others have amply demonstrated, is to validate at the highest cognitive level of metaphysical intuition, the true subject of human experience, the one who acts in transcendence of all the *re*-actions that make up our psycho-physical existence. It is this self that true art addresses in its effort to wrest consciousness from the *nihil* of endlessly mirroring surface phenomena one upon another—whether these be natural appearances or the infra-subjective vagaries of personal psychology. Traditionally, art keeps faith with a perspective that situates and unites man with a cosmic and eschatological frame of reference—not with the objective of robbing the particularity of each thing of its unique qualities, of dissolving *things* into disembodied, abstract conceptions, but the better to allow consciousness to grasp the way in which the particular and transient thing possesses an immutable essence; is a sign, is significant of, a specific quality of the Divine Reality.

At the heart of all cognitive experience there is a link, a reciprocity, between the immutable essence of every object and the intuitive core of every subject, which obliges us to recognize that art cannot properly possess a meaning that is wholly of itself. Arising from just such a reciprocity of object with subject, art applies a prior knowledge and extends an operative skill to ends other than the practice of art itself. Even when we recognize the extent to which art embodies values that are incommunicable by any other means, still it is never the cause of its own significance. Art has to be significant *of* something; it addresses itself to something other than itself. The thesis "art for art's sake"—even in the thousand disguises with which it bedevils our times—cannot escape its pretense that there are creative and imaginative values that are true in themselves without reference to the ultimate nature of the subject to whom they are of value. Valuation itself is inseparable from understanding, just as understanding is inseparable from intelligence. And intelligence demands an adequacy from all things that are placed under its scrutiny.

The chief purpose of the present chapter is to provide something of the metaphysical premises on which the studies in this book are largely based. Each study treats its subject *sub specie aeternitatis,* that is, from the perspective of permanence, and as a series of "places" or "junctures" at which certain artists have responded to the profound mystery of what it means to be a part of the Creation. The genuine artistic impulse springs from and is finally directed toward the metaphysical realm, and it is to that realm that these studies aim to be faithful. That being so each study proceeds from the necessity to have in mind an implied metaphysical context of wholeness and unity without which, as the poet Vernon Watkins observed, the artist works in confusion.

To approach a work of art from this point of view is not, however, to impose unwarranted and irrelevant criteria upon it. To talk, for instance, of the "real" and the "illusory" in connection with a work of art does not oblige one to point to the actual appearance of the terms themselves. Terms like *being, becoming, absolute, contingent,* and the like may not be found there. Nonetheless, that to which such words are directed is present by virtue of the fact that, as we have already argued, any act of human doing and making rests of necessity upon the effective operation of metaphysical pre-conditions. Moreover, to create a work of art is itself to imply, whether by affirmation or denial, that metaphysical assumptions are part and parcel of what it means to be a man as well as an artist. As David Jones insists, "only men are artists and only artists are men." The relevance of the metaphysical for the study and practice of art is no different from what it is for any other branch of knowledge or activity. It is against the background of the Eternal and the Absolute that any temporal and any relative "event" takes place. When the *Garuda Purana* voiced that profound paradox to the effect that it is no use a man reading a book until he has understood it, it underwrote the paradox of all knowledge. In order to understand any one thing we need to understand everything.

It is the eternal soul—that which makes the subject truly human—that mediates the imaginative pattern in accordance with which a man *acts* in transcendence of all the reactions that make up his ephemeral worldly existence. For these reactions have no value when they are considered without reference to the hidden presence of the subject who is the "place" of their existence. It is this fact alone which makes an attempt to arrive at an understanding of this world on its own terms one that is bound to condemn man to the sterility and impotence of endlessly regurgitating the ephemeral contents of a life alienated from the very source of its own reality. If there is to be a true renewal of meaning and value in our lives, and so in our art, it cannot come about simply from arbitrarily rearranging our reactions to life's external circumstances, where, inescapably and remorselessly, we would in any case be obliged to admit to an implied, pre-existing pattern according to which the new arrangement must be conceived. Such a pattern can only be located at its innermost source, where our true subject is rooted in the timeless matrix from which all orientation and renewal proceed.

5

Of Art and Skill

PLATO, in stating in the *Gorgias* that he could not fairly give the name "art" to anything irrational, was no more than restating a teaching of Pythagoras, who is said to have taught that art is a habit of co-operating with reason. Aristotle, in his *Nicomachean Ethics,* extended the same line of thought in teaching that art is a capacity to make, involving a true course of reason. This doctrine makes it clear that the creative principle that is art is a rational habit or disposition of the mind to pursue a true course of action in making something. Thus, art stays inside the artist, being understood in terms of the imposition of form upon substance or matter—sound if he is composer, stone if a mason, and so on. But at a higher level it was understood as an analog of a cosmic principle, whereby the Logos, the Divine Reason, manifests itself in the world of created things. The human artist, by imposing order and beauty upon substance, operates in imitation of how God creates the beauty and order of the world, of how He shapes the order of the Creation from the Divine Intellect according to the cosmic possibilities that properly belong to it and thereby perfect its manifestation.

The teaching that "art" is intimately wedded to reason and rationality was propounded through the centuries in one formulation or another until the Scholastic masters of the Middle Ages. St. Bonaventure's *Retracing the Arts to Theology* was perhaps the last extended treatise to expound the doctrine of art, or making according to skill, as a type of rational wisdom that imitates, ultimately, a divine prototype. But that was then. We live now in different times. Few people today who think of themselves as artists would instinctively associate the practice of their art as being due to a habit of reason that has a cosmic significance.

We can hardly doubt that art, in our time, is widely thought of as something added to life, an optional extra, a diversion practiced by specialists whose products somehow transcend the more mundane requirements needed to sustain our material and economic existence. We are aware that, as if to counter this situation, it is often hinted (at least) that a degree of aesthetic gratification is a necessary part of maintaining our psychological health. This argument sometimes carries with it a tacit denial that such gratification was available to less sophisticated cultures than our own. And this despite the fact that our museums and cultural heritage sites present abundant evidence that culture, belief, vocation, livelihood, beauty, and utility were for these cultures unified to a degree that for us is clearly impossible.

Progressively, since the Renaissance, and as a result of the catastrophic divorce of beauty and utility, art has been both understood and practiced in terms of freely exercising a spirit of individual creativity. Indeed, we have perhaps pursued to its limit the idea that art is the expression of an autonomous principle of creativity owing little or nothing to the demands of reason and intelligibility. But this is all part and parcel of a trend in our time in which every idea seems destined to be tested to point of destruction. We have done this with the idea of art. But we have not cleared away the detritus of what remains. We go on with the practice of art assuming that a meaningful and coherent philosophy underwrites whatever is done in art's name. While at best we are in agreement that art is necessary and desirable, at worst much of what is currently presented as art, if our more avant-garde music concerts and art exhibitions are anything to go by, is little more than a pathology of irrational and abnormal behavior. No doubt this state of affairs has come about under the suasion of a tyranny that urges innovation in defiance of all meaningful criteria.

We have allowed ourselves to become habituated to using the term *artist* to denote one who creates works of art, but without giving much thought to what is intrinsic to the notion of artistry. Instead, we have drifted along with the vague assumption that the word *artist* designates a person of exceptional, aesthetic sensibility; and that whatever someone who possesses such a sensibility conceives and executes must be the thing we are obliged to call "art." But such an assumption will not stand up to scrutiny. Firstly, and most obviously, it makes it impossible to determine who, justifiably, can be said to possess the defining sensibility that is the mark of the artist in distinction from the broad range of people who are not thought to be artists but who nonetheless possess and exercise some measure of aesthetic sensibility in their work. Secondly, and interconnected with this shortcoming, the assumption does not allow for a definition of art itself as distinct from the outcome of any other act of making. These two primary weaknesses grow from the now ingrained acceptance of the idea of art as designating, exclusively, a category of external objects or productions having an aesthetic raison d'être of their own purely on account of the creator's special sensibility. In this view, quintessentially, art is something external to the artist, having been transferred to the object by an acquiescent consent that art is whatever it is that creative artists do. This further assumption gives rise to a widespread and pressing need to answer the question "What is art?"—a question that so readily comes to the surface in almost any current discussion or appraisal of works of contemporary art. This need is felt alike by the expert no less than by the inexpert.

A change in the way in which we think about art would therefore be timely. To this end we could do no better than return to the traditional and universal understanding of art,[1] one that is more faithful to both the nature and function of art itself, as well as to the wider role it plays in the order and maintenance of civilized society. This would mean that whenever we think of art or refer to an artist we ought to make a mental note that the word *artist* refers to one who is a skilled maker and that art itself is the perfection of work. Aided by this habit we would be reminded on each occasion of the primary meaning of the word *art*. Our word *art* comes from the Latin *ars*, "a fitting together." *Ars* also designates "skill" and "craft."

---

1. See the author's *Every Man an Artist: Readings in the Traditional Philosophy of Art* (2005), which, with its bibliography, might serve as an introduction to this wide-ranging subject.

Our word *skill* has come down from the Middle English *skile,* meaning "discernment"/"judgment." We would do well to remind ourselves also that such terms as *artistry, work, craft, masterpiece, vocation,* and *talent* all inescapably imply the sense of a mastery of means applied to a given end: an appropriate and just application of a wisdom that is at once of the mind and of the body to a given, intelligible, and practical end.

To the extent that there is any confusion as to what is meant by the word *art,* that confusion arises from the fact that our use of that term has, as it were, come adrift from its moorings in this primary sense of being the deployment of a faculty that is as much to do with how we think—how we apply the mind—as it has to do with what we apply it to. All too often the intrinsic, time-honored resonances that are implicit in the notion of art as a skill in predisposing the mind to work fruitfully with reason, are absent from our understanding of what art is. This being so we might venture to recover some of these resonances by examining in more detail what is implicit in the notion of skill itself.

To speak of skill is to speak necessarily of something that is exercised in being applied to something other. Skill cannot be exercised in isolation from something that is thereby altered for the better by its application. The change made by the application of skill comes about in some mode or manner according to both the receptivity and resistance of the other. Skill can no more be exercised in the face of total resistance than it would be needed where its application could produce no effect or gain. Therefore, to speak of skill is to recognize a greater or lesser degree of mastery. Such mastery must be present in the one who exercises skill as well as evident in that to which skill has been applied. This in turn means that both that which applies (mental and bodily effort) and that which is applied (intelligible and practical command) face some inherent opposition in the circumstances that require the exercise of skill. In addition it must be recognized that mental irresolution, physical infirmity, and intellectual confusion, as well as the frequent intractability of whatever skill is applied to, all contribute to the conditions under which skill is directed to overcome this opposition.

To be skilled is more and greater than to be unskilled in an order of values established by convention and precedent in any field of applied skill. It is naturally unjust to value and reward unskilled work over and above skilled work. This is due to our innate recognition that skill, in being applied, must in some measure envisage a given result that cannot be achieved without the proper exercise of skill. It is not the moral worth of the desirable end that is in question here, for skill in itself is concerned only with the good of its exercise, not with the good of the end to which it is applied. A just valuation of skill is due because the exercise of skill facilitates the achievement of a given end, not the desirability of the end itself— the production of an efficient murder weapon, for instance. Where would be the justice in rewarding what thwarts a desired end over and above what facilitates it? This principle of just valuation is as true of the skill of the murderer and the maker of chairs as it is of the philosopher.

The implication of all this is that a degree of knowledge and discernment must be possessed by anyone who wishes to exercise skill and that that knowledge and discernment involve a fuller grasp of reality than would exist if that knowledge and discernment were absent. It would be contrary to, and therefore a perversion of, the nature of intelligence to assign a greater significance and merit to the unskillful than to the skillful in achievements of a like nature.

The final goal of skill implies the perfect integration of conception and execution. This presupposes an effective correspondence between the state of mind of the worker and the circumstances that call for skill's application. These circumstances may themselves be of the mind (there is a skill in the proper application of intelligence), or of the handling of the things that make up the practical and material fabric of life. In both cases precedent and convention form the basis on which the exercise of skill proceeds, even though they are not the necessary criteria for artistic value. Precedent and convention must, however, necessarily form the implicit condition for the exercise of skill. No one sets about applying skill at random with a completely blank mind and in a spirit of total innovation.

The aptitude implied by skill presupposes an ability to envisage in the mind appropriate action and effective realization—*what* needs to be done and *how* it can be done. Both are largely cultural acquisitions shaped by past practice and experience. To want always to break with convention (that self-indulgent dream of the avant-garde) in the name of a creative spirit that believes that innovation has an absolute right to impose itself upon the making of anything, is to pursue the chimera of a freedom that is quite literally without meaning. It is akin to believing that to give free rein to a spirit of mischief in changing the shapes of the letters of the alphabet *at will* would increase the expressive powers of language. This in turn would be to pretend that we are obliged continually to invent reality rather than, as our possession of intelligence discovers, reality is that to which we must continually align our experience if we are to understand it. It is here, in the complex interweaving of convention, precedent, memory, and imagination, and much else that is necessary to the practice of any art, that we most clearly witness the impoverishment brought about by allowing the idea that the artist is a skilled maker to be eclipsed by the assumption that he or she is a purveyor of aesthetic sensation and idiosyncratic production.

The fact that skill, as a practical wisdom, necessarily depends upon memory and imagination and therefore upon precedent and convention indicates that skill cannot be meaningful independently of a set of values and criteria that make possible agreement as to the merit and relevance of its exercise. That is to say, for skill to be effective there must be a measure of consensus as to the appropriate occasion and conditions for its application. And since skill is something applied to something other than itself, the merit of its application cannot inhere in skill itself. To exercise skill for its own sake is to make of means and ends one and the same thing. But, properly, the applied end of skill is determined by the values and criteria that themselves determine the merit of its application. Without these values and criteria there can be no assessment of skill since, in the absence of any distinction between means and ends, there is no way to judge how means have served ends. All of which is to say that the exercise of skill implicitly recognizes a standard against which its application is necessarily evaluated, a standard that is independent of the contingencies that warrant its application.

If the artist, as skilled workman, is not in possession of an appropriate skill, the result is noted as a deficiency. By definition a recognized failure to achieve a result cannot be accounted a greater or more complete accomplishment than failure to achieve a best result. Moreover, recognition of deficiency to achieve an end indicates that a desirable outcome must in some sense be discernible. It implies an evaluation against which the deficiency is proved. This evaluation is the measure of the ratio of intention to result. Without it there can be no recognition of the extent to which skilled application has fallen short of an intention to achieve an end result. Without such an evaluation can any artistic judgment be possible?[2]

The standard by which skill is judged must be held in common by both the maker and the informed patron. (There are many occasions when they will be one and the same.) If it is the skill of the maker to operate effectively toward a given end, then it is the skill of the patron to be able to appraise the outcome of the operation—the effectiveness of the means deployed to achieve a given end. The common end of a skilled operation and a desirable result would not be realizable were the value of skill not present in its application. To deploy skill without any conception of a desirable result would be to assume the autonomous value of each and every exercise of skill, as if there could be no comparison of one skilled application from another in circumstances of a like nature. But this is not how we experience the result of skill, where it is clear that some assessment as between one application and another arises naturally from the conditions of the application itself.

The values and criteria by which a legitimate end may be determined cannot include the arbitrary and the unintelligible. How could skill, by its very nature meant to effect a change toward improvement, be deployed toward that which by definition cannot be foreseen or toward that which is incapable of being understood? This would by no means bar the "happy accident," even if it must be

---

2. See Ananda K. Coomaraswamy, "Intention," in *Selected Papers*, vol. 1, *Traditional Art and Symbolism*, edited by Roger Lipsey (1977), pp. 266–75.

recognized that in so far as the exercise of skill is an acquired faculty, we would not undertake to perfect a faculty in the absence of any understanding of its possible outcome? This is tantamount to recognizing at a human level a truth that is equally applicable at a cosmic level whereby, as Plato states in the *Timaeus* (28a), "everything that becomes or is created must of necessity be created by some cause, for without a cause nothing can be created." In relation to skill, what constitutes a cause is a desirable end, and this is by no means limited to the production of a physical object or action. Human needs embrace the mind no less than the body. The skilled formulation of a metaphysical or religious truth is as necessary as is the production of the objects that facilitate daily life: "And I have filled him with the spirit of God, in wisdom, and in understanding, and in knowledge, and in all manner of workmanship. . . . And in the hearts of all that are wise hearted I have put wisdom, that they make all that I have commanded thee" (Exodus 31:3, 6).

We live in a time when the nature and merit of art has never before received so much scrutiny. This in turn generates an unprecedented quantity of evaluation and judgment as to the merit and/or greatness (or otherwise) of art and artists. But in the context of a more or less unrestrained freedom of personal creativity being accepted as the ultimate raison d'être for the practice of art, no standard (other than a consensus of opinion), nothing outside the act of making itself, permits the distinction of means from ends that must be the foundation of evaluation. For evaluation implies the presence or absence of accomplishment, else what would be the purpose of any evaluation? Is there not obviously a qualitative difference between the exercise of skill and random activity? No supposed artistic judgment pretends to make a valuation on the basis of effort alone. This would be to measure behavior rather than accomplishment. What draws us to a work of art (accomplishment) is not, or should not, be the personality of the artist, but the work's achievement in the context of conventions and precedents already established. There is no shortage of evidence to demonstrate that the tyranny of unrestrained innovation that is supposed to legitimize the spirit of creative freedom has in our time replaced the idea that rational habits of mind are the necessary predisposition for the practice of any work of skill. (To the extent that, for instance, it is now common for "conceptual artists" to exhibit work under their own name which they have not themselves executed.) This change in the way we think about art could have come about only by ignoring the fact that established conventions and precedents must be the implied cause of any attempt to break from or replace them. The creative strategy of an avant-garde amounts to moving continuously forward into a judgmental vacuum where criteria and values can have no applicability. In effect it is an attempt to repeatedly wipe clean the slate of past experience and wisdom—never to let it accumulate.

No real and effective assessment of the merit of a work of skilled making can be undertaken where the end to which the means of skill is applied is not in some sense disclosed by the work itself. This fact is as fundamental to any understanding of what has been lost by art when it is practiced in isolation from the normal context of the work and skill that supplies the needs of livelihood. It is also central to the problem we allude to whenever we ask of a work of art we do not recognize as such, "What is it?" We all know what a cup, or a chair, or an icon, or a cathedral is, and are able to recognize the value of their kind. In the sphere of the arts this act of cognition requires a generic identity for it to be meaningful. Without this identity we cannot know *what* is intended and all grounds for critical evaluation are thereby undermined. If "creative activity" is exercised without the objectivity generic identity provides, then it is difficult to see how any accomplishment can be measured. What are we to make, for instance, of a room where, simply, the light goes on and off, exhibited as a work of art? Any real and effective standard of art must in some measure be in conformity with past accomplishment and experience. This is no more than a recognition that each thing made by true art has a generic reality; a reality that is disclosed *by* the work of skill itself. No meaningful work of skill is undertaken without some knowledge of this generic reality, just as no art, whether it be that of farming, motherhood, the sculpting of statues, or the making of poems, is practiced on the supposition that the result is never seen, used, or appreciated by someone other than the artist.

In *re*-minding ourselves, then, of the tradition of thinking of art as a skilled making, "involving a true course of reason," we note that it is neither exclusively nor specifically the task of the maker to determine the appropriateness or otherwise of the need that calls for the production of a work of art. But it is specifically the maker's task alone to judge finally the success or otherwise of *how* a thing is made. The appeal to an unqualified and self-governing spirit of "creative freedom," however, cannot help but obscure the interrelation of productive method, accomplishment, and responsibility in the way that it obscures the distinction of means from ends. It is certainly unwise for man to be without all sense of responsibility for the results of his actions in any sphere. But in matters that concern the artist's responsibility for the outcome of his art, this clearly requires a legitimate objectivity in the deployment of means to achieve a given end: an objectivity that must by its very nature rest upon an adequate distinction of means from ends.

To suppose that art is the product of "creative freedom" alone, subjectivizes the richly complex process whereby a work of art comes into being, is comprehended, and valued. It does so by tacitly claiming that it is the inalienable right of the artist to set the terms of the wisdom and discernment that both the practice and understanding of art (skill) demand. But the complexity of this demand cannot do otherwise than accumulate deposits in convention and precedent, the disowning of which, in the name of innovation, is made in the face of the obvious truth that art (skill) is the means to effect an end that cannot be art itself.

Such confusions no doubt feed the current trend whereby artistic assessment and judgment seem to be largely in abeyance. Everything, it seems, has become grist to the mill of the "creative freedom" of the much-vaunted contemporary artist for whom "anything goes." Nothing can fail or be judged to be inadequate in such circumstances. This, in reality, is a state of self-imposed intellectual vacuity in which it is impossible to objectively establish the need, intelligibility, and valuation of the work in question. If the purpose of art is simply to exercise a creative freedom (in effect a license to indulge unintelligibility), then that exercise itself becomes both the means and the end of the experience that is "art." In which case how can what that exercise produces be justifiably offered for objective appraisal? Surely such an exercise would be its own reward regardless of anything incidentally produced in its name?

Nothing that has been said above should be interpreted as arguing that the exercise of skill is sufficient of itself to produce works of artistic quality. The doctrine of art as a discernment that remains in the artist certainly argues that skill is a necessary cause of works of art. It does not argue that it is the sufficient cause. In so far as the doctrine may act as a guide to the wisdom or otherwise of man's making and doing it might be said to guard against the inevitable productive and aesthetic impulses of man being given free rein in isolation from the practical condition of his environment on the one hand, and the integral requirements of his spiritual constitution on the other. For these are the polar axes between which the human state functions normally. The traditional doctrine of art as a pre-formal habit of reason undoubtedly implies that the production of works of art without skill is impossible. It says nothing about skill being an arbiter of taste. Who cannot call to mind many examples of art that exhibit a high degree of applied skill, yet are nonetheless repellent or perverse? There is, after all, such a thing as virtuosity just as there is decadence. The two are causally linked where skill conveys an impression of superfluity and uselessness. In such cases it can be a question of unintelligence and sentimentality over-playing the expressive means beyond what is sufficient for the formal demands of the production in question. The extravagances of the Baroque are hardly lacking in skill, even as their overweening embellishment suffocates the need for intelligent restraint in the expression of piety. Bad taste has to do with the artist not treating the substance he works with the integral truth due to its qualitative properties: objectively, an abuse of the material substance or subjectively, a perversion of the normal requirements of intelligence and sensibility—the sculptor who strives to make stone simulate as near as possible the sensuous quality of flesh, or the poet who plays upon base sentimentalities to secure the reader's sympathy for instance. Certainly skill is a dimension of the beauty of art since skill is needed to bring a work of art to its formal perfection, which must include the sense of its being fitted exactly to good and appropriate need and use. Excessive skill becomes bad taste precisely when it gives evidence of an element of deception—as we see hinted, albeit distantly, in the word *crafty*.

Nothing in the traditional doctrine of art as skill forbids or excludes the possibility, the desirability—even the necessity—of innovation. It certainly denies that innovation is itself the purpose and justification for art, which it does in the context of an understanding that sees innovation as naturally arising out of any particular need to guide the application of skill toward the realization of an idea. But innovation in this case would have no license to do more than what is required to realize the perfection of the idea in question. This integral perfection is not only what is compromised whenever innovation is pursued for its own sake; it is also what is absent from the pursuit of "creative freedom."

6

Man and Nature
as Polarities of the Sacred

For the invisible things of him from the creation of the world are
clearly seen, being understood by the things that are made, even
his eternal power and Godhead.

ROMANS 1:20

IN ANSWERING the question why it is we have the arts at all few
would disagree that they are practiced for the good of life. This is to
imply that the good is in some sense more than what life would provide without art. And a life without art would surely be little more
than the exercise of our animal faculties for the sake of pragmatic
utility. But on the evidence of the past we can recognize that the arts
normally function as the means to draw man toward the summit of
his full potential. Finding ourselves among the contents of many of
our modern art galleries, with their idolatrous displays of psycho-
effluent, we might well ask if this function is any longer being
served. Here we might well conclude that the arts, or rather the artist, has lost his way and has become the victim of his own cultural
decline. How has this situation come about?

It should be self-evident that art is being steadily depleted of
human relevance, meaning, and value, so that it is no longer
thought to occupy a central position in relation to our need to
engage with the presiding truths. It has to a large extent been marginalized by the sciences. Nonetheless, we are not entirely comfortable with this state of affairs, and remain suspicious of where
science might lead us. In other words, although we no longer use
the phrase, the "two cultures" debate is still with us. The effective
substance of this debate, that of one mode of discourse in conflict

with another, has as its tacit proposal that there are some people who possess what we might call a "scientific consciousness" and others who possess what we might call an "artistic consciousness," and these two types of consciousness never share quite the same view of reality.

In this supposed division of the arts from the sciences what has been left out of account is man himself, more precisely the nature of man in relation to the totality of the Real that at one and the same time surrounds him and permeates his being. So, to express the same problem more conventionally, we are here dealing with the division of mind from matter in the modern consciousness, a division that has forced apart the subjective and objective poles of consciousness. It is this final and radical division that has allowed the sciences and the arts to become two irreconcilable ways of viewing reality that in their combined effect tend on the one hand to abstract man from the outer world of his creaturehood, and on the other to foreclose on the inner world that is the domain of his imaginative and spiritual being.

What has happened to shape these two irreconcilable views? In relation to the "scientific consciousness" what has happened is that, with the all-pervasive influence of materialist thought-processes the modern mind equates those dimensions of reality that are perceived by the discursive faculties as actually corresponding to reality as such. By this means rational thought is permitted to impose its own patterns of logic upon the nature of reality, a process in which all supra-mundane qualities are, when they are not denied outright, pushed to the very periphery of consciousness. In effect any inquiry along these lines into the nature of reality becomes little more than a sort of eavesdropping onto the activity of observable phenomena while maintaining the pretense that the presence of the observer has little bearing on what is observed. Thus, for the scientific consciousness, mind becomes a sort of epiphenomenon of cognition faced with a fugitive "reality" that it attempts to shape and chart by a series of statistical and quantitative formulas. Outside the circle of those who are professionally concerned to promote this quantitative view of reality, the vision of life it presents is remote, intimidating, and of incomprehensible complexity. Such a view seems to suggest that man has been born into the world lacking the means to evaluate an experience of life necessarily defined in some measure by love, beauty, goodness, justice, and the like. That is to say, by truths inaccessible to the empirical proof the practice of science demands. In other words, the worldview of materialist science simply fails to satisfy what seems to be the integral need of our intelligence: to discern the ultimate nature of the identity and destiny of our common humanity.

Now, what has happened in relation to the "artistic consciousness"? Following in the wake of nominalism and the collapse of the Scholastic synthesis in the fourteenth century, gradually, European culture instituted a mode of perceiving reality as if it were no more than the rational and sensory perception of phenomenal appearances. Henceforth, immediate, sensory perception of outward appearances, and the rationalization of the knowledge this gave rise to, was to be the arbiter of truth. Reflecting this transformation of consciousness the task of artistic expression came to be that of representing outward appearances and (as if in summons to some principle of complementarity), the evocation of inner emotional states. In either case, the stimulation of aesthetic experience for its own sake was seen to be the justification for artistic expression. This development had two effects. Outwardly, it lead to a sentimental attitude toward nature, while inwardly art came to be thought of as designating a category of aesthetic objects set apart and in contrast to merely utilitarian things. This aesthetic category of "art objects" was isolated from the total context of human life and the means to livelihood, and by degrees took upon itself a raison d'être that appealed exclusively to the refinement of sensibility. The abnormality of this exclusively aesthetic view of art is evident from its tendency to regard human creativity as an autonomous need in man. It makes art a self-referring activity which is supposed to serve the "good of life" in a context in which there can be no other criteria of the good beyond that of aesthetic pleasure.

This development, over four centuries, had the effect of foreclosing on man's inner potential in such a way that the spiritual orientation of the soul has no integral part to play, either in the practical activities that comprise his livelihood, or in the aesthetic experience of the sensory data of his daily life. From the perspective of this "artistic consciousness" man is, as it were, compressed wholly into the passional dimension of his being, while nature itself becomes, finally, more or less redundant except as a repository of sensory stimuli. As a result, both the full reality of man's being and the full reality of nature are impoverished by a division in which man's spiritual development is curtailed in being set apart from the sacred unity implicit in the natural order of things. This curtailment, formed on the division of art from science, mind from matter, necessarily precludes the integral alignment and harmony of sensory perception, rational thought, and spiritual vision. We shall see in more detail the response of several artists to this state of affairs in Part II of this book, each of them, in their different ways, concerned with the healing of these divisions, a healing that can only come about by way of recovering the human self-image as comprising a threefold hierarchic structure of spirit, soul, and body.

According to the traditional wisdom man is created as a theomorphic being who at the level of his ever-changing bodily existence is more strictly described as a "becoming," and for whom Being itself is located in the supra-mundane origin and unity of all things. This means that from the primordial, metaphysical perspective the Real is located at the highest ontological level of being and not, as is the case with the modern mind, in the most minutely articulated particles of substance it is possible to quantify. Each of the three hierarchic levels or degrees of man's becoming has its *reason* (that by which it is accounted) in the level above it. The very life and essence of each of these levels is therefore under the rule of, and is fitted for, the perfection of the level above it. That this hieratic disposition of our being should have an upward orientation is consistent with its intrinsic order.[1] We can see this by considering the relationship

---

1. The spiritual necessity and the function of this hierarchic structure is explained by Augustine in this passage from his *De musica:* "It is necessary that the soul be ruled by a Superior and rule the inferior. That Superior is God alone; that

between ignorance and knowledge. The state of ignorance is, so to say, a state of unknowingness. Not to know is to suffer the deprivation and absence of what is greater than, what is beyond, any state of unknowingness. But in any subsequent state of knowledge ignorance is shown to be the insubstantial thing it is, rather as a shadow is removed by the introduction of light. In like manner each stage of our progress toward Truth itself is subsumed and included in the level above it until a state is reached where the knower and the known become completely identified and unified. We are here in a realm where, as Toshihiko Izutsu has pointed out, "differentiation or distinction means distance, and distance in cognitive relationships means ignorance."[2]

The three principal levels of the human state receive the *reason* of their being from the level above. That is to say the *reason* ("cause," "motive," or "validation" are all cognate senses here) of a thing is the universal principle and root of that thing. It is of the nature of intelligence to want to know the reason of a thing. To ask of anything "What is it?" is to enquire about the first cause of a thing: it is the act of knowing in drawing the knower toward what is to be known. In the *what* of a thing, in its cognitive essence, is to be found the *why* of a thing. That is, the motive of its characteristic qualities.

In our original threefold nature the highest level, Spirit, receives the reason of its being from that which is uncreated and beyond our being as such. In this uncreated essence the profound mystery of our human identity is finally located in that which is beyond the human. That is the meaning of Christ's words: "No man can be my disciple who hateth not his own soul"; and "he that would save his soul, let him lose it." Eckhart says, the highest point of the soul touches upon

---

inferior is the body alone ... as the entire soul cannot be without its Lord, so it cannot excel without its slave. But, as the Lord is greater than the soul, so the slave is less. And so, intent upon its Lord, the soul understands His eternal things, and then more fully *is*. The more also its slave *is*, in its kind, through the soul. However, on the other hand, neglecting the Lord, the soul, intent upon its carnal slave by which it is led into concupiscence, feels its movements which the slave offers to it and it *is* less." Quoted from *The Essential Augustine*, selected by Vernon J. Bourke (1971; repr., 2007), p. 47.

2. Toshihiko Izutsu, *The Concept and Reality of Existence* (1971), p. 9.

God. Thus, to the degree we are capable of the spiritual vision that is integral to this level of our theomorphic nature we are able to glimpse the *reason* in which all subsequent spiritual possibilities must be subsumed, the summit to which all religion and all art ultimately seek to draw us. This is the source of all things in that from it directly stems the first principle of the one sacred unity that in its transcendent aspect governs the order of all things, and in its immanent aspect is like a super-essential light at the core of all things.

The soul has its life from Spirit. In this middle realm the light of Spirit is reflected as in a mirror: the Divine reflected in the soul. Here, in the intuitive vision that is appropriate to its state, the gods and the angels come face to face with the human. But in addition, in the soul, rational (that is discriminative) knowledge has its seat, and by this knowledge we are not only aware of our own "personhood" but we are also able to recognize it as possessing the possibility of being greater than what constitutes merely our personal individuality.

The primary faculty of the soul is that of imagination, the soul's organ of cognition and vision, with its ability to form distinct images in imitation of sensible appearances in order to embody supra-mundane values and meanings. But the soul acts both as a mirror and as a window. The imagination is not limited solely to reflecting images from the natural world, for it is situated between the levels of sensory data beneath it and perfect cognition above it. Seeing that the vital operation of the soul is to draw us ever upward to this perfection it is its proper nature to reflect, this operation is the equivalent of polishing the surface of the imagination to the point where, rather than reflecting the images of the sensorium as in a mirror, it becomes transparent, like a window, so that we see *through* the images that are present there, and see them anew as illuminated by the light of the Spirit that now penetrates them. In this way imagination assumes its role of being an organ of active, spiritual perception that draws us beyond the transient appearance of things so as to enable us to contemplate their permanent, life-giving energies.

At the lowest level of our three-part nature the substance of the body is illuminated by the soul. Though it is renewed and sustained by physical matter as the organic sheath of the individual life nonetheless, the body gathers the life and reason of its purposes from the soul. Itself unilluminated the body is only properly at one with the world it inhabits when it reflects its actions and its appetites back in the direction of that which gives them meaning and value. The soul, in other words, is the repository of the reason or significance of whatever the body seeks to attain. Which is not to say that the body is of no importance or in any way to diminish its value. It is simply an acknowledgment that the direct and immediate experiences of the body, through the beauty and ugliness of its perceptions, the joy and pain of its transient passions and appetitive experiences, are only recognized as having these properties in the soul itself.

What possible use could we have for the "good" of art and nature were this not so? In the delight and immediacy of sensory experience—because it is a mode of knowledge—is nurtured a consolation for the lost paradise, that momentary freedom from restriction, a lifting of the burden of that corporeality which is inescapably the condition of our bodily existence in the world. "The road of excess leads to the Palace of Wisdom," wrote Blake. There is no joy in art or nature that is not in some sense a pre-figuration of the final triumph of the spiritual over the bodily.

In his commentary on the Book of Genesis, Eckhart reminds us of the earlier tradition of interpreting the story of Adam and Eve symbolically. He quotes Augustine to the effect that according to this interpretation the serpent signifies the sensitive faculty we share with the animals; Eve is understood as the rational faculty, or inferior reason, that is directed toward external things, and Adam the rational faculty, or superior reason, which adheres to God. Eckhart goes on to explain that "in the words 'serpent, woman and man' are expressed the substantial being and nature of the human creature and how it is constituted in relation to its principles and their natural properties."

This symbolic interpretation establishes at once the hierarchy of the faculties of our threefold state as well as implying the three ontological levels of reality to which they correspond: the Divine (sapiential wisdom), the intellectual (discriminative understanding), and the animal (sensory perception). These three levels can also be thought of as the divine, the intellectual, and the animal activities of the soul. As we shall see, this interpretation not only has profound implications for our understanding of the relationship of art and nature to our human vocation, it also offers a similar insight into the nature of the much-debated "dominion" that man is given over nature in Genesis, as well as the relationship between man and woman.

From a Christian perspective the Creation can be seen as a sacred utterance. According to the Gospel of St. John, "In the beginning" [in *principio*, in the first principle] "was the Word and the Word was God. . . . All things were made by Him . . . in Him was life; and the life was the light of men." Also, in Genesis, it is said that God created the heaven and the earth. Moreover, at its completion, it is said that "God saw everything that he had made, and, behold, it was very good." But in order to bring the Creation to its fullest completion— that it should reflect and realize the fullest potentiality inherent in it—God created Man "in our own image" from the same "dust of the ground" of which the earth and the other creatures were created. God "breathed into his nostrils the breath of life; and man became a living soul."

We see immediately that there can be no division of man from nature. Both are of the same "dust" as both are of the same "breath" that is the Logos, the primordially uttered Word which already was when all things began (which is to say, as all things begin nowever), and which therefore underlies all things, and which is the same breath as that of the life of man. The Word or Logos can also be thought of as a supra-luminary energy that, by degrees of emanation from its uncreated source in the Divine, is at last manifested in the corporeal light that illuminates the natural world, as well as irradiating each level of the threefold hierarchy. By this light each level is given its life. The light of Truth is reflected at the level of intellect, the light of understanding at the level of knowledge, and the light of beauty at the level of the created order of the world, finally becoming palpable as the light that permits us to witness the objects of nature.

Before the temptation (which is to say in the first principle of our constitution) Adam witnesses the Creation as a paradise, a living theophany in which the spiritual vision of pure intellect—the knowledge of the fully awakened soul—and the sensual experience of the life-given body are illuminated from a single, divine source enabling him to see and understand all things through the contemplation of the highest glory that is God. Thomas Traherne speaks from this perspective in his poem "Wonder":

> How like an Angel came I down!
> How Bright are all things here!
> When first among his Works I did appear
> O how their Glory did me crown!
> The World resembled his ETERNITY,
> In which my Soul did walk;
> And evry thing that I did see
> Did with me talk.

William Law also speaks of the "superior reason" of this act of visionary cognition in which the Creator and the Creation are seen in the light of their divine reciprocity:

Man, though fallen, has this strong *Sensibility* and reaching *Desire* after all the *Beauties* that can be picked up in fallen Nature. Had not this been the Case, had not *Beauty* and Light, and the *Glory* of Brightness been his *first State* by *Creation* he would now no more want the Beauty of Objects, than the *Ox* wants his Pasture enclosed with beautiful Walls, and painted Gates.[3]

After the Fall it was necessary for Adam to contemplate God through the things of created nature, the "inferior reason" of the perspective of earthbound cognition—the polarity implying division of subjective and objective experience—the necessity of which, Eckhart, elsewhere, explains: "If (the soul) could know God without the world the world would not have been made for her sake."

All this is to say that in the essential threefold structure of our being (we must remember it is a continuous and never-ending cre-

3. [From Law's "An Appeal to all that doubt, or disbelieve the Truths of the Gospel."—Ed.]

ation, its origin and end as near to us now as ever it was or is), aesthetic experience, discursive thought, and spiritual vision are ultimately strung together on a single golden thread; are ever the properties of the outflowing universal principle whose reason, or root, is the radiance, the breath of the divine substance. In the order created by this emanating principle we note that Adam and Eve, spiritual vision and rational thought, at this pre-temptation stage (we might say at this degree of being), are still "as one flesh," both "naked and not ashamed," as stated in Genesis.

Surely this has profound significance for how we interpret that much-disputed passage (Genesis 1:28) wherein Adam and Eve are granted "dominion" over "every living thing." This dominion was granted before the expulsion from Paradise, so we must acknowledge that their dominion has only an efficacy in virtue of the dynamic unity of spiritual vision and rational thought—in other words, the understanding of all things through the contemplation of God. Which is also to say that the governance of man over nature is granted in virtue of man's deiformity. Because man *was* once "naked and unashamed" he is (nowever and essentially) a unity with the cosmic, subtle, and phenomenal levels of the Creation. It is this centrality of his place in the order of created things that enables him, as it were, to transparentize the existential world and to transform its seeming solidness, to have the measure of its contingency in relation to the absolute its transience implies. In his dominion over nature man is not called upon to act *as if* he were God, but to act *in God's image*—to be witness to the sacred theophany that God saw was "very good."

The primordial human pair were created *after* God had made the world and all it contained. The sequence here is crucial. In creating the world God of necessity has to create a witness to the divine act of his creativity (which amounts metaphysically to saying that in the infinity of the principle there must be included the very possibility of an external witness to the principle itself, its own self-reflexive limit, created nature). Why else would there be a Creation? Man alone knows that created nature is dependent upon powers beyond nature itself. Which means that his "dominion" over nature must be responsible to those powers in virtue of the complementarity of his and its hierarchic constitution. It is this complementarity that proves the centrality of his position in the created order of things and bestows the right of his "dominion."

Man must act *in* nature. He cannot act neutrally as if outside of it. He has no liberty to absent himself either from the outcome of his actions or from the commonality of created things. Actions have outcomes, which in turn entails the possibility of success or failure. But by what criteria can he possibly deduce that he has failed or succeeded if the only standard he has is taken from nature itself; is already in nature? It is man's cognizance of powers beyond the Creation that lends the burden of his responsibility to, and must ever temper his dominion over, nature. Man, then, has no freedom without consequence to dispose of nature according to an arbitrary willfulness. He is such a creature that his freedom is to conform his creaturehood according to the order and luminescence of the sacred substance he recapitulates.

But we should not see a type of determinism in this orientation of man's freedom. Rather, it is man's deiform constitution that necessitates a share in the divine freedom. To Adam, as to Eve, and in distinction from all other creatures, is given the freedom of will to choose whether or not to eat of the fruit of the Tree of Good and Evil. In this freedom of choice is located the source of original sin. Adam is warned that eating the fruit will cause his death. That is, the faculty of spiritual vision not only proceeds from, but is nourished by, the Divine so that it sees all things as they subsist in the eternity of their original glory. But this vision of the ineffable is occluded whenever the soul's cognition is deflected so as to attend exclusively to the external, transient forms of created nature—phenomenal appearances. Eckhart points out that the highest part of the soul, intellect, the light of spiritual vision, exchanges a "mutual glance" with God. This is the natural origin of truth, founded in the root and source of all good. The pre-fallen pleasure of Adam in the Garden of Paradise is just such a "mutual glance," just as the "sorrow" and "desire" (mentioned in the Biblical account) of the fallen state of Adam's expulsion is Adam's apprehending the consequences of his dust-formed creaturehood.

We must remember that the precipitation of the Fall begins at the lowest level of man's threefold state, the serpent's temptation to Eve. This is the appeal of the faculties of "inferior reason"—sensory perception—to consider the fruits of this world as sufficient unto themselves. There would have been no substance, as it were, to the temptation were it not for this promise to the rational faculty that it would become divine in its vision—an inversion, be it noted, of the threefold hierarchy. That was the temptation; the promise that "ye shall be as Gods," and the creature of earthbound cognition should possess all things and be granted the vision of eternal simultaneity. Discriminative knowledge, then, foreclosing on its dependence upon the rule of the higher faculties of the spirit, is promised a vision of things as if it possessed God's eye-view of the Creation, that of the very weaver of the fabric of opposites; of good and evil, light and dark, heaven and earth, night and day, man and woman, life and death. That the warp and woof of this fabric is unknown to Adam and Eve before the Fall is signified by their being "naked and unashamed." Which is to say they know nothing of the cognitive division that is the polarity of past and present, male and female, subjective and objective worlds. In their pre-fallen state they possess a direct vision of the Divine Unity as it subsists within the division and refraction that is the multiplicity and concatenation of opposites. Adam is said not to have any sight until his eyes were opened after eating the fruit. His "closed eyes" thus indicate the interior gaze of the highest intellect upon the Divine Principle itself—the very source of the duality of things. It should not escape our notice that it is only after the expulsion that Adam and Eve *knew* the division of their sex.

Adam's act of free will, as it were willing his own death, and at the initial instigation of the serpent, begins the inversion of the proper order of the faculties. Now each level is in thrall to the ontological state of the level beneath it. The divine order is overturned; the primordial sin is instituted (*sin*, from the word for dis-ease, thus a disorder or dis-ruption in the qualities of a thing that prevents the perfection of the nature of that thing). Eckhart glosses the word *evil*: "It is order that makes something good, so that it is impossible for there to be good outside order and conversely for there to be evil where order exists." Having no longer the vision of the Divine Unity contemplated only in the perfect alignment of the threefold hierarchy of states of being, Adam's and Eve's eyes are opened outward to a recognition of their carnal nakedness, the imperfect state of their humanity, and their dependence in common upon the properties that constitute the lowest level of the triad of faculties. Adam, after eating the fruit, is said by God to have "become as one of us." Thus it is the expulsion that sets the seal upon Adam's loss of contemplative vision. Thereafter the Divine is not directly manifest to the eyes of flesh which must now attempt to trace the sacred luminosity from the shadows of the things of this world. All this comes about because, as God says (3:17) "thou hast harkened unto the voice of thy wife"—the inferior reason of the rational faculty directed to outward things. This occlusion of vision is nothing less than discriminative knowledge and aesthetic sensation given rein to function seemingly of their own accord, an illegitimate autonomy that isolates them from the superior reason that ultimately lends intelligibility to their actions. (The significance of this usurped function might be glossed with these words from the first chapter of Romans, "they . . . became vain in their imaginations, and their foolish heart was darkened.") The consequence of this occlusion of cognitive vision is that in the state of our creaturehood the conforming of our nature (the pattern or exemplar *after* which it is shaped), is never achieved without a sacrifice that is perfected by Grace. And that is the paradox of the human state, that in order to become fully human we must transcend our "humanity," a path that takes us beyond the level of our psycho-physical selfhood and all that accrues to it. Only by relating everything to the deepest interior principle of our subjective being can we become "objectively" what we truly are. Only thus can we avoid the anomaly of seeking to be wholly our "self" by means of habits of thought and action we know that "self" to be the author of.

The serpent is not evil in its acknowledgment of the sensual world, but in its resolute attachment to it. In Adam the Divine Substance becomes man that man may become divine. Which is to say, in his integral deiformity man returns all things to their just measure. But to the extent of his attachment to the things of this world, so the path by which the way of return is traced becomes effectively obscured—phenomenal appearances lose their transparency so that, cognitively speaking, the knowing subject is faced with a *res* it cannot unite with.

The first act of the primal One, the Creation *in principio*, must by definition be created out of a state of nothingness since its advent precludes any existent thing out of which it could be formed. This cosmic principle is at the root of all manifestation. Nothing is explained by reference to the same ontological level of reality of that which is to be explained. Nothing material is explained materially. The origin of the world is not explained by reference to any of its manifest aspects. The world is nothing if not an appearance and logic demands that every appearance is of something—a prior reality.

From a Biblical perspective the creation of the world is also the articulation of a thought—a word uttered in the void of the divine potentiality. This prior potentiality is no "thing" as such but is the "nothingness" on which all things are formed. It is the Cosmic Dream that dreams us, as Shakespeare's Prospero saw—

> the great globe itself,
> Yea, all which it inherit, shall dissolve,
> And, like this insubstantial pageant faded,
> Leave not a rack behind: we are such stuff
> As dreams are made on . . .

The articulation of the one Divine Substance at the level of sensible manifestation is the "hidden" reason or root—the intelligible principle—of every part of its multiple reflections in the world. Each and every minute particular, in other words, is a reverberation, a replica that harks back to the One that is the prior Divine Unity. Why else would Blake ask us to see "a world in a grain of sand," and "heaven in a flower"? This principle of replication is mirrored in the fact that everything we re-cognize in this world is one in so far as it is itself in its abiding sameness. Thus every one thing, rightly perceived, is a window onto the "veiled" reality of the primordial Oneness from which it emerges. This cosmic veil that is the multiplicity of things is the screen or surface onto which each thing, as a cognizable image, is projected. Without the single, anterior veil of creat*ive* nature onto which they are projected the multiple things of creat*ed* nature would not exist, would have no reality, just as the images of a film projected into darkness would disappear for want of a reflective surface to receive them, to permit them to appear.

The intelligible principle of a thing, that which makes our cognition of it possible, is the *form* of a thing—that *on* which and *after* which a thing is formed. The word *form* and its derivatives, *formulate, conform, deform, reform, inform, transform, uniform*, all imply a pre-existent type or model of which the thing in question is a re-presentation. The form of a thing is what it *is*. This is no less true of works of art in that they are the outward articulation of an image or idea first held in the artist's mind. Every work of art, everything made, is a representation of its form. And it is this form that we seek when we ask, for instance, of a thing we have not previously seen, and so do not understand, "What is it?" Or of a person we have not previously met and so ask, "Who are you?" We are asking to *know* the form or identity of an appearance we see but cannot recognize. The phenomenal appearance of a thing is, then, a resemblance of something that is more than simply what is outwardly manifest. The resemblance tells us *that* a thing is but not *what* or *who* it is. This is how, for instance, he or she appears to be. Indeed, the word *person*, from the Latin *persona*, a mask, itself suggests something concealed by an external appearance; an appearance that personifies and thus makes evident a veiled or hidden reality. Only with reference to the ontological root of their being, their form, can we find the who or what of an individual's existence. Without this form there would be no person to put in an appearance.

It is the same with the appearance of the world. We cannot discover the *why* of the world's appearance because we are able to examine—whether minutely through the microscope, or comprehensively through the telescope—every characteristic of *how* it behaves. This takes us no nearer the *form* which is "hidden," and is undiscernible by those faculties that allow us to comprehend the fact of its phenomenal appearance. For this we must develop the faculties of the soul appropriate to the level of reality to be discerned. For this we need what Traherne called "virgin apprehension": an innocence, a purity of internal vision that is such a stillness at the root of our being—without disturbance or taint of any created thing—that it can be likened to the soul's becoming a polished surface on which is clearly reflected the ineffable life of a thing as it subsists in the original glory of its being in the unity of all things beyond generation or decay. This is what Blake referred to when he wrote: "There exist in that Eternal World the Permanent Realities of Every Thing which we see reflected in this Vegetable Glass of Nature. All things are comprehended in their Eternal Forms in the divine body of the Saviour . . . The Human Imagination."

The deiformity of man's threefold constitution makes of him just such a creature as has to inquire after the hidden *forms* of things. Seeing that this necessarily implies that what is known can only be known in the mode of the knower—that like is known by like—this amounts to our asking the question "Who am I?" (*Who*, rather than *what*, as Richard of St. Victor reminds us, since it is a person who answers to the question.) Man is haunted by the knowledge that the things of this world are not sufficient in themselves; that things are not entirely what they appear to be. It is man's vocation to trace their origin, to uncover their true reality. Man has to ask of all that surrounds him, *what* is incontrovertibly true of that which appears to be so? It is of the very essence of his being that he asks why is there anything at all rather than nothing.

In so far as man looks outward onto the world with his sensory faculties he sees objects, colors, shapes, movement. But he does not *see*, with his eyes of flesh, that which permits the appearance of each thing; he does not *see* the light of which colors are a refraction; he does not *see* the space that shapes articulate; he does not *see* the time in which movement takes place. So far as the senses are concerned light, space, and time are non-existent, even though they are the hidden veil that make sense data possible, the "illusion" that permits man's discovery of the Real. To find the hidden dimension, the implicit context of his apprehensions, he must turn inward and begin the ascent of his faculties, referring the beguiling and manifold attractions of outward appearances back to the One that is implied by their manifoldness.

It is precisely at this sensory level that the perception of beauty is located in its immediacy. And it is our love of beauty that motivates our search for the perfection of its source where it no longer bears the shadow of transience. In other words, and because extremes meet, in the perfect, sensory beauty of a flower, for instance, we have an intimation of the sacred order of things: at the level of sensory appearances we have a prefiguration of that "very good" that God "saw" (sees) in His Creation. It is here that the enkindled soul begins its ascent, through the rational levels of cognition, beyond thought to the heart's intuition of its transcendent origin. Eckhart comments: "Man's sensitive faculty is more excellent than those of all the other animals by reason of its participation in the rational faculty." For man alone sees the *ratio* of all things, thus in him alone among the creatures is there the possibility of an unerring cognition and this, finally, is the only justification for his "dominion . . . over every living thing that moveth upon the earth" (2:28).

But at the rational, discriminative level of our apprehensions, however clearly we may see the things of corporeal vision, nonetheless we possess at this level only a partial grasp of their complete nature. Here we can only in limited measure grasp the being that objects re-present; the time which allows movement to be witnessed; the light that colors participate. Here the full measure of what being and time harbor is not yet laid bare. We see things coming into existence, their growth, decay, and death. We recognize their fleeting passage as the future ceaselessly flowing into the past. So we come to understand even time as an "appearance," a fleeting "seeming to be" from which something of us escapes. If there were not a part of us untouched by time it would not be possible for us to witness the passage of time. Movement is only measured by something static, something that is not totally identified with the properties of movement. As William Law observed, "What could begin to deny self if there were not something in man different from self?" The world of appearances is everywhere impermanent. But yet we have the idea of permanence. And so we recall Augustine's observation that "the world was not made *in* time, but *with* time." Thus, man's deiformity, the fact that he is created in God's image, lends him, so to say, the possibility of adopting God's eye-view of the world. That is, his ultimate being shares in the reality, the *in principio*, that *is* before the flow of time begins.

To pierce to the root of Oneness, the all-comprehending stasis that makes this dance and play of multiple seeming possible ("mirror on mirror, mirrored is all the show," is how Yeats described it), requires a stillness of being that is beyond the rational, discriminative faculties. We must have divine assistance; we must see with what Traherne calls "Celestial Eyes." Here the Adam of our nature is called upon to recover its original innocence. Here is our utmost assent to the fullest radiance of our being, here we exchange that "mutual glance" with God; Serpent, Eve, and Adam; spiritual, rational, and aesthetic faculties finally in mutual harmony.

What comes first must take priority. What comes first must be most eminent. What comes first all subsequent things are ordered to and all faculties are governed by. It is finally light—the "light that lighteth every man that cometh into the world"—in whose illumination we are transfigured (*trans*—to go across, over, beyond) by the Divine Substance that is the "object" of our redemption and the "subject" of our "dominion." The true perception of nature's beauty, and the joy of making what conforms to our true being, draw us to this summit. The making of the Creation is the divine play, necessary in that there should be an outer witness to the inner beauty and goodness of its Creator. And art, in imitation of His "sport," is man's making of the things that are needed to bring him to the state of inner witness. Thus the creature works in the mode of the Creator that the Creator can work in the mode of His creature— He knowing Himself in us and we knowing ourselves in Him.

7

Work and the Sacred

Man is a slave in so far as alien *wills* intervene between his action and its result, between his effort and the task to which it is applied.

This is the case in our day both for the slave *and* for the master. Man never directly confronts the conditions of his own activity. Society makes a screen between nature and man.

SIMONE WEIL

WORK, whether as a topic of discussion, a fact of daily experience, or merely as a mental preoccupation, touches the lives of all of us. We argue endlessly over who should do what and how much; about what are the appropriate conditions for the performance of work; and above all what is the just reward for its accomplishments. We live in a society that has for some time now devoted a considerable effort to the eradication of work—at least as physical toil—only suddenly and paradoxically to discover, at a time of unemployment, that we need the dignity of work. Certainly we are heirs to the problems that work poses, even to the point of wondering whether it has a future at all. But in the midst of all the activity and preoccupation it engenders we seldom pause to reflect upon the essential nature of work.

Toward the end of her book *The Need for Roots* Simone Weil observes of modern civilization that "it is sick. It is sick because it doesn't know exactly what place to give to physical labour and to those engaged in physical labour." This may seem at first hearing a somewhat unusual diagnosis of the malaise and alienation common to our age. But remember the phrase *physical labor*. It is physical labor—merely quantified human effort, unrelieved by any qualitative satisfaction to transform it—that to Simone Weil is the essence of our sickness. She goes on:

Physical labour is a daily death.

To labour is to place one's own being, body and soul, in the circuit of inert matter, turn it into an intermediary between one state and another of a fragment of matter, make of it an instrument. The labourer turns his body and soul into an appendix of the tool which he handles. The movements of the body and the concentration of the mind are a function of the requirements of the tool, which itself is adapted to the matter being worked upon.

She ends her book with the following two sentences: "It is not difficult to define the place that physical labour should occupy in a well-ordered social life. It should be its spiritual core."

This seems an audacious claim until we recall that meaningless work and soulless work are one and the same thing. Work imposed upon our lives so as to be meaningless we feel to be a burden that is contrary to our inmost nature—in some sense a denial of our very being. Yet work is man's very signature. It is said that by his fruits we might know a man. So the question we have to ask is not "What does a man get *for* his work?" so much as "What does he get *by* working?"

To speak of there being a "spiritual core" to work is not only to invoke a certain image of man, it is also to hint at the existence of a subtle thread that joins the sacred to whatever demands are made upon man in order that he sustain his physical existence. It is to presuppose, in some way or other, that the spiritual forms the implicit context of our lives and that our being is not fully real without this hidden context. If this is not so then we would have to face an awkward question: how it ever came about that, in order to sustain his earthly existence, man should be obliged to follow a course of physical action that seems a direct denial of his deepest nature, as if by some ghastly mistake of his Creator it is man's destiny to follow a direction that leads him away from the very thing it is his nature to be? If we are to avoid such a dilemma, we must conclude that in some way work is, or should be, profoundly natural and not something that must be avoided or banished as being beneath our dignity. So, we are here concerned to inquire whether, in what ways and under what conditions, work possesses a contemplative dimension.

If we are to fully understand this dimension of work, we must lay bare its essence; what it is *before* it is conditioned by any social, moral, or economic prescription. We must apprehend it as an inner experience prior to any productive outcome it may have. We must isolate it from all the modes it assumes as a consequence of our presence in the world and which result in the obligations society imposes on us; obligations we discharge by working. These obligations can make such totalitarian claims upon us that we tend to lose sight of the immaterial significance that lies at the very heart of work.

The modern habit of equating work with time-consuming toil makes us prone to forget that it is *man* who is the instrument and the agent of work. Only man works. A horse may toil, as may a beaver. But only man can be liberated or "uplifted" by working. Only man can be demoralized by work. And herein lies the danger of the work ethic of mechanized industry; that it makes an ethical absolute of our social and economic necessity to make and do things. In having no real and effective use for the intangible and pre-productive impulse that is at the core of work, modern industry loses the spiritual function of work. And in its tendency to push man to the periphery of the productive process it effectively loses man as well. In an environment in which man is subordinated to mechanical techniques it is all but impossible to experience the physical effort of work as the natural and inevitable medium through which body and soul effect the transformation of matter.

The problems and paradoxes of work that are all too evident in our society will only be resolved if and when we are willing to return to a spiritual anthropology, when we are willing to acknowledge our theomorphic self-image and restore our traditional constitution as beings that possess an integral threefold structure of spirit, soul, and body.

In our threefold constitution all three states of the human microcosm are thought of as receiving their life and illumination ultimately from that which is uncreated and therefore "above" that process of continual change and development that is manifest life. At the highest level the spiritual faculties of the soul act as a mirror reflecting the archetypal realities of the Divine Intellect. It is in the light of this level of reality that we contemplate the mystery of our subjectivity and discover it to be finally irreducible as an identity within the Divine itself. In the middle realm the faculties of the soul are bipolar; they act like a window that in one direction looks "above," or inwardly, onto what is beyond our subjectivity as such. In the opposite direction they look "below," or outwardly, onto our sensory experience in order to localize or "clothe" and give continuity to our psychological life. By means of these two directional impulses of the soul we map out the intelligible value of all our experience.

Finally, even though the substance of the body, as the living, organic sheath of our individual life, is renewed by physical matter, it nonetheless gathers the reasons of its purposes from the soul. Itself unilluminated, the body is the sustaining instrument of material transformation. But its bodily nature is only in harmony with the material world it inhabits when it is empowered to relate its actions and its appetites directly to the higher levels of being which give them meaning.

Work is the chief means by which the focal point of consciousness is concentrated "outside" the individual's subjectivity. The effort of work is an act of transformation in which the worker has the possibility of rising to the level of those values and meanings that transcend the operations of physical life. It is this potentiality for transmutation that we should at all times keep in view in any consideration of what constitutes the essence of work. Whenever this potentiality is not present in the effort of work then our physical engagement with the world of matter becomes no more than a burden, and we become merely brute instruments in the manipulation of material substances. If this were not the case we could not even conceive of, much less experience, joyless, soul-destroying work. And such an experience is no less possible in the most mechanized and hygienic industrial workplace than it is in the most unremitting physical drudgery. However much we increase the effort, and however much we elaborate the mechanical means of shaping matter in the pursuit of production, we cannot escape the paradox that at its most meaningful and its most accomplished, work can provide us with an *inner* harmony and balance when those means are kept relatively simple and direct.

This paradox poses an important question in relation to the fact that the manipulation of matter exacts its price in the expenditure of both material and bodily energy. (The Latin *homo,* for man, incidentally, is closely linked with *humus—of* the earth—from which we derive our words *humble* and *humility.*) Should we not see, then, in this expenditure of energy, an in-built correlation between the finite material resources of the world and the physical limitations of the human body? Should not this consumption of bodily energy awaken in us a recognition of and a humility toward our physical limitations, thereby setting a limit to our exploitation of the living body of the earth? In other words, ought we to consider whether there is a natural, integral correlation between the limitations of our bodily energy and the degree to which we should consume material resources in order to sustain ourselves—a correlation that should not be betrayed by any means of production that does not take account of the *inner* meaningfulness of work?

One of the most pernicious ideas that prevents us from realizing the intimate relationship that should exist between work and our spiritual nature is an idea that has seemed almost impregnable to attack in western thought over the last three centuries, and even now shows little sign of exhausting the springs of absurdity it constantly draws on. It is the idea that art and work are and must be separate categories of activity. We have got into the habit of thinking of art as a separate category of aesthetic *feeling,* and so have also got into the habit of acting as if art were a separate category of *making* that is not directly related to the immediate demands of our physical life. We have forced an artificial division between the "outer" and the "inner" man which amounts to sustaining a pretense that human kind constitutes two races: that of man as artist and that of man as workman—as non-artist.

This is to fly in the face of common sense. Neither can it be said that the work of the workman—that is the work of utility—that it is necessarily non-beautiful in contrast to the work of the artist. Nor can it be said of art—that is works of refined sensibility—that it serves no human need. If we admit that man is a spiritual being then it is clear that he has needs and requirements beyond and in addition to his bodily needs. It is also clear that the integral wholeness of his being demands that he should not be divided within himself so as to serve his spiritual needs with one sort of activity and his physical needs with another. For the work of utility rightly done may result in a type of beauty that is informed by a refinement of sensibility, just as art inevitably involves some form of making and utility such as is characteristic of practical work. Just as there is no art without work, so there should be no work without art, so that all who are actively involved in work should be in some sense artists. All artists are workmen. At least to the extent that each seeks to achieve some mastery over his material, to effect its transformation, and to the extent that such transformation, properly accomplished, will involve mastery over oneself. If we are to save ourselves from any division between our making and our thinking, in which our houses, the fixtures and fittings in them, our everyday utensils, our clothes and all the things we use daily are one part of life (produced industrially with the minimum of human agency), while we have a few "art" objects (that are the expression of nothing more than the sensibility of the person who made them) to "transform" another part, we must see such a state of affairs as profoundly unnatural and demoralizing. Can we really believe that a visit to an art gallery, in our "spare" time, is sufficient to compensate us for the meaninglessness of a humdrum experience of work unrelieved by any personal satisfaction?

If we are to recover the "spiritual core" of work we should not only remember that to accept a division between art and work is to falsify our true nature, we should also remember that it is with man himself that any reform must begin, for man is greater than what he creates. In Philo's words, "Even a witless infant knows that the craftsman is superior to the product of his craft both in time, since he is older than what he makes and in a sense its father, and in value, since the efficient element is held in higher esteem than the passive effect." In reminding ourselves in this way of the anteriority of man's being to his work we also catch a pre-echo, as it were, of the relationship between the human context of work and the archetypal nature it mirrors. As Plotinus wrote: "All that comes to be, work of nature or of craft, some wisdom has made: everywhere a wisdom presides at a making."

Once we have recovered the idea that there is no unbridgeable gulf between art and work we can go on to consider the ways in which man is linked by his spiritual nature to the work of his livelihood. For if the sacred is not present in things at hand it is unlikely to be present at all. It does not function only in exclusive categories of thought and spirituality. The numinous, sacred essence of things is nearer to us than is our jugular vein—to borrow a phrase from the Qur'an. How can this be? Let us examine some of the words we habitually use when we discuss the relation of work to life. Wisdom so often works in words like a preconscious, directive energy.

It is still just possible to speak of the workman as having a trade, or as following a vocation. The etymology of the word *trade* is uncertain but its root is possibly *tread*. What we tread is a path—a walk toward some goal. A trade, then, is a form of work or craft, an occupation conceived as a walk in life. From this we can see that the idea of a manual trade contains the sense of a vocation, and as such possesses the possibility of some form of realization, by way of conforming a set of external circumstances to an inner imperative, an inner voice.

A vocation is, of course, a calling, and functions by virtue of an inner summons (and, incidentally, raises the question of *who* is summoned by whom?). The etymology of the word *work* implies the expenditure of energy on something well or finely made— made with skill. As such it points toward a kind of perfection of attainment in the human artificer. So, hidden in the word *work* we come again upon the idea of realizing or attaining something above or beyond the mere expenditure of physical energy. Moreover, this attainment implies not only the rejection of certain possibilities and the adoption of others, it also implies (as Plotinus suggests) an inherent wisdom to make the choice that will permit the effective realization of whatever is to be attained. Now, since strictly speaking there is no perfection in the created order of things, this perfection toward which skill inclines must belong to another order, a supra-natural order of things; precisely that toward which man is called.

The abstract Greek noun *technē* gives us, in its Latin equivalent, *ars,* meaning, in one of its general senses, a way of being. From the Latin *ars* we derive our word art. The Indo-European root of *art* means to fit together. *Technē* has the same root as the word carpenter (in Old English a skilled worker is especially one who works in wood). The carpenter is one who fits things together. *Technē* means a visible skill in craftsmanship. But in Homer it is used in the sense of something in the mind of the artist—what later comes to be called imagination. And this sense of art as being a mental predisposition that stays in the artist was deeply embedded in our language until the seventeenth century, when it began to be applied to a select category of things made. So, permeating all the meanings that accrue to the language of work and art we have the sense of one who fits things together: one who fits the domain of manual necessity to the order of a higher imperative. Certainly the symbolism and the mythology of the various sacred traditions, as they are connected with the arts and crafts, indicate that such is the case.

To stress the idea of art as an effective reasoning of the person who makes things, rather than applying it to an exclusive category of aesthetic objects, is not to suggest that there is no difference between say, the art of cathedral building and the art of the potter. (The difference is one of degree rather than one of kind.) That is not the point: which is that in all cases (and who would care to decide which was the most important art between, say, cathedral building, motherhood, and agriculture), human making is a wisdom. In each an art is involved, and in so far as this involves the expenditure of effort, both mental and physical, it is a sacrifice— and one of the meanings of sacrifice is "making holy," to perform a sacred ceremony.

The primordial meaning of human work, then, is to be found in the fact that it is not only a skill about doing, but that it also embraces a supra-human wisdom about being. Or, to put it another way, the act of making has a contemplative foundation at the heart of our being. And when we turn to the sacred traditions, whose expression in human artifacts is a constant source of wonder for their beauty and skill, we find that the workman or craftsman or artist does not receive his vocation from the material circumstances of his life but that his calling is from the highest source.

In the Indian tradition the source and origin of the craftsman's calling is derived ultimately from the divine skill of Visvakarma as being revealed by him. The name for any art is *silpa*, a word that is not adequately translated by our words *artist*, or *artisan*, or *craftsman* since it refers to an act of making and doing that has magical powers. In the context of the Indian tradition works of art imitate divine forms and the craftsman recapitulates the cosmogonic act of creation as the artifact itself recapitulates the rhythms of its divine source. By his action of making, and in conjunction with his practice of yoga, the craftsman as it were reconstitutes himself and thereby goes beyond the level of his ego-bound personality.

In the craft tradition of Islam certain pre-Islamic prototypes were preserved and came to be connected with parables in the Qur'an and with certain sayings of the Prophet. Speaking of his ascent to heaven the Prophet describes an immense dome resting on four pillars on which were written the four parts of the Qur'anic formula— In the name—of God—the Compassionate—the Merciful. As Titus Burckhardt has pointed out, this parable represents the spiritual model of every building with a dome. The mosque in Islam is the symbol par excellence of the Divine Unity, the presiding principle of Islam itself. The mosque thus acts as the center toward which the arts and crafts of Islam are orientated in virtue of its involving so many of them. From the construction of the mosque the crafts, as it were, flow, since architecture, along with calligraphy, is the supreme art of the Islamic revelation.

In Islam the crafts were organized around guilds which were themselves closely connected with Sufism, the esoteric dimension of the Islamic faith. Similarly, the guilds of medieval Christendom employed a symbolism and a knowledge of a cosmological and hermetic nature. The symbolism of the crafts in the Christian tradition take as their starting point the person of the Christ who was himself a carpenter. (The Christ of the trades appears as a carving in many English parish churches.) It may be argued that the highest sacred art of Christianity is the icon—the representation of the Divine Image. But alongside this is the craft tradition, pre-Christian in origin, which is above all cosmological in its symbolism, beginning with physical space as the symbol of spiritual space, and the figure of Christ as Alpha and Omega, the beginning and the end, the timeless center whose cross rules the entire cosmos.

Such symbolism is innate to the arts and crafts—which is to say, the livelihood—of past civilizations, and has a ubiquitous presence in the physical artifacts of people's lives. All crafts and trades, from ploughing to weaving, carpentry to masonry, metal work to poetry and music, are traditionally interwoven with their transcendent principle. Here is one such witness to the fact, from K. R. T. Hadjonagoro's *Batik: Fabled Cloth of Java*:

> [Batik] was a vehicle for meditation, a process which gives birth to an uncommonly elevated sublimity in man. Truly realised beings in the social fabric of Javanese community all made batik—from Queens to commoners. . . . It is almost inconceivable that in those days batik had any commercial objective. People batiked for family and ceremonial purposes, in devotion to God Almighty, each man's endeavour to know God and draw near his spirit.

According to Genesis, work is the result of original sin. Nonetheless, for the Christian there is always the exemplar of God, "who made the world and saw that it was good." Against this there is the counterpoint of a recognition that His Kingdom is not of this world, so that man, who has some remembrance of the Divine Paradise of his origin, retains the possibility in his work of traveling the path back to God, for "there is no faith without works" (James 2:26).

Between these two perspectives the earthly destiny of man takes place. What proceeds from the Divine Principle is good; the archetype of perfection is the unmanifest reality of the Divine Principle: "Every perfect gift is from above, and cometh down from the father of lights" (James 1:17). The following passage from H. J. Massingham's *The Wisdom of the Fields* (1945), indicates something of the remarkable longevity of this idea:

> The most eloquent example I know of this inborn and indwelling principle comes from Droitwich where lives a cabinet maker named Fowkes. For in him it has become conscious and part of his philosophy of life. He made a small oval hand-mirror in mahog-

any scrap-wood for the wife of a friend of mine. When my friend called for it, he disclosed his belief that the crafts were originally divinely bestowed and the gifts had ever since been passed on from father to son. In support of this hereditary theory he told my friend that his grandfather on the mother's side was renowned in his day as being one of the finest workers in veneer and inlay in England. He himself had known nothing about veneer work. One day he "felt the itch" to do it and immediately and with ease, so he said, accomplished it. Having discovered that no trial and error nor self-teaching were necessary he derived his proficiency from his grandfather.

In all human work the archetype is a prior knowledge or wisdom in which resides the divine prototype or perfect model of any particular act of making.

The vision of the divine prototype as a wisdom inherent in the actual tools of trade is beautifully evoked in Exodus 25, where, after describing in some detail the making of a sanctuary, Moses is urged that it be done, "According to all I shew thee, after the pattern of the Tabernacle, and the pattern of the instruments thereof even so shall ye make it." But on the indefinite number of possibilities capable of being realized it is the burden of work to place a limitation, since all work involves a pre-conception or image that is subsequently shaped to a determined end. Without this pre-conception and its subsequent determination there would be no distinction of means from ends. Work would be sufficient unto itself. But as Aquinas points out, "As God who made all things did not rest in those things . . . but rested *in* himself *from* the created works . . . so we too should learn not to regard the work as the goal, but to rest from the works of God himself in whom our felicity lies."[1] Work is the imposition of order on matter, matter transformed by human intention and will. The true workman does not work merely to perfect the operations of work itself but according to an inner order that is his perfect nature. That is why the worker must be free to become the very thing he makes. As Eckhart says, "The work that is 'with,' 'outside,' and 'above,' the artist must become the work that is 'in' him,

1. [Thomas Aquinas, Commentary on the *Sentences*, 2d. 15, 3, 3.—Ed.]

taking form within him, in other words, to the end that he may produce a work of art in accordance with the verse 'The Holy Spirit shall come upon thee' (Luke 1:35), that is, so that the 'above' may become 'in.'"[2]

It follows that if the artist or the workman is to achieve perfection in his making he must let nothing come between his conception of what is to be done and its execution. And this conformity of his being to the final realization of the work is the primordial model of human workmanship. It implies that work is, in essence, for the sake of contemplation, just as much as it implies that the perfection of work is achieved only at the expense of self-consciousness. As the Japanese potter Hamada puts it: "you have to work when you are not aware of self." In work perfectly realized there is no thought of reward, no love of procedure, no seeking after good, no clinging to goals, whether of attainment or of God Himself.

Eckhart, in a sermon on justice, gives a further clue as to how our work and our being are interwoven; how, essentially, our work is to *be* and our being *is* our work:

> The just man does not seek for anything with his works, for those who seek something with their works are servants and hirelings, or those who work for a Why or a Wherefore. Therefore, if you would be conformed and transformed into justice do not aim at anything with your works and intend nothing in your mind in time or in eternity, neither reward nor blessedness, neither this nor that; for such works are all really dead. Indeed I say that if you make God your aim, whatever works you do for this reason are all dead and you will spoil good works. . . . Therefore, if you want . . . your works to live, you must be dead to all things and you must have become nothing. It is characteristic of the creatures that they make something out of something, but it is characteristic of God that He makes something out of nothing. Therefore, if God is to make anything in you or with you, you must beforehand have become nothing. Therefore go into your own ground and work there, and the works that you work there will all be living.[3]

2. *Treatises and Sermons of Meister Eckhart,* translated by James M. Clark and John V. Skinner (1958), p. 251.
   3. Ibid., pp. 53–54.

As if to expand and annotate this passage from Eckhart we find at the end of Plotinus's *Fourth Ennead* the following:

> All that has self-consciousness and self-intellection is derivative; it observes itself in order, by that activity, to become master of its Being: and if it studies itself this can mean only that ignorance inheres in it and that it is of its own nature lacking and to be made perfect by intellection.
>
> All thinking and knowing must, here, be eliminated: the addition introduces deprivation and deficiency.

None of this is in any way meant to deny that our acting upon a material substance is conditioned by that substance proceeding through our senses. But at the very core of the act the senses are not consciously involved and there is an immediate and unconditioned intuition in the soul of the timeless source of action: something that is not part of the act of making as the dead center of a hub does not take part in the rotation of the wheel. And no degree of perfection in work is attained that does not touch upon this stasis of Perfection itself. That is the spiritual function of skill. No perfection is embodied in that which is unprepared or insufficient, for like is known by like, and skill in the execution of work is first of all a skill residing in the workman. The skilled maker intuitively knows that the perfection of his work rests upon his own being and is not determined by external circumstances. It is the worker's own lack of self-discipline that prevents the perfect realization of his task. It is just this interior perfection of being that the crafts, with their tools as an extension of the physical body, serve and which the machine destroys. The tool nurtures the integral relationship that lies at the heart of all work; the total freedom of potentiality in physical effort corresponding with the necessary determination inherent in perfectly realized workmanship. Such is the "spiritual core" of work. H. J. Massingham recorded the living process in his *Shepherd's Country* (1938); watching a craftsman who was making a traditional Cotswold, five-barred gate or "hurdle," he wrote: "The intrinsic contact with his material must and does humanize him and unseal the flow of the spirits. He seemed to be talking to his wood as well as to me, and sometimes he forgot I was there. . . . It would be meaningless to say

that such a man as Howells loved his work: he lived in it." We mentioned earlier that the word *homo* (man) is connected with *humus,*
and has important ecological implications. Man is quite literally "of
the soil," his life is sustained hourly and daily by what the soil provides. All traditional cultures have been sustained by the crafts,
especially agriculture. By virtue of their being intimately rooted in a
specific geographic place, and so to the specific set of social, material, and ecological circumstances that provide the formal occasion
and substance of the means of livelihood, the crafts conserve the
natural environment. This is so because the crafts are in turn tool-
based. The tool is a conservative instrument of manufacture precisely because of its intimate relationship with the bond that unites
hand, eye, and the intuitive sources of skill.

Skill is to some extent cumulative. It is born of circumstances
that are relatively stable and it flourishes in the context of tried and
tested ways of doing things. We can only measure skill against a
given set of conventional procedures and a pre-determined end. We
cannot determine whether a totally new procedure is skillful since
the novelty of the method required for its accomplishment will be
outside any convention and will be unique to the occasion. The
worker cannot test himself against a set of circumstances that are
unknown to him. For which reason the constant search for novelty
and innovation in work demoralizes the worker (as indeed it has
demoralized the "artist" in our time). Constant innovation must
eventually undermine the conventions and social occasions that
unite the worker and his patron—not forgetting that all workman
are also patrons.

There are profound reasons why the crafts tend not to elaborate
the means of production away from the elementary procedures of
hand-tool skills. To do so has the effect of diverting the operation of
the worker's skill away from the perfecting of his inner resources,
and diverting it toward the external, instrumental circumstances of
the means of production. When this happens, as we see today in the
almost total uniformity of the machine-made infrastructure that
surrounds us, the natural world that sustains us is eventually
reduced to no more than so much raw material, to be plundered
regardless of any ultimate outcome. We should not be surprised that

such an amoral and indiscriminate view of the material context of work has slowly led us to poisoning the environment. The crafts, on the other hand, are far more likely to be materially sustainable. They tend not to work against the interests of man and nature but integrate the rhythms and substance of both while at the same time opening a door internally upon states of mind and of beauty that transcend the necessarily physical conditions by which life proceeds.

The fact that in the mechanized, industrial milieu men confuse *needs* with egotistical appetites and have great difficulty in imposing any restraint upon them is itself a demonstration of that same milieu's amoral irresponsibility in seeking infinite expansion of consumption in a world of finite resources. When we speak about our needs we have to remember that they are determined not by our appetites but by our nature as spiritual beings. It is in virtue of the intuition of our spiritual nature that we understand who we are. Which is to say we understand that we are not, as creatures, sufficient unto ourselves but are beings who are called to perfect ourselves. That we are able to regard our appetites, our passions, our desires, objectively as *part* of our nature proves the possibility of our being raised to a level above them. And this obliges us to recognize that whatever is required to bring about our human perfectibility constitutes our needs. As Plotinus says, "In the matter of the arts and crafts, all that can be traced to the needs of human nature are laid up in the perfect man."[4] To labor is to pray. When work is truly for the sake of contemplation it carries the same import as a passage of scripture. The work of Gothic cathedral builders speaks with the same voice as Gothic spirituality. There is as much a message of non-attachment to the ego in a Sung vase as there is in a Zen text.

To make something by hand is a relatively slow process, it requires commitment, patience, aptitude, and skill such as is usually gained over a period of gradual mastery, during which the character of the worker is also formed. The tool draws upon the unwritten and accumulated wisdom of past usage. The hand, and its extension, the tool, challenge the inner resources of the workman in a direct way. His mastery of the working situation must operate so

4. *Fifth Ennead,* ninth tractate.

that there is a vital accord between mental concentration, physical exertion, and the material properties of the substance worked to the degree, as we have seen, that the workman lives *in* his work. What he produces is vibrant with a life and a human signature that is missing from the uniform products of the machine. Why else should we feel nostalgia at the artifacts of the past but for the fact that they have been invested with a quality of human involvement that is so evidently absent from the mass-produced products that surround us? We feel in such artifacts something of the pulse that is common to the pulse of our own being.

By contrast, the mark of the machine product is its uniformity. To the rhythms of life and the rhythms of nature the machine is indifferent, if not disruptive. Although the development of the machine is based upon a cumulative, technical knowledge, for the machine operator there is no wisdom of past methods of production. The machine has no "history" since it is continually updated by technical innovation, so that it cannot be an instrument of human continuity. The organic link that binds one generation to another in mutual interdependency is thus severed by a quantitative mechanization that responds only to the economic imperative. The continual technical development of the machine projects forward to an uncertain future and is disruptive of those natural rhythms of renewal and consumption that tend to be conserved by the tool. In a craft culture, which is in a sense a flowering of nature that addresses itself to heaven, production fosters the primary human qualities of resourcefulness, self-reliance, and moral integrity in the context of man's obligation and responsibility to his natural environment. What in the tool is the possibility of a reciprocal rhythm of exertion and contemplation open to the spiritual dimension, becomes with the machine a sort of diabolic ingenuity and contrivance that stifles the soul through an inimical, mechanical pace. In other words, and by way of summary, the tool produces *according* to human needs, the machine *regardless* of human needs.

Nothing is easier than to point to the many ways in which life has been made easier by the machine. But are these benefits such that we may have full confidence in the direction and final goal toward which the machine blindly forces us? There is little point in arguing that life is now more comfortable and convenient for the mass of men and women (which is far from being incontrovertible in any case) than it has ever been before if we do not consider at the same time the ultimate price of this achievement. Our progress is toward a future that no one can accurately envisage, let alone claim to determine. Are we to accept unquestioningly this blind enterprise?

In looking back to the craft cultures; in recognizing the essentially spiritual character of the arts and crafts of the sacred traditions; in studying tool-made artifacts as a repository of wisdom through the means of symbolism and initiative practices, there is no need to deceive ourselves that such things can be re-instituted by our simply wishing it to happen. We know that this cannot be the case. Our world has not yet finished with its self-mutilation. But in so far as we are human and able to recognize for that very reason that we are made for that which is greater than our own productions, so we must address ourselves to the truths above and beyond the fact of our historical circumstances. By that much we may avoid falling victim to historical fatalism.

If we are to seek some ultimate cure for the sickness Simone Weil spoke of then surely we must first establish the nature of the disease. The very least we might achieve in taking stock of past cultures of people for whom work and the sacred were an organic unity is to have, in a positive sense, some measure of what we have fallen from. Rather this, surely, than to conclude negatively that we are merely the victims of events we have neither the power to control nor the will to understand. The dominant forces at work in our society would have us believe that the next step in our technological development will rid us of our work altogether. That such a utopian dream should go hand in hand with the possible destruction of man himself is no coincidence. It is certainly the projection of a false image of our nature. If we are to offer any effective resistance to this dream it can only be on the basis of our understanding of how the "spiritual core" that is the heart of workmanship both fosters and safeguards the inter-relationship between man and the sacred.

8

Standing on Earth:
Wendell Berry and the Two Economics

If reason was all, reason
would not exist—the will
to reason accounts for it;
it's not reason that chooses
to live; the seed doesn't swell
in its husk by reason, but loves
itself, obeys light which is
its own thought and argues the leaf
in secret; love articulates
the choice of life in fact; life
chooses life because it is
alive; what lives didn't begin dead,
nor sun's fire commence in ember.

From "The Design of a House"

WENDELL BERRY's writings are the voice of a life lived integrally. To read him, therefore, can be a disarming experience. Everything he writes, essays, poems, novels, short stories, is faithful to the particularity of its occasions, acutely aware of the danger—at a time of cultural and communal disintegration—of all argument and judgment not based on direct experience. Hence the clarity and certainty of his vision. Berry would certainly disclaim the title of theologian or philosopher, but seeing that his attempt to comprehend a "Biblical ecology" must necessarily point in the direction of principles and doctrine, then to that extent we can see that his "philosophy" is, as it were, a rediscovery of the perennial principles of "right livelihood." It is not only Christian for it draws, in addition, upon a body of traditional wisdom that extends beyond the realm of long-held Christian belief. In his effort to understand the way in which "principles are clarified by their practical effects," so he has found himself obliged to formulate a religious language that is faithful, at one and the same time, both to the outcome of his practical concerns and the "philosophy" implicit in them.

An introduction to a selection of his essays—because they are chosen from a much greater body of work in which not only essays but poetry, novels, and short stories form a unified whole—might, then, usefully highlight the "philosophic" background against which the particularity of his concerns is placed, especially as this "philosophy" is far from being common currency. Indeed, the contemporary world that Berry's polemic is focused upon is largely the outcome of this "philosophy" having been set aside, and without its having been replaced by a kind of wisdom that could serve the same need. Men and women cannot live without principles. If they will not have true principles then they must, willy-nilly, suffer the punishments of accepting false ones, with whatever distortion and falsification that that entails.

It is part of conventional, unquestioning thought that we live in an age of materialism. Accordingly, and in so far as it is a view unconsciously held, to all intents and purposes the fruits of our manipulation of matter form both the incentives for our actions and the goal of our enterprise. We approve of whatever succeeds in producing a material benefit or advantage. That our success does not of itself provide us with the criteria wherewith to judge our actions—for good or ill—we prefer not to notice. That such actions can be shown to have a measurable effect in material terms is sufficient. That is the hallmark of our age. We see the degree of our dominion over the material realm as the measure of our mastery over it. Ours is a civilization of validation by success. Our so-called materiality is our faith and success is our religion.

Our concern and involvement with matter should have, then, all the signs of a loving, nurturing relationship, seeing that it is the common substance of which we are made, and of which we partake. If we are, as we unconsciously presume, materialists, then surely matter itself should be accorded the highest esteem and reverence of which we are capable. Indeed, should it not be for us almost akin to the divine as the object and utmost focal point of our worship? Yet the very opposite is the case.

The truth is that the implications of a totally materialistic view of things are never fully embraced, and the fact that material existence is seldom the real basis of our thought and actions is rarely acknowledged. That is the crux of the paradox by which we try to live. In the human economy by which we conduct our daily lives we have instituted our dilemma. Berry writes:

> The so-called materialism of our time is . . . at once indifferent to spiritual concerns and insatiably destructive of the material world. And I would call our economy, not materialistic, but abstract, intent upon the subversion of both spirit and matter by abstractions of power. . . .
>
> For human beings the spiritual and the practical are, and should be, inseparable. Alone, practicality becomes dangerous; spirituality, alone, becomes feeble and pointless. . . . Each is the other's discipline, in a sense, and in good work the two are joined.[1]

When Berry points to the marriage of the spiritual and the practical as the ultimate term of our material livelihood he is bridging a chasm that has been yawning in our path for some four centuries. It is the chasm of post-Cartesian man's dualism in which he is pulled apart by two irreconcilable extremes of thought. At the one extreme he must preserve in his thought the unity of the rational thinking ego, a unity which must then become a mental concept empty of life. At the other extreme, he is left to gain knowledge of the world on the model of the reasoning self, only to find that he is finally overwhelmed by the plurality of the specializations that such an approach to the multiplicity of things demands. In proposing the

---

1. [All Berry essay quotations are from the volume of essays, edited by Brian Keeble, which this piece introduces. See the list of sources in the back matter for details. —Ed.]

Logos as the only adequate unifying principle Berry is able to make use of a deeper logic than that reached by rational thought:

> My purpose . . . is double, I want, first, to attempt a Biblical argument for ecological and agricultural responsibility. Second, I want to examine some of the practical implications of such an argument. I am prompted to the first of these tasks partly because of its importance in our unresolved conflict about how we should use the world. That those who affirm the divinity of the Creator should come to the rescue of His creature is a logical consistency of great potential force.
>
> The second task is obviously related to the first, but my motive here is somewhat more personal. I wish to deal directly at last with my own long held belief that Christianity, as usually presented by its organization, is not earthly enough—that a valid spiritual life, in this world, must have a practice and a practicality—it must have a material result.

Our abstraction has, then, closed off the channels of the numinous in the natural world and as a consequence we live in an environment that has become a prison of our own making, a prison whose particular punishment is the threatening Vision of finally depleted "resources." The systematic application of this abstraction, its rationale and the conclusion toward which its relentless functioning drives us, condemn us to a loveless cycle of depredation and diminishing returns. William Blake described the process in the two series of his *There Is No Natural Religion*: "The bounded is loathed by its possessor. The same dull round, even of a universe, would soon become a mill with complicated wheels." Berry, as it were, extends the theme:

> The Creator's love for the Creation is mysterious precisely because it does not conform to human purposes. The wild ass and the wild lilies are loved by God for their own sake and yet they are part of a pattern that we must love because it includes us. This is a pattern that humans can understand well enough to respect and preserve, though they cannot "control" it or hope to understand it completely.

We have lost the true mirror of our being; that immemorial wisdom and knowledge that allows us to recapitulate our abiding nature as creatures made in the image of God, and as a consequence we have also lost our proper place in the order of created beings. And with that loss has gone a culture capable of revealing to us our constant dependence upon the mysterious, unmanifest sources of life itself. We have forgotten that the "human" is inexplicable without the divine. As a consequence of this loss we have become good (beyond our understanding) at being *in*-human. It is as if, having seen that we are what we have made of ourselves, we have abandoned all that is "given" us from what is beyond us. We have acted, and continue to act, as if death, evil, sin, and all manner of human inadequacy were matters we could, with a little more "research" and adjustment, more or less reckon without in the course of our being and doing. The model of our self-knowledge has been nothing more than the sum of our actions. We have derived our self-image and defined our humanity in terms of nothing more substantial than those transient theories and cultural acquisitions that the passage of time makes obsolete. The result, in retrospect, seems all too predictable:

> In the hierarchy of power among the earth's creatures, we are at the top, and we have been growing stronger for a long time. We are now, to ourselves, incomprehensibly powerful, capable of doing more damage than floods, storms, volcanoes, and earthquakes. And so it is more important than ever that we should have cultures capable of making us into humans—creatures capable of prudence, justice, fortitude, temperance, and the other virtues. For our history reveals that, stripped of the restraints, disciplines and ameliorations of culture, humans are not "natural," not "thinking animals" or "naked apes," but monsters—indiscriminate and insatiable killers and destroyers.

As a result of our divorce from nature, in the void of our abstraction, we have a culture unimaginably impoverished of those modes of knowledge and levels of experience that would save us from the destructive vision of man and nature as things asunder; as separate elements of a reality open to the possibilities of endless human interference and exploitation:

> Before the specialization of the disciplines that accompanied the industrial revolution, one of the dominant strains of Western cul-

ture was a concern for the limits of responsible action. And these limits were defined primarily by the human place, below the angels and above the animals, in the hierarchy of created things. To act in violation of these limits is to invite consequences that cannot be controlled, and may not be survived.

To behave as if we are the "sovereign lords" of nature's processes instead of being God's vice-regents on Earth is, in the industrial economy, our unavoidable proclivity. It is clear that our relationship with nature must keep a fine balance; for men and women cannot live apart from nature and so must in some way alter it:

> If they choose to make too small a difference, they diminish their humanity. If they choose to make too great a difference, they diminish nature, and narrow their subsequent choices; ultimately, they diminish or destroy themselves. Nature, then, is not only our source but also our limit and measure.

Characteristically, Berry does not seek to prove the point by way of those accumulations of facts and statistics and charts beloved of a certain sort of ecologist, but by way of a poet's intuitive insight. An earlier poet, admired by Berry, had already seen that this fine balance men must keep in and with nature is manifestly a form of the divine justice:

> As the poet Edmund Spenser put it almost four hundred years ago, Nature, who is the "greatest goddesse," acts as a sort of earthly lieutenant of God, and Spenser represents her as both a mother and judge. Her jurisdiction is over the relations between the creatures; she deals "Right to all . . . indifferently," for she is "the equall mother" of all "And knittest each to each, as brother unto brother." Thus, in Spenser, the natural principles of fecundity and order are pointedly linked with the principle of justice, which we may be a little surprised to see that he attributes also to nature. And yet in his insistence on an "indifferent" natural justice, resting on the "brotherhood" of all creatures, not just of humans, Spenser would now be said to be on sound ecological footing.

Contemporary man is not so much caught up in the simple dichotomy of "faith" and "reason" as caught up in a confusion of the two—a blind faith *in* reason. He has not relinquished the idea that God has control of the destiny of things in order to settle in easy acquiescence for the idea that nobody, or nothing, controls that destiny. He has ended up with the false belief that rationality is the supreme arbiter of knowledge and intellect; in other words, he believes that he himself has such control. But only in abstraction do men dream this sort of omnipotence. Men and women make *specific* acts that have *particular* results, more often than not with spiritual, moral, and physical consequences. That we do not take account of this in any sort of self-reckoning not only shows how eroded has become our sense of responsible action, it is to fly in the face of the humility necessary to our sustainable existence: it is hubris. Thus, what emerges from the moral neutrality of technological innovation is the application of the philosophy of self-validating success: if it can be done it will be done! Nuclear energy, genetic engineering, space conquest, bespeak our hubris. Wendell Berry has the measure of such arrogance:

> The hierarchical order of Creation, the Chain of Being, is being broken; humans have usurped powers that belong only to God; and the consequences are therefore neither foreseeable nor controllable.
> The antithetical theme—the antidote—is spoken by MacDuff in the third scene of Act IV [*Macbeth*]:
>
> > Boundless intemperence
> > In nature is a tyranny.

In such allusions to the doctrine of temperance in the old poets there is at work what I think can justly be called an ecological intelligence: a sense of the impossibility of acting or living alone or solely in one's own behalf, and this rests in turn upon a sense of the order upon which any life depends and of the proprieties of place within that order. Without this intelligence, temperance can govern no act for it cannot be defined. As MacDuff speaks of it, temperance is no abstract or ideal virtue, but the enactment, the practice, of the understanding that one lives within an order of dependence and obligation superior to oneself. It is the practice of decorum.

If the theme of abstraction and its ramifications can be said to form the wider backcloth of Wendell Berry's thought, then that of "the effort to describe responsibility" is his specific foreground subject. "My work has been motivated by a desire to make myself responsibly at home both in this world and in my native and chosen place," he has written. This theme has, as it were, two prolongations each of which is continually being reconsidered and illuminated in the light of the other. One is the recognition of, and insistence upon, the value of the body. The other, touched upon already, is that the whole world of human thought and action is enveloped in the mystery of the unknown.

It should be quite clear that man does not come to understand nature by domination of it. He does not draw close to the mystery of created things in any attempt to subjugate them for his own ends. On the contrary, it is only by assimilating his inmost being to the norms and rhythms of nature that he may come to be its intimate participant. Only by means of this contemplative process can the assumption that nature is somehow "outside" and "other" than man be overcome, and nature reveal itself as a source of spiritual illumination. Just as it is necessary for man to realize that he cannot be fully human apart from God—and in that realization see nature as part of the process of human redemption—so it is also necessary for us to see that God is in some way deprived of his necessary self-manifestation when the divine is set apart from man and nature. In this sense nature, as God's creature, can be looked upon as the "second revelation."

This metaphysical perspective is the implicit, central premise of Wendell Berry's "Biblical ecology," and we should not fail to see this central premise of his thought simply because of his continual concentration upon those more tangible realities that form the immediate bodily context of man's physical existence. For Berry there is no meaningful way of grasping the bodily context of our earthly existence without allowing for the unseen and unknowable Mystery that both envelops man and is within him like a nascent seed. This Mystery and the body must be interactive at all times:

> In affirming that there is a necessary and indispensable connection between language and truth, and therefore between language and deeds, I have certain precedents in mind. I begin with the Christian idea of the Incarnate Word, the Word entering the world

as flesh, and inevitably therefore as action—which leads logically enough to the insistence in the Epistle of James that faith without works is dead.

> For if any be a hearer of the word, and not a doer, which is like unto a man beholding his natural face in a glass:
> For he beholdeth himself, and goeth his way, and straight way forgetteth what manner of man he was.

The essay "The Gift of Good Land" represents Berry's most concentrated attempt to explore the implications of this doctrine from the standpoint of his "long held belief that Christianity—as usually presented by its organizations—is not earthly enough," while at the same time wanting "to see if there is not at least implicit in the Judeo-Christian heritage a doctrine such as that the Buddhists call "right livelihood" or "right occupation." Berry does not, in characteristic fashion, tackle the problem head on, preferring to draw together the strands of his own practical experience by means of its illuminating connections. Certainly whatever is most compelling and convincing in his argument, in his exemplifications and elucidations, in no way contradicts the immemorial wisdom inherent in the doctrine. Berry concludes:

> To live, we must daily break the body and shed the blood of Creation. When we do this knowingly, lovingly, reverently, it is a sacrament.... To use knowledge and tools in a particular place with good long-term results is not heroic. It is not a grand action visible for a long distance or a long time. It is a small action, but more complex and difficult, more skillful and responsible, more whole and enduring, than most grand actions. It comes of a willingness to devote oneself to work that perhaps only the eye of Heaven will see in its full intricacy and excellence. Perhaps the real work, like real prayer and real charity, must be done in secret.

In the interchange of man's presumption toward nature, and rebellion on nature's part as a result, a vital paradox becomes obscured: "the natural forces that so threaten us are the same forces that preserve and renew us." Berry sees the development of this obscuration as in part the responsibility of Christianity's failure to "provide us with a precise enough understanding of the commonplace issues of livelihood." And his insistence that Christianity has not been earthly enough is an insight that both qualifies the condemnation and circumvents many of the crudities of argument that proceed on too narrow an interpretation of Genesis 1:28. In the essay "God and Country" the author glosses this passage as indicating the inescapable teaching, that since the world is, in a sense, God, He can never relinquish title to it:

> He has never revoked the conditions, bearing on His gift to us of the use of it, that oblige us to take excellent care of it. If God loves the world then how might any person of faith be excused for not loving it or justified in destroying it?

With this question Berry aligns another closely related thought that pre-occupies him; that Christianity has been responsible for a too great "disembodiment of the soul." And he concludes that,

> to lay up . . . treasures in heaven (Matthew 6:20) cannot mean to be spiritual at the earth's expense or to despise or condemn the earth for the sake of heaven. It means exactly the opposite: do not desecrate or depreciate these gifts, which take part with us in the being of God, by turning them into worldly "treasure"; do not reduce life to money or to any other mere quantity.

Christianity has indeed forced a polarity of the material and the immaterial in its emphasis on the division between the natural and the supernatural, with the consequent tendency to concentrate on the salvation of the soul as a movement away from the world. Moreover, this tendency has de-emphasized the spiritual significance of—as we ought properly to call it—created nature by its distinction between grace and nature. Hence the urgent need, in a time of materialistic abstraction, as Berry argues, to re-instate the spiritual value of the bodily. The terminology is important and precise. Matter is diffuse (and ultimately unknowable). Body is local and of intimate habitation: "To be in place is good and to be out of place is evil, for where we are in respect to our place both in the order of things and on earth is the definition of our whereabouts with respect to God and our fellow creatures." If the body is wrested from its ordered place so as to seem independent of its natural environment so the soul will be, as it were, unfocused for the want of all those attachments to particular times, places, and things, and that precise configuration of circumstances that releases and directs the delight that is its energy. If the body atrophies out of failure to complete the cycle of renewal and expenditure of energy proper to its actions, then the soul becomes self-regarding out of failure to enact the cycle of transformation which is its vision of the mutual interpenetration of spirit and matter.

The ramifications of this rupture of bodily reality and immaterial truth are nowhere more explicitly examined than in one of Berry's most trenchant essays, "Two Economies," where the discussion is couched in terms of the Great Economy and the human economy. In its full implication Berry's effective ideal of a natural and harmonious relationship between man and his place, both in the order of creatures, as well as geographically and locally, echoes the goal of the Taoist sage:

> The clear understanding of the virtue of Heaven and Earth, is what is called "The Great Root," and "The Great Origin";—they who have it are in harmony with Heaven, and so they produce all equitable arrangements in the world;—they are those who are in harmony with men. (Chuang-tzu [Zhuangzi], translated by James Legge)

The term and concept of the Great Economy Berry uses as a more "culturally neutral term" for the Kingdom of God. Thus, it is, like the Tao, or the Kingdom of God,

> both known and unknown, visible and invisible, comprehensible and mysterious. It is, thus, the ultimate condition of our experience and of the practical questions rising from our experience, and it imposes on our consideration of those questions an extremity of seriousness and an extremity of humility.

The Great Economy originates values that are primary, or given. It also originates materials and powers that are transformed in the human economy. When the human economy functions properly it does so acknowledging its dependence upon the Great Economy. As an example Berry gives, not surprisingly, that of topsoil:

> We cannot speak of topsoil, indeed we cannot know what it is, without acknowledging at the outset that we cannot make it. We can care for it (or not), we can even, as we say, "build" it, but we

can do so only by assenting to, preserving, and perhaps collaborating in its own processes. To those processes themselves we have nothing to contribute. We cannot make topsoil, and we cannot make any substitute for it; we cannot do what it does . . . a handful of the real thing has life in it; it is full of living creatures. And if we try to describe the behavior of that life we will see that it is doing something, if we are not careful, we will call "unearthly": It is making life out of death.

Willingness to ignore this limitation of the human in the face of the "unearthly" is an example of our hubris. If the traditional role of the spiritual and ethical virtues is to weave the fabric of our humility, then the role of the arts is to provide a context for its practical realization in the human economy. Art is of secondary value in relation to what is "given" in the Great Economy. The human economy originates, manages, and distributes secondary, or added, values and is mainly concerned with husbandry and trusteeship. When the virtues are practiced within sight of the Great Economy they lead to action-work performed as art: the labor of some particular and necessary task (traditionally, the proper occasion of art) for the good of the thing to be done. It is the specific "habit" of art to take up a material thing or circumstance and to bring it to as complete a state of its potential, inherent perfection, in relation to the whole, as is possible. The responsibility of the artist (in the broadest sense) as steward of the Earth is, in Berry's words, to "safeguard God's pleasure in His work. And we can do that . . . by safeguarding our pleasure in His work, and our pleasure in our own work." In this way the Wheel of Life comes full circle: what is made according to the inherent gifts of human hand and mind (as opposed to the application of the mechanized, impersonal powers of machine technology), nurtures in the artist the very image of his deiformity. To fashion outwardly in matter is thus to form inwardly the very substance of spiritual being. The beauty and pleasure of human work (art) is our guarantee of it.

The signature of human wisdom is so to manage the human economy that it is sustained in a state of harmony with the Great Economy; in relation to those values and powers it is beyond human enterprise to provide. To sin against the Great Economy is to attempt to found the human economy as an autonomous economy; as the only economy, and so to act in isolation from the supreme order of the Great Economy. The industrial economy is such an "invasion and pillage of the Great Economy" since it tends not to account for its indebtedness to the materials and powers of the Great Economy. The human economy does not, for instance, create life, intelligence, health; those things by which it is sustained. Moreover, the industrial economy must promote the function of production and consumption as though such indebtedness represents a sustainable human value:

> When humans presume to originate value, they make value that is first abstract and then false, tyrannical, and destructive of real value. Money value, for instance, can be said to be true only when it justly and stably represents the value of necessary goods, such as clothing, food, and shelter, which originate ultimately in the Great Economy. Humans can originate money value in the abstract, but only by inflation and usury, which falsify the value of necessary things and damage their natural and human sources. Inflation and usury and the damages that follow can be understood, perhaps, as retributions for the presumption that humans can make value.

Because humans are only able to clothe, feed, and house themselves on a sustainable basis by means of the acquired wisdom of their cultural heritage Berry concludes that the human good is effectively situated, *ultimately*, beyond the human as such. In so far as nature *has* to be the means and utility for any human economy, then the human subject per se must be seen as an epiphenomenal "I" faced with the multiplicity of external objects that make up material reality. This interfacing relationship will function only imperfectly and partially as a reflection of the values and powers of the inclusive wholeness implicit in the Great Economy. Yet on this very imperfection and partiality the industrial economy is founded, by virtue of the fact that it is itself nothing other than the extension and application of the scientific consciousness, a consciousness whose hypothetical paradigms of truth and value are made on the basis of envisaging man as not much more than a "self-conscious" subject more or less isolated and apart from the object of knowledge it wishes to grasp. Yet the implicit oneness and wholeness of the

Great Economy preclude such divisions of subject from object, knowledge from reality, man from nature, that is the characteristic of scientific consciousness. And this is why, as a model wherewith to establish the human economy, and thus to sustain the human good, the industrial economy is bound to come to grief, since it proposes the abstract autonomy, not only of the sources, but also of the application of human reason when faced with the multiplicity of external material things. This pretended supremacy of rationality must have the effect of stimulating the mind—in its efforts to grasp the diversity of the reality it is faced with—to dominate the object of its attention. And this it does by means of quantification, enumeration, and measurement only. Given this condition of its operation, reason is bound to usurp the powers and values of the Great Economy and come to see created things as subject to its authority. Created things, in this light, very soon become "resources." Resources father material goods—merchandise! Reason, harnessed to human appetites thus creates patterns of production and consumption which eventually grow beyond any reasonable control. Berry sees clearly what must follow:

> Because we are always setting out to control something that we refuse to limit, we have made control a permanent and helpless enterprise. If we will not limit causes, there can be no controlling of effects. What is to be the fate of self-control in an economy that encourages and rewards unlimited selfishness?
>
> More than anything else, we would like to "control the forces of nature," refusing at the same time to impose any limit on human nature.

That it is part of the "hidden agenda" of the industrial economy that it should come to "control the forces of nature" is yet another symptom of the crisis of abstraction whereby rationality is faced with the necessity of attempting to control the very thing on which its existence and functioning depends. It does so by making an abstraction, in this case a disembodied appetite, of the body, and removing it from the circuit of renewal and return. The body, as a mere mode of consumption, is displaced to become the victim of the disordered human economy where everything is out of place so that eventually even the body seems to have no place in it. The greatest triumph (and the greatest absurdity) of the industrial economy would be to have unlimited control over the means of consumption and profit while at the same time eliminating their dependence upon the human body. In the final analysis it is only disembodied appetites that "consume." Wendell Berry points to the historical context wherein this process began:

> Sometime between, say, Pope's verses on the Chain of Being in *An Essay on Man* and Blake's "London," the dominant minds had begun to see the human race, not as part of a member of Creation, but as outside it and opposed to it. The industrial revolution was only a part of this change, but it is true that, when the wheels of the industrial revolution began to revolve, they turned against nature, which became the name for all of Creation thought to be below humanity, as well as, incidentally, against all once thought to be above humanity. Perhaps this would have been safe enough if nature—that is, if all the rest of Creation—had been, as proposed, passively subject to human purpose.

For the human economy to displace itself in relation to the powers and values of the Great Economy is thus to turn against the divine unity that is the ground of the interconnectedness of all living things. Driven to the goal of its own logic, in this displacement, it is finally for man to turn against man. For in the spurious autonomy of human rationality all value judgments seem open to subjective manipulation, all natural, objective restraints open to challenge:

> That we can prescribe the terms of our own success, that we can live outside or in ignorance of the Great Economy are the greatest errors. They condemn us to a life without a standard, wavering in inescapable bewilderment from paltry self-satisfaction to paltry self-dissatisfaction. But since we have no place to live but in the Great Economy, whether or not we know that and act accordingly is the critical question, not about economy merely, but about human life itself.

In his insight that the actions of man toward nature are dependent and determined by human culture Wendell Berry in effect proposes that any reform in man's use of nature must begin with the reform of our self-understanding—it is a call for the re-examination of the human self-image. For the de-sanctification of nature has followed on, first from man's attempt to live as if he were only human, and then from his radical de-humanization. But in addition, behind Berry's call to acknowledge the mutual interdependence of culture and agriculture, must be the broader implication that man has to recover a sense of the unity and harmony of the divine and the natural, each sharing the ebb and flow of the one life; the one meaningless without the other:

> What the old believers in the Chain of Being have to say to us is that if we conceive ourselves as the subjects of God, whose law is in part the law of nature, then there is some hope that we can right ourselves and behave with decency within the community of creatures. We will be spared the clumsiness, waste, and grave danger of trying to make up our own rules.

Surely there is now evidence beyond measure that man's "emancipation" from a spiritual culture has made him more rapacious rather than more realistic in his attitude toward the material world:

> Whereas animals are usually restrained by the limits of physical appetites, humans have mental appetites that can be far more gross and capacious than physical ones. Only humans squander and hoard, murder and pillage because of notions.

And such "notions" are cultural phenomena. They are a measure of the health of our culture. There can be no such thing as a healthy attitude toward nature presiding alongside an unhealthy culture.

> If we corrupt agriculture we corrupt culture, for in nature and within certain unvariable social necessities we are one body, and what afflicts the hand will afflict the brain.

The self-indulgent specializations of modern culture are mirrored in the over-indulgent specializations of modern agriculture. The former is founded upon the idolatry of sensibility while the latter is founded upon the inversion of a sentimental attitude toward nature, and both are coupled with the debasement of work by mechanization. Both are the expression of an industrial economy that has supplanted the cultural tools and methods with which we might foster an organic and sacramental approach to the powers and sources that sustain us. Our most urgent need, then, is for culture-borne instructions about who or what humans are and how and on what assumptions they should act. The Chain of Being, for instance—which gave humans a place between the animals and angels in the order of Creation—is an old idea that has not been replaced by an adequate new one. It was simply rejected and the lack of a new one leaves us without a definition.

How, then, can these divisions be healed, these diminishments be enlarged? How are the abstractions of our specializations to be transformed to become the substance at hand of a necessary good?

> I think it is love. I am perforce aware how baldly and embarrassingly that word now lies on the page—for we have learned at once to overuse it, abuse it, and hold it in suspicion. But I do not mean any kind of abstract love, which is probably a contradiction in terms, but particular love for particular things, places, creatures, and people, requiring stands and acts, showing its successes or failures in practical or tangible effects. And it implies a responsibility just as particular, not grim or merely dutiful, but rising out of generosity. I think that this sort of love defines the effective range of human intelligence, the range within which its works can be dependably beneficent. Only the action that is moved by love for the good at hand has the hope of being responsible and generous.

Here, finally, the abstractions from reality, endemic in our culture, are overcome. Particular love unites God and man, knower and known, man and nature, men and women, body and soul, work and worker, producer and consumer. It, like action, cannot be abstract. It proposes intimate attachments, it disposes an open generosity in its responses, it exposes kinships of common wealth, it opposes distances and qualities such as threaten the subtlety of its continuance. It does not harbor regret at the unknown or savor expectation of an unfulfilled future, and not least is it impatient of each and every artificiality that divides use from beauty. The life of love flourishes in things at hand:

> Love defines the difference between the "global village" which is a technological and totalitarian ideal, directly suited to the purposes of centralized governments and corporations, and the Taoist village-as-globe, where the people live frugally and at peace, pleased

with the good qualities of necessary things, so satisfied where they are that they live and die without visiting the next village, though they can hear its dogs bark and its roosters crow.

We might conjecture and argue a long time about the meaning and even the habitability of such a village. But one thing, I think, is certain; it would not be a linguistic no-man's-land in which words and things, words and deeds, words and people failed to stand in reliable connection or fidelity to one another.

Wendell Berry is poet, essayist, novelist, farmer, and teacher without division of parts. Only the exigencies of publishing make it necessary to present him here exclusively as an essayist. Among current American writers his is the voice we can least afford not to hear. He is not so much an "American" writer as a writer from a small corner of the Kentucky landscape. The conviction of his insights grows out of his deep attachment to a particular place on earth. However, man and soil being what they are, his concerns are exportable and, sooner or later, must become ours. His response to his own experiences have the measured pace of a man who walks behind the plow. The ground is covered with a gentle persistence and a thoroughness of attention bred by long familiarity. There is no leaping to conclusions unwarranted by what has been encountered on the way. There is no glamor but plenty of nutrients, as Gary Snyder has observed. All our expectations of urban America's opposition to nature are in him overthrown. He helps us in the undoubtedly difficult but unavoidable task of measuring the contingencies of life against the only wisdom that can make such contingencies explicable in any true sense. And in so doing he demonstrates that he knows what and where he is, and that he is what he knows.

9

Are the Crafts an Anachronism?

IN THIS CHAPTER further consideration is given to the question of what might be the deeper implications of the fact that, in a world in which they have only a marginal social role and almost no economic justification, the handicrafts never entirely concede defeat to the by now global industrial method of manufacture. In essence this amounts to asking whether the crafts are an anachronism or whether they have an intrinsic significance for a society that is sustained minute by minute by a highly sophisticated array of technological products that are about as far away from the world of traditional handicrafts as it is possible to get.

Yet that slow, painstaking, time-consuming method of making things by hand will not die even in the face of a system of production, distribution, and consumption that by all reasonable estimates should long ago have eradicated it. Have we not, after all, solved the problem of making sufficient things for our needs? Surely our machines do that for us? And as a result are we not freed to engage with higher things? Somehow a stubborn, nagging doubt persists.

The current state of our post-industrial society would seem to suggest that the "higher" things have eluded our grasp and we have been left empty-handed. There is a widespread sense that the "leisure society" does not provide us with those long-promised—yet so often postponed—life-sustaining satisfactions. And alongside this there is the growing realization that the material wealth of our society has been achieved at the expense of meaningfulness in the workplace.

In asking whether or not the crafts are an anachronism are we not tacitly admitting to the fact that there is something more to them than simply the methods and procedures they employ: that they are more than an outmoded way of making things? For if the whole question of *how* things should be made could be answered without reference to the question, by *whom?* and for *what?* then we would scarcely be interested at all in any particular method of manufacture. Each improvement in efficiency would automatically make any previous method obsolete and, except for a certain antiquarian application, the crafts would certainly have disappeared in the face of two centuries of industrial enterprise and all that that implies.

The fact that the crafts have never been entirely done away with as a way of meeting certain of our needs must suggest that they involve a dimension of human experience that goes beyond the complex interplay of intuitive, imaginative, and manipulative skills which go toward mastering the material substance of the craft itself. And this in turn suggests that our inquiry as to the significance of the crafts must address itself not so much to the actual method of production as to the agent whose task it is to master and deploy the method of skill in question. For a thing to have significance it must signify something. It must be a sign of something and signs point to values. And it is the unique gift of men and women to recognize values and the necessity to act upon them.

In view of our possession of this gift it is little use our arguing that the modern world has progressed beyond a crafts-based civilization, as if the mere passage of time itself were capable of imposing upon human activity a value and a significance it would not otherwise have. For the world that surrounds contemporary urban man is in reality man's own construct, itself the result of adopting or rejecting certain values in favor of others. It cannot be argued that history makes us what we are, unalterably and inevitably, and therefore that history has decreed that the crafts have no necessary place in human affairs. For history is nothing more than the sum of human activities. Any world we make we can just as surely unmake. The fact that we currently express deep misgivings about the condition of the environment, a condition we ourselves have created, points to the fact that we are able to make an objective assessment and judgment from beyond the evolutionary process that is simply historical change as such. We are not, in other words, hapless victims of our time and place; we do have access to a set of values that transcend what would otherwise be our total confinement to historical causality. This tells us more about the nature of man than perhaps it does about the nature of any process of manufacture. And it points to the importance and the necessity of our asking the fundamental question, "What or *who* is man?"

This question, posed in one way or another, has been at the root of that now lengthy and continuing school of radical thought that has seen fit to call into question the direction and goals that industrial—and now by extension, post-industrial—society has set itself. This school of thought has, with reference to the manual trades and handicrafts, challenged the very foundations of modern society, built as it is on the almost total monopoly of industrial, mechanized production. What each of its dissenting voices has sounded is a warning against the danger of allowing the mechanical system a free rein in satisfying our human needs. These dissenters have seen, sometimes wholly, sometimes in part, that it is inherent in the very nature of such a system that it would eventually enslave men to those monetary and quantitative considerations that nourish merely the gods of economic efficiency. Such a system must inevitably lead not only to the dehumanization of man but also to widespread social manipulation of the factors that determine what a "need" is. That their fears were not ill-founded should by now be obvious. In every exhortation, in every forecast, in every appeal from our leaders as they urge us along the path of progress, the inducement is almost always exclusively that of "economic growth." And this in the face of a daily experience of life in which for great numbers of humanity "the economy" is as vengeful a god as was ever dreamed of by our ancestors. (It was recently reported that 1.5 percent of the workforce is displaced annually as a direct result of technological innovation and development.)

Even to pose our initial question is, of course, to admit to our conditioning by an environment which is almost entirely the product of the machine: an environment which harbors an inherent confusion as to the intrinsic merits of art, craft, and work. For industrial man the distinction between art and work is quite clear. Art is the domain of aesthetic sensibility and work is the domain of productive effort. And modern crafts inhabit an ill-defined terrain between the two, uneasily drawing from both. On the aesthetic side, the modern craftsman (seduced by the "prestige" of the fine arts) sees temptation in the fact that the accidents of individual sensibility weigh favorably in the judgment of artistic success. On the side of skill, he recognizes the necessity to demonstrate a disciplined mastery of materials as a mark of mature accomplishment. But because he is forced to operate within a society in which he has no natural patron (one who knows what *ought* to be made), the craftsman is marginalized by two dysfunctional conditions: on the one hand, the wide acceptance that "artistic freedom" has a value in isolation from moral, rational, and practical criteria, and on the other hand, the almost unquestioned assumption in the marketplace that the necessities of life are taken care of by a method of production that places little or no value on manual skills. All this is symptomatic of a conflict in industrial society *because* it is a conflict within industrial man himself For the modern worker is obliged to seek a livelihood in a system where the justice that is due to his humanity is in direct conflict with his economic survival. For we have set in place a society where the artist in us is free to work for the good of his feelings provided he does not expect, in so doing, the right to earn a livelihood. At the same time the workman in us is free to work for the good that is material necessity provided he does not thereby expect the right to an inherent satisfaction from the work he must do to secure a livelihood. What has been made all but impossible by the industrial system is that men and women can attain a livelihood by doing what is both aesthetically and morally sound and economically and practically valid, by a means that allows them both intellectual and spiritual responsibility.

We can perhaps sense more vividly the degree of impoverishment imposed by such a system if we contrast it with the value accorded the handicrafts by our ancestors, whose artifacts fill our ethnographical museums where they are revered for their skill and ageless beauty, and whose concept of the handicrafts is one that grants them nothing less than a sacred function. For it was traditionally the role of the crafts that, over and above serving practical ends, they were to serve the maintenance of the subtle link that binds together beauty and being, the severance of which has had such devastating consequences for the modern world. Unlike the situation that faces the modern worker, in the traditional and sacred context of the crafts each member of society, in so far as he or she practices an art, is responsible as a moral being for the good use of the community, while at the same time being personally responsible for the intrinsic good of the thing he or she makes.

In Ecclesiasticus 38 it is said of the craftsman that in trusting to his hands "every one is wise in his work," by which wisdom he "will maintain the state of the world." We can hardly fail to notice the parallel between such words and those quoted by the Indian scholar Stella Kramrisch, who says that according to traditional Indian belief and practice, every creature has a function (actually a craft vocation) which is fulfilled in the universe and deviation from which "might even endanger the order of the universe." This suggests that if the crafts have become an anachronism in our time this is not due to any inherent weakness or fault in the crafts themselves, but that we have assigned them a status that is considerably beneath the full dignity of their normal function.

The juggernaut of modern industrial enterprise is based upon the moral neutrality of capitalist investment which exploits the nature of usury to exert unrelenting pressure toward a purely quantitative, economic expansion. This essentially "blind" process has created a society in which it is all but impossible to determine what qualitative criteria might apply to the concept of human needs and how those needs might best be met. In other words we are embroiled in a pattern of life that is hardly able to distinguish between what is a real need and what is an artificially stimulated appetite and so cannot distinguish satisfaction from superfluity. This makes it virtually impossible to determine what *must* be done (as opposed to what *can* be done) in order to unite our everyday life of making and doing with the reality that is the ultimate nature of our humanity. Indeed, such a system has an obvious vested interest in seeing that such divisions are never healed, all the better to manipulate the confusion and disharmony that inevitably manifest themselves in a demand for material consolations.

All men and women make things, and it is by skill, by the deliberate intent of the mind and its exertion toward what is other than mind—some occasion or material circumstance outside of the mind—that things get made. And since each and every one of us makes things by the exercise of skill (which is the root meaning of art) each and every one of us is in some degree an artist. But behind our doing and making there is an agent or being who remains free and objective in relation to what is produced by the action that is applied skill. How we do and make does not determine our being so much as how we do and make is the very signature of our humanity. For if by our "fruits" we shall be "known," then work, far from being nothing more than a utilitarian process, must in some sense be capable of revealing the proper nature of our humanity. In other words action follows being. The converse would be to propose that action possesses within itself its own sufficient reason. The metaphysical objection to such a proposition is clearly stated by Eckhart:

> The work has no being, nor has the time in which it occurred, since it perishes in itself. Therefore it is neither good nor holy nor blessed, but rather the man is blessed in whom the fruit of the work remains, neither as time nor as work, but as a good disposition which is eternal with the spirit as the spirit is eternal in itself, and it is the spirit itself. (Sermon 8, Blakney edition)

So we perhaps begin to see that work is not something we must be freed from—indeed cannot be freed from unless we are freed entirely from action—but something we must engage in in such a way and at such a level that it is revealing of our deepest nature. It must contribute to our spiritual life while serving our bodily needs.

The very opposite is the case with the industrial pattern of work which is part and parcel of a social ethos that continually holds out the promise of leisure as the reward for the time and effort put into work. But this escape to a state of freedom *from* work is not offered as something that will serve our spiritual needs. Far from it. The so-called "leisure" of our consumer society is a parody of that spiritual condition of true inactivity, the contemplative interiority of a state of being in which we must finally acknowledge that we are only truly "free" when we are released from the necessity to re-act to the demands of the external world.

The idleness characterizing the leisure society (where no one has time to do nothing) is a condition of sloth in which the will to act to some meaningful end is, as it were, suspended in a state of restless neutrality. The medieval schoolmen understood this to be *acedia*, which, as Josef Pieper explained in *Leisure: The Basis of Culture,*

> means that a man prefers to forgo the rights, or if you prefer, the claims, that belong to his nature. In a word, he does not want to be as God wants him to be, and that ultimately means that he does not wish to be what he really, fundamentally, is. . . . Metaphysically and theologically, the notion of *acedia* means that a man does not, in the last resort, give the consent of his will to his own being; that behind or beneath the dynamic activity of his existence, he is still not at one with himself, or, as the mediaeval writers would have said, face to face with the divine good within him.

From the Christian perspective the starting point of all discussion of work has to begin with man's expulsion from Paradise—the loss, or rather "annexing," of the spiritual domain entailed by our being brought into our bodily life. Here the "sweat" of labor is made necessary by our material needs and is suffered in the knowledge that it may form a channel or path along which the original undivided unity of being of our nature may be traced and re-made whole. In this primary sense the work of right livelihood (it is the traditional role of the crafts to foster and preserve the sanctification of labor) is analogous to adopting the vocation of the contemplative life of prayer: the life of true inactivity. Work is prayer. Man at prayer and man at work, both turn in an inward direction away from the diverging, multiple impulses of the external world in order to effect a convergence of the soul's faculties toward a state of equilibrium that is an internal act of harmony and unity.

But whereas the "work" of contemplative prayer is a withdrawal from the world, the work of making and doing necessarily involves us with the world. It is given to very few to withdraw from the world to live a life of prayer and solitude. The mass of men and women, unable to surmount the inevitable distractions and entanglements of their bodily and social existence, need the concentration and discipline of a practical vocation in order to restore the inner balance and harmony that is their proper being.

So we may recognize that at its highest point of efficacy, inspired work, as with prayer, arrests the scattered sentient powers of the soul so that the workman becomes by degrees dead to his empirical ego as he approaches a state of perfect action. In this convergent movement of his being, initiated by the discipline of a skill (the very words *discipline* and *skill* imply of necessity a mastery over something "other" that is the opposite of *self*-indulgence), the subtle process whereby the workman comes "face to face with the divine good within him" can begin. Thus, by degrees we become detached from the contrary states that constitute the dualistic nature of our existence; life and death, spirit and matter, inner and outer, subject and object, pain and joy, so we are less the passive recipient of these contrary demands and more the instrument of the harmony and balance that transcends them. Thus conformed to the intelligible order of the Logos within, we become more the subject and vessel of the Creator and less the object of external contradictions. To use apophatic, Eckhartian terms, it is already a step toward God to see the Creation as His abundant gifts to us. It is another step nearer to want Him more than his gifts.

But, it is one thing to allow that because the mass of men and women are more or less excluded from the state of contemplative perfection, so they must be allowed the relative "freedom" of exploring their creativity, and quite another to claim that such creativity must proliferate on its own terms. For human action, let it be repeated, cannot be its own justification. For man is, primarily, called upon to understand the reason for his existence. Without such an understanding he cannot hope, beneficially, to relate his thoughts and subsequent actions to the underlying order of the reality of which he comprises only a part. Action cannot be free from the rigor and necessity of the primordial qualities of beauty and perfection if it is to take account of the "divine good within."

All traditions speak of human intelligence as having a sacred function precisely because the human per se is indefinable except in terms of the Divine. Suspended as he is between celestial and diabolic forces it is in turn only man's capacity to recapitulate what transcends him that grants him a legitimate dominion over the world of nature. Which is why only man can conceive of an earthly paradise and why, conversely, in denying what is above him, only man can create a hell on earth.

While it is certainly true that the crafts, in their material aspect, have their foundation in the external necessities of our existence which demands that we feed, shelter, and clothe our bodies, nonetheless, the origin of the crafts is rooted in the cosmological idea that the very substance of the world, in virtue of its being part of the Creation, is the "body" of God, the manifest aspect of the unmanifest Divine Principle. It is the reflection of this on the human plane that permits the analogous symbolism of the craftsman as one who creates in imitation of God's act of creating the world. The sacred crafts re-enact, at the existential level of the material creation, the primordial act of cosmogenesis. That is to say, on the human plane, perfect doing and making consist in the true alignment of mind, eye, and hand as a recapitulation of the divine perfection of the world that is the true alignment of the spiritual, the psyche (of the soul) and the bodily in a movement from potentiality to act.

If the crafts were not able to effect such a true alignment then we would not find in all traditional texts (such as we have already quoted from Christian and Hindu sources) passages that speak of the craftsman as upholding and maintaining the order of the universe. What is implied in all such texts is the idea that one's first and immediate duty and one's last or ultimate end must become coincident as comprising a unity. *Justice* is that which is conformable to a law, or to a rule, *order* is due place or rank, and *proportion* a due share or order of a part in relation to a whole. These ideas are semantically related in signifying a relationship of harmonious unity among disparate parts, a unity that reflects the equilibrium of the universal order. Obviously there can be no right livelihood in the things of injustice, disorder, and disproportion any more than it is conceivable that men and women could consecrate to God work that is flippant, indulgent, and superfluous.

Even the most cursory glance at the contents of our ethnographical museums will give abundant evidence of the symbolic aspect of the crafts. For not only in those things produced by the crafts—pottery, weaving, building, clothes, carpentry, and so on—but also in the very instruments of the crafts themselves, we find a rich language of symbolism indicative of their spiritual status. For instance, Christ, as the incarnate Divine Principle, and thus "in whom all things are made," was a carpenter—one who works wood.

Owing to its ubiquity as the primary substance to be worked in meeting so many practical and material needs, as well as its plasticity in accepting so many diverse forms, wood symbolically conforms to the *prima materia* of the Creation. (Swedenborg received a revelation of wood as the symbol of the celestial goodness in its lowest corporeal plane.)

St. Bonaventure points out in his treatise *Retracing the Arts to Theology*, that St. Augustine said the Son of God is the "art of the Father": through whom, it may be added, we are enabled to see the beginning and end of all things; that is, what is right and true. As St. Bonaventure also points out, one sense of the word *right* is that a thing's middle is not out of line with its extreme points. In the similar way a carpenter works a piece of wood, checking to see that it is *true* (from "fidelity," "trust," OE *tréo,* giving English *tree*—"as firm and straight as a tree"), by the use of a *rule* (from "regular," measuring bar, pattern of conduct, a discipline) that tells him if the middle is aligned with its beginning and its end. His tools are no less symbolically assimilable to the divine process or causes that shape the *materia* of the universe. Moreover, Christ, as the "beginning" and "end" of all things, was sacrificed on a wooden cross, in turn assimilable to the Tree of Life or world axis that holds heaven and earth together. The richness of such symbolic correspondences, which could easily be elaborated, should be sufficient to illustrate the cosmic function of the craftsman.

What we do not find is that the mass of men and women in remote ages satisfied their material needs in some unsophisticated and brutish fashion with an eye only to efficient and pragmatic solutions. On the contrary, in serving material needs the maker keeps his ocular vision on the immediate and contingent requirements of the task at hand. But at the same time he keeps the inner eye of spiritual vision on those things that relate to his final end— the fact that he is a created and creative part of that sacred reality that is the world. By so doing he produces an environment that forms the living context for the human spirit to participate in the cyclic rhythms of nature that are themselves a reflection of the cosmic rhythms of the universe. For just as the principle of nature is rhythmic organization and order, so the principle of manufacture is the ordering of matter according to an intelligible pattern. By his most common and repeated actions the craftsman integrates himself with the vast, powerful, fructifying sources of reality so that his individual existence is not projected into a meaningless expanse of time and space. For, essentially, the arts and crafts are the application of a science of rhythm, as René Guénon has pointed out; the phonetic arts being the application of the rhythm of succession deployed in time and the plastic arts being the application of the rhythm of simultaneity deployed in space. By contrast, in the industrial milieu, time is speeded up and space becomes merely indefinite extension. In so doing they erode, and eventually abolish, the meaningful relationship of the temporal with the eternal and the finite with the infinite. Time and space lose their spiritual significance as the primary ordering principles of orientation for the "place" and "direction" of human vocation and destiny.

The technological environment projects man into a progress that disrupts the cyclical and periodic rhythms of time, to replace them with the open-ended future of an indefinite development. In such an environment, space that is normally experienced as locally qualified extension—as the "container" of events—becomes the generalized field of a "freedom" paradoxically experienced as oppressive and where man is subject to the forces of inertia and compression in the physical realm and acceleration and dispersion in the psychological realm.

The sacramental and ritual character of the traditional crafts, on the other hand, actualizes the numinous context of time and space by formalizing and embodying the link between the inner contemplative domain of the soul on the one hand and the outer active domain of the body on the other. These two domains are, however, not discrete or disjunctive but complementary, dual facets of the one same reality in its transcendent and immanent, objective and subjective modes. This sacramental character places a heavier emphasis on the agent of action—the quality of the humanity of the maker—in the productive process than it does on the technical means of manufacture. This is again quite the opposite situation facing the industrial worker whose complicity is with a mechanized technique in which almost his entire work function has been systematized as a result of someone else's conception and design. This is to devitalize the work process, emptying it of precisely those external, manipulative challenges and internal, psychological satisfactions that give meaning and value to the experience of work. And what else could what we call soul-destroying work be but just such an absence or devitalization? Seen in this light we can better appreciate what is lost in the progressive model of industrial production, where the worker is always prey to the indiscriminate development of the working environment, a process that anesthetizes his soul as the price demanded for its own survival.

With the traditional crafts the means of production are kept as close as possible to the fundamental interaction of hand and mind, with the eye as intermediary, sight being the agent of both perception and action. This economy of instrumental means allows the manipulative and visual faculties their closest collaboration with the intellect, which then acts as the motive source of the worker's skill.

The intimate link between the crafts and ritual, work and prayer, action and spirituality, has been fostered and transmitted by the guild societies in all traditional cultures. In India, for instance, the presiding god of craftsmen is Visvakarma, sum total of consciousness, knowledge, and inspiration, the architect of the universe, in whom resides the divine skill that is revealed to the craftsman through the sacred texts and oral transmission of traditional doctrines and disciplines.

In the Christian tradition, all wisdom, knowledge, and ability ultimately descends through Christ, from the Father. St. Bonaventure, for instance, conceives the mechanical arts as resulting from the illumination of knowledge, which illumination (or light) is, in the final analysis, coterminous with the Divine Light that is the Logos, which illumines each and every being and goodness present in the world.

From the Islamic perspective, the arts and crafts are like so many formal crystallizations in the realm of multiplicity of the Divine Unity that is the inner reality of the Qur'an made manifest by the Prophet and his companion 'Ali, the founder of Islamic calligraphy and patron of all the guilds.

The existence of the guilds, in both East and West, was for the purpose of nurturing and sustaining an initiatory knowledge in which art, craft, work, science, mechanics, dynamics, geometry, and so on are all categories of thought and forms of wisdom-*sapientia*. This illumination of the mind corrects and perfects the intuitive knowledge of a thing's essence and how it is to be realized in some outward form and is analogous to the trans-mundane light of the Divine Intellect throwing an illuminated pattern on the mirror of the human intelligence. The rays or threads of this transcendent light can be likened to translucent states of being held in hierarchic suspension from their ultimate source in the infinite perfection of the Divine Principle that is the spirit of God.[1] The purpose of the activity that is the particular craft skill is to follow the rigors of a discipline such that, in accomplishing inner and outer mastery, there is a perfect integration of bodily activity, imaginative conception, and spiritual illumination—wholeness of being, in fact. This traditional practice of the trades presupposes that each thing to be made, each action to be undertaken, has itself a norm of perfection—that which enables it, through the agency of intellectual determination and manual skill, to attain its true and essential nature.[2]

From the foregoing observations it will be clear that an answer to the question "Are the crafts an anachronism"? cannot be simple, for it depends upon what we admit is involved in their practice. If we see all work as simply the pragmatic means by which we satisfy our material needs, then of course the crafts are outmoded as a way of

---

1. That such a doctrine was still dependably current among his readers could be assumed by George Herbert when in the 1630s he wrote in the last stanza of his poem "Mattens,"

> Teach me thy love to know
>   That this new light, which now I see,
> May both the work and workman show:
>   Then by a sunne-beam I will climb to thee.

However, by around 1810 perhaps fewer of William Blake's readers would have recognized the allusion to the same doctrine in these famous lines:

> I give you the end of a golden string,
>   Only wind it into a ball:
> It will lead you in at Heaven's gate
>   Built in Jerusalem's wall.

2. "The Tea Ceremony signifies that we ought to perform all the activities and manipulations of daily life according to primordial perfections, which is pure symbolism, pure consciousness of the Essential, perfect beauty and self-mastery. The

producing the necessities of life. But any study of the traditional conception of the crafts, and of the human self-image that is integral to them, reveals a more complex picture; one that touches upon spiritual factors that at best have been obscured or debased in the way work is understood in the modern world. However, such a study obliges us to recognize that there are social, economic, as well as spiritual conditions required for the traditional conception of human vocation to function properly; conditions hardly in providential alignment in the modern world. Indeed, it should be said that the modern world is the result of having these conditions misaligned. But that does not permit us to dismiss as speculative fancy what a study of the crafts is capable of revealing, both about the nature of the human agent of the crafts and about the spiritual milieu the crafts are capable of embodying. From the standpoint of contemporary conditions we are in the position of one who, faced with a mountain and not having the full means to ascend it, is nonetheless neither in a position to deny that the ascent is possible, nor to deny that the view from the summit is what it is.

The story of the Fall, of man's expulsion from the Heavenly Paradise, is the story of man's having to live "by the sweat of his brow." That much is inescapable. But does it follow that we are condemned to a life of brute exertion without redemption? Machines may have relieved us of a good deal of physical hardship but at the price, to say the least, of introducing a scale and pattern of work that makes for much soulless drudgery. And we know ourselves to have a soul as surely as we register when our soul is not given its due. As to our redemption, from the standpoint of a study of the crafts as the

---

intention is basically the same in the craft initiation of the West—including Islam—but the formal foundation is then the production of useful objects and not the symbolism of gestures; this being so, the stone mason intends, parallel to his work, to fashion his soul in view of union with God. And thus there is to be found in all the crafts and all the arts a spiritual model that, in the Muslim world, often refers to one of the prophets mentioned in the Koran; any professional or home-making activity is a kind of revelation. As for the adherents of Zen, they readily seek their inspiration in 'ordinary life,' not because it is trivial, to be sure, but because—inasmuch as it is woven of symbolisms—it mysteriously implies the 'Buddha nature.'" Frithjof Schuon, *The Eye of the Heart* (1997), pp. 140–41.

instrument and repository of sacred culture, the answer is unequivocal. In their natural habitat the crafts presuppose an analogical and
effective relationship between labor and spiritual edification in
which work has both dignity and sanctity. To work in this context is
to seek purification through discipline. And because there is no
freedom without discipline, so it is possible for our vocation to be
exemplified in the mastery of a practical skill as the best and most
natural means to dispose our salvation.[3] This makes it possible for
our first duty as spiritual beings to be coincident with our responsibility as social beings. For as surely as "rights" incur responsibilities,
so ultimately we can only concede our neighbors' "rights" on the
basis of their spiritual freedom to realize his or her deiformity. We
are surely entitled to ask whether the industrial system presents a
more dignified, and in the end, a more realistic paradigm.

But if we insist that the answer to our initial question—Are the
crafts an anachronism?—is yes, then what have we admitted? We
have admitted to there being no possibility of an inner perfection in
whatever we labor at. With that confirmed and in the name of consistency, we must go on to admit that labor is a monstrous encum-
brance without value, and that learning is a mere gathering of
information without meaning, the final goal of both being mechanical efficiency. In which case both had better be dealt with by
machines, as indeed we see is attempted, by the "leisure industry"
on the one hand and by the computer on the other. But this does
not answer, so much as shelve, the question of *why* we should labor
and think at all! As we have already suggested, it is precisely spiritual
and qualitative values and meanings that determine what *ought* to
be done as opposed to what simply *can* be done.[4]

---

3. "Let every man abide in the same calling wherein he was called. Art thou
called *being* servant? care not for it: but if thou mayest be made free, use *it* rather."
1 Corinthians 7:20–21.

4. To mean something is to have in mind a cognitive intent. Hence it is to signify the actual and effective penetration of the intelligence by a cognitive value. The
value of anything implies an equivalent exchange of something; here a cognitive
worth that enters a given state of being by that which is adequate to it. In such an
effective penetration Beauty, Goodness, and Truth presuppose the possibility of
our elevation from lower to higher states of being.

The extensive range of mechanized contrivances we call modern industry assumes the destruction of the crafts as inimical to its survival. Such indeed is its very raison d'être. It is not in the interests of such a system to awaken in those it enslaves any intimation of possibilities the system itself cannot satisfy. There is an exact common measure between the fact that in the post-industrial society the body, no longer challenged as the instrument of creative work, has become a complex of organs appealed to only in as much as they are able to *feel*. How else can we explain that the blandishments of the advertising industry are directed almost exclusively toward convenience and gratification—the stimulation and indulgence of bodily sensation. A consumer society such as we know it could not function except in a world where the body has little to do but concern itself with its appetites—and these a mere palliative.

What alienates us from an environment made up almost entirely of the products of industrial technology is the fact that such products could not exist except by means of a system of manufacture that is first and foremost founded upon the destruction of the sacred status of human vocation. And, as an entailment of that destruction, the erosion and eventual obliteration of the natural context of that vocation—the direct, vital experience of birth, death, generation, the natural and lunar cycles, the whole panoply of the heavens and the earth, water, land, river, tree, stone, and flower through which the order of the sacred is mediated to man's experience.

If we look to the beauty of the crafts and all that they have engendered, it is to seek liberation from the enslavement of our own misdoings. Nothing is more natural to man than that he should achieve a lasting standard as a bulwark against the inevitable transience of his earthly life. What is that standard to be? That is the real question posed by the crafts.

Why do the crafts continue to occupy our attention? Surely it is because we are still capable of recognizing in them a mirror image, however faint, of what it is we might yet become. We do best to honor that image by acknowledging that, in all but abandoning the crafts in favor of industrial means of production, we have lost a significant portion of what it means to be fully human. The anachronism of the crafts is achieved at the cost of our own disfigurement.

PART II

Word Made Flesh:
Modern Artists and Tradition

10

Eric Gill and a
Holy Tradition of Working

ERIC GILL was born on February 22, 1882, at Brighton. A talent for drawing led him to Chichester Art School, after which he was apprenticed to a London architect. Under the influence of W.R. Lethaby and Edward Johnston he took up letter carving, receiving his first commission in 1901. In 1913 Gill and his wife entered the Catholic Church, by his own admission the most important event in his life. With Hilary Pepler he formed a Craft Guild Community at Ditchling (1916–24). For four years he had his workshop at Capel-y-ffin in the Welsh Black Mountains. His final workshop community was at "Pigotts" near High Wycombe from 1928 to 1940, the year of his death. In everything he did he was concerned to know and to live sacred principles common to man and the matter of human work. Those who knew him intimately attest to the integrity of vision and wisdom with which he realized his intention.

When Gill died at the age of fifty-eight he left behind a dozen or so books and many shorter polemical writings, over a thousand wood engravings, nine typeface designs, a considerable amount of sculpture, stone and wood carvings, inscriptions, some of the finest nude studies of this century, as well as designs for postage stamps, coins, books, at least one clock, a church, and much else besides. No wonder that those who have written about him since cannot agree in their judgment as to the most enduring part of this legacy. About this perhaps Gill had his own ideas. David Jones reports that Gill had once said to him: "What I achieve as a sculptor is of no consequence—I can only be a beginning—it will take generations, but if only the beginnings of a reasonable, decent, holy tradition of work might be effected—that is the thing." Moreover, his friend and mentor Ananda K. Coomaraswamy wrote, "He invented a human way of working, and found that it was that of all human societies. . . . This amounts to saying that Eric's was not a personal point of view, but simply a true one, that he had made his own. He was not 'thinking for himself' but assenting to credible propositions; and he was; accordingly, a man of faith." There is a precedent then for pointing to Gill's doctrine of the norm of workmanship as the most singular part of his achievement.

Since his death, none of Gill's books has been reprinted. This has not deterred his critics, a good many of whom have had their own ideas of what he stood for. There is almost a folklore—in which fact and fiction are knit together—surrounding the memory of the man. Few bother to find out what he actually said. There is a consistent and coherent doctrine scattered among his writings. It needs extraction. This anthology attempts to present that philosophy essentially and integrally rather than exhaustively.[1] It is time, once again, for Gill to have his say.

Eric Gill was all of a piece. You must take him whole or not at all. You can no more detach his doctrine of art from his doctrine of work than you can detach his morals from his religion. They all go together. He cannot be tried against the prevailing conditions or the "inevitability of history" or against the acceptance of human culpability without those things thereby being seen the more clearly for what they are. His appeal is always to necessity and good sense.

Almost invariably, his past detractors have failed to perceive the level at which his thought moves. This failure on the part of many of his critics springs not so much from a mere disagreement about the purpose and direction of our civilization as from their unwillingness to accept the degree to which Gill's views are at one and the same time "absolute" and "radical."

Gill refused to put together a philosophy by way of small adjustments and accommodations to any of the modes and disguises with which the doctrine of a godless scientific and economic progress infiltrates the mental and physical life of modern society. Perhaps

---

1. [See the list of sources of this book's chapters, at the end of the book, for details about the anthology referred to here. —Ed.]

the more common form of capitulation to this "progress" is the passive acceptance with which it is believed that "machines are here to stay!" That Gill saw no such necessity, and that he saw their eventual demise as being due to their fundamental incompatibility with the proper nature of man has caused some of his critics to accuse him of wanting to go back to the Middle Ages. This criticism persists in spite of the fact that he has specifically written that there can be no putting back of the clock and that we must make the best of modern conditions on the basis of sheer reasonableness. Where the critic wants the convenience of what is familiar, and the compensations of "art," Gill simply wants truth and consistency. Gill had his sights on the heavenly Jerusalem: his critics have theirs on England today, or perhaps tomorrow. It is the perpetual clash of interests between the politics of eternity and the politics of time.

This clash of interests, having engaged Gill's critics in the past, must certainly engage his reader today. There have been two permanent stumbling blocks between Gill and his reader. The two interlock. The first is the obvious need to come to terms with the absoluteness of his image of man: his quite literal belief in the fact that man is created in the image of God. If you believe this to be true, and you examine the consequences that follow from it as rigorously as Gill did, your conclusions as to the nature and purpose of human life must be totally different from those you would hold if you believe that man is a mere "higher," more clever primate, a more or less haphazard system of appetites, instincts, and energy drives and the like. This latter view is so obviously incompatible with the whole spectrum of Gill's thought that the reader must either learn to accommodate Gill on this point or admit that he desires other things and pass on.

The second stumbling-block—the assumption that the "progress" of technological development is inevitable—we have already touched upon. But the following must be added. If you assume that the whole of man's experience does not go beyond the world of time and space then you must believe that all development will take place within the confines of that world. In which case there can only be an exploration of the extent of space and—since the horizontal movement of time is ever forward—development in future time. The pull of the future must seem inevitable in such circumstances. It is hardly coincidental, therefore, that the philosophy of materialism (which rests upon such assumptions) should, as Gill says, "click" with an industrial world, and that in the nature of things it must issue in an ever greater degree of technological sophistication. But this did not prevent Gill from seeing the inconsistency of such a belief with free will (with its concomitant of intellectual responsibility), and with the ultimate spiritual nature of man.

The two presiding principles along which, as it were, Gill guides his thoughts on the nature and purpose of human making are those of "beauty" and "art." Let us look at his notion of beauty first. Here Gill's point of departure is St. Thomas, quoting St. Dionysius the Areopagite: "The Beauty of God is the cause of the being of all that is."[2] Thus beauty is an absolute and has to do with cognition. Absolute Beauty is the very cause of the perfection of things and as being is coincident with the Good, is the end to which the nature of things tends. The Scholastic doctrine of beauty as a transcendental, an objective property in things—the splendor of intelligibility—can be traced back through St. Dionysius and St. Augustine to Plotinus and eventually to Plato's formulation of beauty as the radiance of truth. It was this tradition that St. Thomas built upon, while giving beauty a more immediate and subjective emphasis when he described it as "that which pleases when seen." But we must not assume that St. Thomas's deceptively simple description identifies beauty with that pleasure, that quickening of the aesthetic senses that is felt in common delight. Gill reminds us that what sees is the mind, the "inner eye" of the mind. Though the outward senses are the channel through which what pleases must pass, nevertheless in seeing beauty the mind acts and apprehends in the self-same act Being Itself. In that act the *thing* that presents itself is not diffused or dissolved away into abstraction. It remains in the perfection and order proper to itself, a thing of greater clarity, a thing without which no beauty is seen at all. And this perfection and clarity is nothing less than the thing's essence, its form, the qualitative imprint, as it were,

---

2. [See the citation for this quote in the introduction to this book, where the translation differs from that which is used here.—Ed.]

stamped on the created thing by its creator. Thus in the measure that a thing seen reflects the beauty proper to itself, so the mind sees what that thing is without adulteration and privation.

By analogy the same is true of works of art as things made, since whatever is made is first conceived in the mind of the artist. It is the intelligibility of this formative process in which the work of art is made in imitation of its mental prototype that the beauty of art consists. Just as the beauty of natural things is in accordance with the perfection of their being as part of the whole of the created order of things, so the beauty of a work of art is inseparable from its occasion and purpose as a thing called forth by intelligible need. Beauty cannot be said to be a property belonging to works of art exclusively, and the artist or workman does not proceed *directly* to "make beauty" any more than he works to "produce pleasure." The beauty of works of art is not aesthetic (as is our pleasure at the resultant thing), but cognitive and in accordance with the goodness and truth with which the said work fulfills what it is its nature to be. For this reason a work of art (or nature) is inseparable from its creator's intention, always remembering that as it is not part of God's intention to create natural things for the sake of idle curiosity, but to lead us on to higher things, so it should never be the intention of the artist to create meaningless luxuries which it is beneath man's natural dignity to tolerate.

The complementary principle to beauty in Gill's thought is that of art. Traditionally and normally, the notion of art is part of a body of wisdom according to which things made attain to the proper perfection of their nature. Man, considered in the light of an inverse metaphysical analogy whereby he is the reflected image of God, in fashioning an object materially at the same time fashions himself spiritually. By the same process of analogy in the act of creating God externalizes Himself, whereas the artist or workman in the act of making internalizes himself—by making outwardly, in an act of pure worship, man fashions his own internal essence. That is to say, he returns to the perfection of his own nature. Here we have the perennial idea of human vocation as part of the conformity of all things to their true nature as an expression of the divine will. Only he can attain perfection who is integrated with the causes and ends

of things. This way he incurs no sin—sin being defined as a departure from the order to the end. We might recall that in his *Republic*
Plato described justice as the freedom of men to do and act according to what it is their nature to be. And in connection with works of
art Gill wrote: "We've got to make things *right*. Beauty consists in
due proportion. We have got to give things the proportion that is
due to them. It's a matter of justice."[3] The artist works, then, in imitation of the true nature of things. He does not imitate God's works,
for that would be to make copies of copies, but imitates God's manner of working as it is inherent in his nature so to do.

The word *art,* in the Scholastic formulation of the traditional
wisdom, refers to that operative habit of the intellect by which the
artist possesses what is the proper perfection of work to be done.
This formulation takes as its point of departure Aristotle's description in his *Ethics* of art as the innate condition of the mind by which
a man proceeds upon a rational course of action in the making of
something. Art is an inner skill, not mere outward dexterity. By the
light of art the workman sees *what* is to be done; by the operation of
art he knows *how* it shall be done. As the operative agent of art the
workman's only concern is for the good of the work to be done. In
departing from the perfecting of his art the workman sins *as an artist.* Art, then, stays in the artist and is not personified by the artist.
David Jones observed of Gill that he worked as though a tradition
existed. He meant that Gill worked assuming that these conditions
and values both applied and were true.

With the division of "art" from "work" and "beauty" from "use"
in the modern world, art comes out of the artist and gets attached,
so to say, to the work of art itself. The creator of "art," now called an
"artist," personifies art and is given the sole prerogative of its production. Beauty too comes out of the thing made to be an aesthetic
sensation desired for its own sake. No longer the property of a thing
that shows forth the fullness of integrity, harmony, and intelligible
clarity due to its being; no longer identified with goodness and
truth, beauty is now associated with a select category of things
made. As an aid to emotional stimulus, beauty is freed from the

3. *Letters of Eric Gill* (1947), p. 200.

process of rational manufacture so that art has become "pure" or "fine" and as such is treated idealistically. The workman is no longer expected to be in *possession* of his art; "art" and "work" are distinct, even opposed, orders of making. Moreover, "art" becomes a snob value and the word *art* actually comes to denote the objects that comprise this artificially isolated category of things whose value is maintained in the interests of social prestige. Indeed, the modern world speaks of "art" instead of "works of art" because this artificial isolation makes it necessary to distinguish "art" from "non-art" in the category of things made.

All this Gill called "art nonsense" and he sought to debunk it in so far as it makes a "false mysticism" of man's creative spirit and distorts the proper order and status of intelligent workmanship.

Gill's indebtedness to the English tradition of radical thought, whose roots go back beyond William Cobbett to Blake and reach forward through Carlyle, Ruskin, Morris, and on to his contemporaries and friends W. R. Lethaby and Edward Johnston, has always been acknowledged. Indeed, Gill's critique of the modern industrial world and his re-affirmation of the dignity of human labor must be set against the perspective of such thought as his achievement must be seen to be cumulative in respect of their example.

Gill always acknowledged a degree of kinship with William Blake, though he was far from sharing Blake's visionary sense of the imagination. But just as Blake was the prophet of the then industrializing English nation, so Gill may yet be seen as the prophet of post-industrial England. Blake was an artisan engraver in late eighteenth-century London, a time of decline in many such trades. The influx of population drifting away from agricultural subsistence in the fields and villages of rural England had come to form the mass of dispossessed and unskilled proletariat of the new centers of mechanical production. In the wake of this upheaval came the erosion of craft skills, and to Blake this fact highlighted the destructiveness inherent in the process of mechanization. Blake saw this process not indeed primarily as destroying muscle and bone (though it did that well enough) but as destructive of the inner man—*homo faber*—the "Poetic Genius" in every man. "A Machine is not a Man nor Work of Art; it is destructive of Humanity & of Art," he declared in his *Public*

Address of 1810. He had already, in about 1788, in his two tracts *There Is No Natural Religion* and *All Religions Are One*, found it necessary to point out that the nature of man is Infinite, in opposition to the encroaching philosophies of the mechanic system based exclusively upon a knowledge derived wholly from the bodily organs of perception. This bounded universe, as he saw, would be "loathed by its possessor," for in denying man the Infinite that is connatural to him it binds him to the Ratio merely of his own ego.

In these tracts Blake settles once and for all the terms of reference for the ensuing radical debate on the destructiveness of the mechanical system. When Gill claims that "death is the actual aim of industrialism, its diabolic direction," it is nothing new. Blake had seen it a century earlier and had spoken out against it in a powerful passage in his *Jerusalem*:

> ...all the Arts of Life they chang'd into the Arts of Death in
> Albion.
> The hour-glass contemn'd because its simple workmanship
> Was like the workmanship of the plowman, & the water wheel
> That raises water into cisterns, broken & burn'd with fire
> Because its workmanship was like the workmanship of the
> shepherd;
> And in their stead, intricate wheels invented, wheel without wheel,
> To perplex youth in their outgoings & to bind to labours in Albion
> Of day & night the myriads of eternity; that they may grind
> And polish brass & iron hour after hour, laborious task,
> Kept ignorant of its use: that they might spend the days of wisdom
> In sorrowful drudgery to obtain a scanty pittance of bread,
> In ignorance to view a small portion & think that All,
> And call it Demonstration, blind to all the simple rules of life.

This passage anticipates a good deal of the thought Gill expressed a century later after the same system had consistently proven its social and human divisiveness as well as its spiritual impotence.

Cobbett rode on horseback over the southern counties of the same England that Blake knew. A prodigious worker himself, Cobbett knew the importance to a just society of a right and responsible livelihood for its people. He witnessed the rural aspect of the social upheaval created by the drift of population to the "Great Wen." For him its effect was not only social but was recognizable in the fact that it laid waste the land. Cobbett had a hatred of unproductive land. For him, where beauty and utility had been put asunder there could be no natural beauty in a situation that was morally unacceptable. He poured his inimitable scorn on those responsible for the enclosure of the common land. The consequent lack of ownership of the means of subsistence meant that the dispossessed agricultural laborer was as much the slave of the "Lords of the Loom" as was the factory worker. Cobbett saw, and knew that he saw, the germinating seeds of the modern consumer society. His denunciation of the increasing self-sufficiency of the body of *idlers and traffickers* who create the modern marketplace, keeping apart those who produce things and those who have need of them, had its basis in the observation that, in such conditions, both the producer and the consumer must gradually relinquish control over the means of production in favor of the "middle-men, who create nothing, who add to the value of nothing, who improve nothing . . . and who live well, too, out of the labor of the producer and the consumer." Cobbett was no less aware of the effect of all this upon the mass of city slaves. Here his analysis of the "calamity" occasioned by the mechanic invention pre-figures Gill's concern that the machine is only acceptable if wholly owned and directed by the worker himself, who must also have the benefit of the profits that accrue to its working: "We must have the machine at home and we ourselves must have the *profit* of it; for, if the machine be *elsewhere*; if it be worked *by other hands*; if other *persons* have the *profit* of it . . . then the machine is an injury to us," he wrote in his *Rural Rides*.

Beyond recognizing the dignity it may lend, and the injustice, when its fruits are withheld, that labor may occasion man, Cobbett said little about the inherent nature of work. But Thomas Carlyle went further. In the chapter "Labour," in his *Past and Present*, he saw that "there is a perennial nobleness, and even sacredness in work." Moreover, "a man perfects himself by working," for "even in the meanest sorts of Labour, the whole soul of a man is composed into a kind of real harmony."

Carlyle saw into the center of the active life of the working man. Recognizing a sort of Platonic justice there, he wrote, "Blessed is he who has found his work" for in "the inmost heart of the Worker rises a god-given Force." For him the only knowledge is that which holds good in working—the rest is "hypothesis of knowledge." In such thoughts Carlyle comes close to expressing the traditional notion of the marriage of wisdom and method in all vocational endeavor— "Admirable is that of the old Monks, 'Laborare est Orare,' Work is Worship"—a balance of the contemplative and active life of the intelligence and the will, the harmony of reposed soul and dynamic body. In Carlyle we have a foretaste of Gill's thought that as man is the summit of nature, so his art improves on nature, and that every man is a special kind of artist. In the same work Carlyle wrote, "He that works, whatsoever be his work, he bodies forth the form of Things Unseen; a small Poet every Worker is." The humblest platter, the Epic Poem, these that Nature has not yet seen he creates—to Her a "No-thing!"—these the worker summons from the Unseen, "in and for the Unseen." He who looks to the powers of this world must ever play at the deceiving of his true self—the unspeaking voice of conscience, the silent reverberation of perfection in his nature. The worker who, for whatever reason, looks to "the world and its wages," works at a "Sham-thing" which is best not done. Thus Carlyle saw, before Ruskin, that the tragedy of industrial work, "under bondage to Mammon," was the enforced idleness of "the rational soul" it induced in the worker, stopping the springs of charity and thus destroying the moral basis of human intercourse.

If the ultimate nature of Carlyle's religious notions was somewhat vague, there was no mistaking the "true Deity" of his age: "Mechanism." Under this secular god men no longer feel the pull of the "internal perfection"; their faith, as he wrote in his essay "Signs of the Times," is "for external combinations and arrangements, for institutions, constitutions,—for Mechanism of one sort or other, do they hope and struggle. Their whole efforts, attachments, opinions, turn on mechanism, and are of a mechanical character."

The wellsprings of faith in the "Deity of Mechanism" had been pinpointed by Coleridge in his *Statesman's Manual* of 1816, some thirteen years before the prophetic text of Carlyle's essay. The mechanic philosophy, Coleridge wrote (elaborating on Blake's tracts, as it were), "demanding for every mode and act of existence real or possible visibility, knows only of distance and nearness, composition (or rather juxtaposition) and decomposition, in short the relation of unproductive particles to each other; so that in every instance the result is the exact sum of the component quantities, as in arithmetical addition. This is the philosophy of death, and only of a dead nature can it hold good." This "philosophy of death," founded on the mechanism of Hobbes, the empiricism of Locke, and the economics of Adam Smith, had issued in a

> commercial spirit, and the ascendancy of the experimental philosophy which . . . combined to foster its [the discursive understanding's] corruption. Flattered and dazzled by the real or supposed discoveries, which it had made, the more the understanding was enriched, the more did it become debased; till science itself put on a selfish and sensual character, and *immediate utility*, in exclusive reference to the gratification of the wants and appetites of the animal, the vanities and caprices of the social, and the ambition of the political, man was imposed as the test of all intellectual powers and pursuits. *Worth* was degraded in to a lazy synonym of *value;* and value was exclusively attached to the interest of the senses.

Carlyle, in his moment of vision in "Signs of the Times," caught an echo of the warning sounded by Coleridge: that the mechanical model by which men hoped to shape the world shapes man in its turn. Men come to conceive and understand themselves on the model of external circumstances. Cultivated on exclusively mechanical principles, the inward is finally abandoned and the mind is emptied of any significance other than that of evincing the mechanical method. This undue cultivation of the outward overrides and considers as nothing the "Dynamic," as Carlyle called it, in man's nature: "the primary, unmodified forces and energies of man, the mysterious springs of Love, and Fear, and Wonder, of Enthusiasm, Poetry, Religion, all which have a truly vital and *infinite* character." More and more, development comes to mean something external and measurable; social virtues are equated with political and economic expediency. "Men are to be guided only by their self-interests." The cash nexus that binds the worker to his employer becomes the standard by which men measure all effort and reward. When the sufficiency and corruption of public laws prove their inability to maintain an effective balance of "self-interests"—or it is the law of the new political economy that property should be concentrated and protected—exploitation comes as naturally as fruit to the tree.

With regard to the ethical neutrality of a system of manufacture in which work had atrophied to a mere mechanical function, Ruskin, as Gill acknowledged in his essay devoted to him, saw "clearly that the roots of human action, and therefore of human art, are moral roots." Just as, in the face of the rapid advance of the new system, Carlyle had found it necessary to point to the contrast between the "Dynamical" and the "Mechanic" method, so Ruskin in his turn points to the moral contrast in the division of society inimical to the "Mercantile Economy"; the economy of "pay" signifies the legal, moral, and social claims made by the few upon the labor of the many: poverty and debt on the one side, riches and right on the other. But for one who had seen that "there is no wealth but life" the iniquities of the disproportion in reward between employer and employed were less important than those of a system that could manufacture anything "except men." It was not so much the division of labor or the "degradation of the operative into a machine" that the system had achieved but the division of men themselves, "broken into small fragments and crumbs of life," as he put it in *The Stones of Venice.*

Like Carlyle before him and Coomaraswamy and Gill a century later, Ruskin had glimpsed the truth that every man was a special kind of artist and thought the task of the reformer was to rekindle in every laborer that "power for better things," the *"thoughtful* part" of him which must be prized and honored even in its imperfection "above the best and most perfect manual skill" such as the mechanic system produces. This way he would be "made a man," whereas before he had been a mere "animated tool." In *Unto This Last* Ruskin had castigated his uncomprehending contemporaries for their unquestioning reliance upon the modern political economy itself built upon the premises of Mill, Malthus, Ricardo, and so on. What the new science had left out of account was precisely the "motive power of the soul." It was this very unacknowledged quality, the soul, that seeped into every quantitative calculation of the "political economist's equations, without his knowledge, and falsifies every one of their results." Work is best done, not for pay or under pressure, but "only when the motive force, that is to say, the will or spirit of the creature, is brought to its greatest strength" by the "social affections"—precisely what the political economist is likely to see as merely "accidental and disturbing elements in human nature." Blake, Coleridge, Carlyle, and then Ruskin, each struggled to keep open a sense of the soul's worth in the face of its gradual occlusion by the closed system that accepts as its sole province the domain of what can be measured and weighed.

But Ruskin, though he had seen that the work of mere utility— the "dishonour of manual labour"—must be done away with altogether, showed the impotence with which Gill charged him when it came to the question of the beautiful. With the eye of an aesthete whose vision is formed on an inverted materialism he wrote in *Modern Painters*: "Any material object which can give us pleasure in the simple contemplation of its outward qualities without any direct or definite exertion of the intellect, I call in some way, or in some degree, beautiful." For Ruskin the beautiful was always something incidental, something added, like a sheen or gloss to the being of a thing, not a light within it. Never a cognitive principle, beauty is always an affective impulse and is sensational as to its object. It is thus not surprising that "art," for Ruskin, far from being the rational principle of normal workmanship, was not much more than whatever elicits his deepest feelings at delighted observation—and the artist is, for him, one who can depict such feelings. Attempting to unite beauty and workmanship, in a passage in *The Two Paths*, he wrote: "Beautiful art can only be produced by people who have beautiful things about them, and leisure to look at them; and unless you provide some elements of beauty for your workmen to be surrounded by, you will find that no elements of beauty can be invented by them."

William Morris's wrestling with the divisive monster of beauty on the one hand and utility on the other took a different form yet again from that of his predecessors. He saw through the fallacy of the Protestant ethic—used as an expedient to bridge the divide—that work, *any* work, because it serves "the sacred cause of labour," is good in itself. This same fallacy Carlyle had come close to advocating. For Morris, the evil shadow of the industrialized system obscured the light of an obvious truth: there are, he wrote in *Useful Work versus Useless Toil*, "two kinds of work —one good, the other bad; one not far removed from a blessing, a lightening of life; the other a mere curse, a burden to life." The work it was manly to do has hope in it, a threefold hope—"hope of rest, hope of product, hope of pleasure in the work itself." All other work "is slave's work— mere toiling to live, that we may live to toil." Such was the heritage of the dispossessed peasants of the eighteenth century who became the proletariat of the nineteenth—"a great mass of slaves, who must be fed, clothed, housed, and amused as slaves, and that their daily necessity compels them to make the slave-wares whose use is the perpetuation of their slavery." This fact remained fundamental to Gill's view of contemporary society. He too saw that the tyranny of the modern marketplace consists in the fact that the buyer, far from being an enlightened patron (which he could still in a measure be at the country fairs Cobbett saw must be destroyed by the increased trafficking of middle men in shops), is no more in possession of an educated taste and discretion that any other consumer of those goods which are called into existence for no other reason than to serve as the very lifeblood of the system of their production. For Morris the smart of injustice was in the enforced degradation of man at this "tax of waste," this treadmill futility that is a trading on the ignorance of the productive masses by the profit-gathering minority who have "the power of compelling other men to work against their will." For Gill (who transposed many of Morris's observations into the terms of his own philosophy), no less than for Morris, this imposition upon the worker to labor against his will was by necessity inherent in the mechanical system; the necessity to destroy in the worker any real intellectual responsibility he might have for what he makes. As Morris put it in *How We Live and How We Might Live*: "They do not know what they are working at, nor whom they are working for, because they are combining to produce wares of which the profit of a master forms an essential part, instead of goods for their own use." Moreover, "they will be in fact just a part of the machinery for the production of profit; and so long as this lasts it will be the aim of the masters or profit-makers to decrease the market value of this human part of the machinery." This is easily recognizable as the foundation of Gill's mature view of the question of the modern worker being merely the sentient part of the machine who has only his energies with which to trade his life and whose life must be put at its lowest acceptable value by his masters.

In seeking a solution to the redistribution of justice as well as profit, like Ruskin before him, Morris was to founder on the rock of beauty, which was for him a subjective addition to life and its necessary utilities. Hence, as Morris supposed, if the worker is freed from the iniquities of a system that encroaches at every moment upon his work and his leisure time as well as his artistic and his moral accountability, he would make things at a sufficient pace of leisure that the work of his hands (it would come to this), in harmony with his pleasure at creation, would add beauty to his products. Thus would come about the "pleasant life," a sort of paradise on Earth whose occupants would have; "First, a healthy body; second, an active mind in sympathy with the past, the present, and the future; thirdly, occupation fit for a healthy body and an active mind; fourthly, a beautiful world to live in."

Given Gill's integrated religious and metaphysical viewpoint, it was inevitable that he would come to reject this vaguely humanist dream of a paradise whose raison d'être is curiously absent: inevitable that he should see that Morris's politics were those of time and not of eternity. Gill, in judging Morris, applied the same principle as on so many occasions and went straight to the heart of the matter: "He saw no being behind doing." Morris's predominant concern was for the fact that, by the mechanical system, the workman is robbed of the pleasure and satisfaction of free creative effort, and a just reward for his labor. But Gill's concern was for the fact that the worker, in being robbed of intellectual responsibility, is also robbed of the possibility of apprehending the holiness of the Creation and of his own being by means of a life of work as prayer; a norm of manufacture connatural to man's rational intelligence. Even though he was prepared to concede that art cannot flourish in the hands of a coterie of specially gifted men, Morris nonetheless thought that art must be the outcome of a vaguely humanistic aspiration toward what he called the "beauty and true pleasure of life." Despite his undoubted personal skills in the many crafts he practiced, Morris had no proper doctrine of work. When he came to describe his vision of the social revolution he had called for—which revolution was no more than "a stage of the great journey of evolution that joins the future and the past to the present"—we find that vision trailing off into an increasingly attenuated generalization: "I console myself with visions of the noble communal hall of the future, unsparing of materials, generous in worthy ornament, alive with the noblest thoughts of our time, and the past, embodied in the best art which a free and manly people could produce." The artist's role in the construction of such a society was to produce no more than "beauty and interest."

It is significant that both Ruskin and Morris believed that greater leisure and a higher standard of living would lead to the restitution of the arts among the people. By contrast Gill called for a "holy poverty" as the only rational attitude to material things; hence his criticism of Morris that "he saw joy in labour but no sacrifice." What is more, Gill foresaw that in the Welfare State the "factory hand" would come to despise the culture of "higher things" for which he is supposedly made free by the mechanical system.

Although he had learned much from Morris, Gill rejected him. It was as much a rejection of the arts and crafts movement as a whole as of Morris himself. Gill also rejected the socialism that went with their vision, on the grounds that they had no effective answer to the system they affected to despise; a system which perpetuated the moral irresponsibility of the capitalist investor on the one hand and the intellectual irresponsibility of the worker on the other.[4] Whereas the arts and crafts movement had merely established a vogue among the rich for sentimentalism, socialism, because it had failed to see anything wrong in the industrial system of production as a solution to the problem of human need, as a political movement was, as Gill wrote, "hardly more than an attempt to re-order the distribution of factory products and factory profits."[5]

Of this failure of socialism it fell to Morris's disciple W. R. Leth-

4. *Autobiography* (1940), p. 270.
5. Ibid., p. 140.

aby to make the obvious point. Now that the conditions of labor had been bettered by the rise of trade union power—and seeing that mechanized production cannot form a sufficient basis for human conduct—the task of the unions must be to attend to the "element of quality in workmanship." Indeed, "As work is the first necessity of existence, the very center of gravity of our moral system, so a proper recognition of work is a necessary basis for all right religion, art and civilisation. Society becomes diseased in direct ratio to its neglect and contempt of labour." Like Carlyle, Ruskin, and Morris, Lethaby too looked for his bearings to the unified tradition of art and workmanship that was the natural expression of the mind of the Middle Ages: "The most distinctive characteristic of the Middle Ages was the honourable position in the State then taken up by labour."

But Lethaby went one step further along the road uniting beauty and use, art and work, by being more explicit and concrete in his definitions. In Lethaby we find a good many of Gill's mature conclusions on the nature of beauty, art, and workmanship, in at least a verbal form that is close to Gill's own. It was Lethaby who wrote in his book on architecture; "we need not trouble about beauty, for that would take care of itself." Among his papers on art and labor (published in 1922 as *Form in Civilisation*), are aphoristic distillations of thought that might almost have come from Gill's pen: "Beauty is that which when seen we should love"; "Beauty is the 'substance' of things done"; "Beauty is the flowering of labour and service"; "Beauty has to come by the way"; "Appreciation of Beauty should be one with our judgement of essential quality. . . . The sense of Beauty is the work-conscience."

For Lethaby, art is "the right way of doing right things." Art is "ordinary manipulative skill." It is "*service* before it is delight; it is *labour* as well as emotion; it is *substance* as well as expression." "A work of art implies workmanship." "What I mean by art, then, is not the affair of a few but of everybody."

Like Gill, Lethaby, theoretically at least, fused yet did not confuse art and utility. He was fully aware of the transcendental origins of human workmanship and had written widely on themes of myth, symbol, and cult related to what he called in his essay "The Centre of Gravity," "the 'revelation' of the crafts to men." Gill, during his formative years, had been closely associated with Lethaby and would obviously have absorbed much of his teaching. Yet for all the similarity of Lethaby's final position to that of Gill in the theory of beauty, art, and workmanship, there remains the feeling that it is just that: theory. We cannot find anything like the same degree of personal, manipulative, as well as theoretic integrity in Lethaby that we find in the life and work of Gill. Although Lethaby could situate the proper place of beauty in art, art in workmanship and service, he lacks Gill's depth of resonance and conviction in being able to inter-relate spirit and matter, being and doing, man and society, art and utility, beauty and holiness to an adequate metaphysical structure. And this reservation could apply equally well to all but Blake of those precursors of Gill that we have examined. But to the list of Gill's masters there is one more name to be added. In some ways it is the most important.

It was the mastery of Edward Johnston's calligraphy that first gave Gill a direct experience of what was meant by work conceived and executed out of the living unity of beauty and utility. The excitement of the experience was, he wrote, "as of the intelligence discovering the good . . . and finding it desirable." The aesthetic "shock" at first seeing Johnston's writing transported the younger man: "I was caught unprepared. I did not know such beauties could exist. I was struck as by lightning, as by a sort of enlightenment: . . . and for a brief second seemed to know even as God knows."[6]

Much of what Gill himself was to absorb from Johnston's teaching remained axiomatic: *Making* refers to the material object, *doing* to action and intention; the worker is one who works in substances, and these substances demand a special method. Thus the substance impinges directly upon the form of the thing to be made. The worker thinks of substance, object, and design as inseparable factors in the process of workmanship. The product of work is substance brought to life—and that which is thus brought to life is the very mark of the worker's being. The primary occasion of work is use.

6. Ibid., pp. 119–20.

Good work is fit purpose. Use and purpose determine the proper treatment of the object. The worker aims at beauty only indirectly as attaining a measure of divine reward. Use and beauty define the axis of embodied truth—usefulness being the end most immediately and commonly apprehended. It is use that curbs the three sins to which the workman is prey: lack of resolve, meaningless imitation, and affectation. Such thoughts of Johnston's, learned as the practical wisdom of human facture, lasted Gill all his life.

In an important passage in his *Autobiography*, Gill makes a confession and in so doing makes an important and fundamental distinction, one that helps us to understand the complex process of absorption and rejection in his approach to his masters: "My socialism was from the beginning a revolt against the intellectual degradation of the factory hands and the damned ugliness of all that capitalist-industrialism produced, and it was not primarily a revolt against the cruelty and injustice of the possessing classes or against the misery of the poor. It was not so much the working class that concerned me as the working *man*—not so much what he got *from* working as what he did *by* working."[7] Thus, for all their concern at the social injustice of the mechanized system, for all that they had shown themselves sensitive to the archetype of beauty, arguing for its return at the heart of human labor in the face of the increasing dehumanization of mechanical production, Gill's precursors had not got to the root of the matter, They had not questioned consistently, deeply, and vigorously enough the nature of man's being.

It is Gill's insistence on starting nearly every argument with the implied question "What is man?" and following up with penetrating clarity its necessary and rational corollaries that distinguish him from his masters. In recovering the norm of human workmanship on the basis of the whole meaning of life Gill avoided the fallacy (one to which modern man is particularly prone) of attempting to establish the criteria for the active life in the productive outcome of the active life itself. The depth and conviction of Gill's achievement is present in virtue of his total response to the truth of those

7. Ibid., p. 111.

metaphysical doctrines he made his own but which were no less the possession of the perennial wisdom that at nearly all times and places has been the normal spiritual legacy of man.

What of Eric Gill today? It would be all too easy to dismiss him as a nostalgic reactionary who, in looking back to the ideals of an earlier age, placed himself out of court in so far as the problems of late twentieth-century society are concerned. But such a judgment would not only be superficial, it would also be wrong. Gill, by the absolute categories of his thought and by his constant appeal to reason placed himself at the center of things. The problems that engaged his mind are still with us. Far from being resolved, they have merely been brought, in the years since his death, to a new level of sophistry, becoming an unquestioned part of the social and intellectual malaise. Time and again Gill thinks his way to the root of those fallacies and contradictions upon which modern society unwittingly rests: its social and productive system that has mass leisure as one of its main aims yet which leads to the "tragedy" of state-sponsored idleness; its sentimentalizing of art while dehumanizing work; its pursuit of individualism by means that tend to even greater conformity and standardization; its denial of the place and significance of the Infinite in a world expected to yield "infinite" material development. Only those who have capitulated to the premises on which the current social and economic condition of society rests can afford the specious luxury of seeing Gill as an outmoded figure.

There is now a growing body of opinion that would hold that if the industrialized world is to recover its balance it can only do so on the basis of a re-socialization of work such as Gill points to. A system of production, fueled by a morally neutral capital investment that in turn fuels a technological development which is itself blind in so far as the ultimate goal of society is concerned, can give only the appearance of justice (in improved conditions, higher salaries, etc.), not the reality of it. The driving force of such a society, Gill saw, can lend nothing to a vision of that final end from which man must take the meaning of his existence. If the industrial system frees man for "higher things" by reducing his need to labor, why must there be such an outcry at the consequences of paid unemployment? As Gill observes, slavery may no more be necessarily uncomfortable than freedom comfortable.

Gill's views on economics and politics have been criticized as being naive, presumably by those who would consider the economics of industrial production, with its insatiable appetite for the Earth's resources (not to mention the attendant problems of wide-scale dereliction and pollution), enlightened. Simple and unaffected his views may have been, but never as if unacquainted with evil. Hence, in his observation that the machine is primarily an instrument for producing profits is foreshadowed the observation that the modern economy is primarily concerned to produce *demand*. In seeing the man of business as being at the mercy of "undisciplined fancies," Gill recognized the remorseless circularity of that unique form of modern slavery, "consumerism." He saw that its victim, the "consumer"—that final triumph of "economic man"—has no choice but to roam the marketplace in order to squander the "fee" paid him for the time spent supporting a system whose very existence depends upon contriving ways to stimulate a demand for goods that can never be wholly satisfied. Such is the treadmill of "consumer choice" and hence it comes about that men must serve "the Economy" for the good of a society that has no higher notion of the social good than that of "free enterprise" serving consumer demand. Already, in *News from Nowhere*, Morris had spoken of the inevitable downward spiral whereby "the production of measureless quantities of worthless makeshifts" knew no limit since "the only admitted test of utility in wares was the finding of buyers for them—wise men or fools, as it might chance." Producer and consumer alike, must come to suffer the smart of tyranny when "the Economy" has the power of Holy Writ!

In the field of "art," too, in so far as it is a separate and specialized domain of activity in modern society, Gill's views are no less timely. By insisting on the connatural nature of common sensibility and pure being in the intuition of beauty Gill effectively joined what had for some centuries been artificially separated: Being and knowing, loving and thinking, living and making. His assimilation of beauty to truth and goodness, moreover, provides a path between the twin (from the traditional viewpoint) heresies of post-Renaissance aesthetics. The first heresy was the seemingly irreversible persuasion of some four hundred years during which "art" had taken the imitation of appearances as a yardstick for expression. The invention of photography "killed" this heresy, but the counter-measure of the modern movement—an emphasis on the abstract nature of aesthetic values—opened up an equal and opposite heresy. The heresy of naturalism falsifies the nature of reality by tending to limit it to appearances, forgetting that, logically, appearances are of something. The heresy of abstraction falsifies the nature of intelligence in supposing that reality is all in the delight the mind feels in its own correspondence to certain values of pattern and symmetry. It is perhaps not too difficult to see that behind these twin heresies are two equally partial and unconscious theories of the beautiful—at their crudest, the one exclusively objective and the other exclusively subjective. In the objective view beauty is thought to reside in the appearance of the things we perceive. In the subjective view the objective reality of the thing perceived is granted but beauty is thought to belong to the act of emotive assimilation. The objective view will not accept that the act of perception is adaptive and contributory in the assimilation of beauty while the subjective view will not accept that beauty is not wholly attributable to emotive response. In other words, neither view can accept that beauty is in the order of being. Both forms of heresy tend to overlook the fact that the relationship between mind and beauty—utilizing the simultaneous co-operation of both perception and emotion—is ultimately cognitive and depends more upon the action of the intellect than upon sensory stimulus.

On the basis of Gill's doctrine we might notice how it is hardly a coincidence that in a society which unwittingly subscribes to the notion of art as the province of a special sort of person concerned with beauty, art eventually becomes that hypertrophied banality and crudity with which we are all too familiar. Indeed, a society which unconsciously holds that the pursuit of beauty is the purpose of "art" results in an environment unsurpassed in its dehumanizing ugliness; similarly, the pursuit of leisure as the basis of the good life results in a society in which few people find the time to make what is pleasing to our innate sense of what conforms to a good life.

There can be no mistaking the directional impulse of Gill's thought; it is heavenward. Not so much a heaven "up there" as one with a more local habitation: the kingdom of heaven *within*, which is the kingdom proper to man—that is to man the maker.

11

Archetype as Letterform: The "Dream" of Edward Johnston

DURING the many hours which I have spent in conversation with calligraphers and lettercutters over the years, I have always been struck by the way in which the practicalities of achieving the "perfect" letterform and its appropriate spacing in a given context are at the root of their preoccupation and effort. No doubt this is as it should be. What scribe or lettercutter worth his or her salt would take up this exacting craft and not be haunted and challenged by the idea of perfection?

But what one rarely comes across, if at all, is a serious consideration of *where* the notion of perfection comes from. For it has also been my experience that calligraphers and lettercutters, while pursuing their craft as if some notion of perfection was at least tacitly motivating them, are all too ready to deny that the perfect letterform exists.

What I would like to attempt here, then, is an exploration of the idea that the perfect letterform must be real—for if it were not, then it would not have the power to inspire the hand, the eye, and the mind of the craftsman as often as it obviously does.[1] Perhaps it would be better to say that the perfect letterform has a reality, even if it is never manifest in a material substance, such as ink or stone, or to use more Scholastic terms, that it has *being* even if it does not

---

1. The reference throughout to a perfect letterform is more a matter of convenience than a dogmatic assertion. This same perfection is operative in a whole collection of letters that, cumulatively, have an organic unity, each single letter being in some way modified in accommodation to the whole context of its presence.

exist. But to make this distinction between being and existence presupposes that reality is much more complex and multi-layered than what our everyday consciousness reveals to us.

The reader may be familiar with the old adage that "to work is to pray," a saying which gives some indication of the fact that the crafts were traditionally practiced as if it were possible that they possessed a spiritual dimension and that they might act as a support for contemplation. I believe the writings of Edward Johnston indicate that he exercised his vocation as if this was still a possibility. Even though Johnston's practical example has inspired innumerable scribes to take up calligraphy and lettering, no one, so far as I know, has so far examined this aspect of his work. If it is time to re-examine the legacy of Johnston (as has been suggested by some contemporary lettering practitioners), then this rather more "hidden" aspect ought to be fundamental to that re-examination.

If calligraphy is to be understood and practiced as being more than a game of shape-forming—albeit a very skillful and sophisticated game—then we might look to the example of Johnston to learn more of the depths of this ancient, universal craft. Johnston's was an example that prompted one of his pupils to claim of his inspirational teaching that it came as if out of "eternity and infinity" (L147).[2] That is a very pointed description, whose wording is carefully chosen. Speaking of the ultimate objective of his work, Johnston himself said: "Life is the thing we all want and it is the desire for life that is behind all religion and all art.... Our aim should be ... to make letters live ... that men themselves may have more life" (P88). Again, we note the carefully chosen words. This does not sound like someone advocating the practice of "art for art's sake," or even "craft for craft's sake."

If you look at a copy of Johnston's *Writing and Illuminating, and Lettering*—that is, if you have an earlier edition—you will find

---

2. The abbreviations used throughout are an initial followed by the page number of the following books by Johnston: F = *Formal Penmanship and Other Papers*, edited by Heather Child (1971); L = *Lessons in Formal Writing*, edited by Heather Child and Justin Howes (1986); P = Priscilla Johnston, *Edward Johnston* (2nd ed., 1976); W = *Writing and Illuminating, and Lettering* (1906), and reprinted many times.

three quotations given prominence on a page facing the author's preface.[3]

Now from all that we know of him we can certainly agree with Eric Gill's assessment that Johnston was "deliberate of speech and equally deliberate of thought." We know that Johnston was a deeply religious man, and it is therefore impossible to believe that he lived his life keeping his vocation as a calligrapher and his religious experience in separate compartments. So we must believe that these quotations were chosen with great deliberation by a man who claimed that the "one thing I care most about" is "to search out and live the truth" (P34). We must also remember that Johnston thought sufficiently of the following passage to write it out at least twice in 1934, one of these being for presentation to no less a master craftsman than Alfred Fairbank. Of this Johnston said, "in many ways the ms is yet my best" (L35). The last of the three quotations reads as follows: "In that communion only, beholding beauty with the eye of the mind, he will be enabled to bring forth, not images of beauty but realities (for he has hold not of an image but of a reality), and bringing forth and nourishing true virtue to become a friend of God and be immortal, if mortal man may" (Wx).

This extraordinary passage, taken from Plato's *Symposium* and given such prominence by Johnston, needs to be examined carefully. I say "extraordinary" because it is by no means representative of the habits of mind and thought that have shaped and which energize the modern world, referring as it does to the intelligible realm of archetypal Ideas. Indeed, it is precisely because Johnston placed at the head of his treatise a quotation which does not underwrite modern assumptions as to the nature of reality and the mind that we must look at that quotation in some detail.[4]

---

3. I have a copy of the twenty-third edition of this book in which this page was still included. At some later date it was withdrawn.

4. For instance, we find the following "Argument" in Johnston's *A Carol and Other Rhymes* (1915), pp. 48–50, which gives some indication of the nature of his thought in this matter: "We see the light of the stars, not the stars themselves: we see the light reflected from a piece of white paper, not the paper itself. In other words, we see what things are *doing* rather than what they *are*. But as light takes

The passage occurs in that part of Plato's dialogue where Diotima is elaborating for Socrates her teaching that Love is "a great spirit between divine and mortal." She says that it is possible for men to gaze on Beauty's very self, unsullied, "not dogged with the pollution of mortality and all the colors and varieties of human life." Diotima insists that, only when men discern heavenly beauty itself—face to face—through what makes it visible, will they have hold of the true.

The quotation begins, "In that communion"—that is to say, in the mind's *contemplation* of beauty, and continues, "beholding beauty with the eye of the mind." When he speaks of "mind" here Plato does not, as might be assumed, mean the rational mind—that part of our common-sense consciousness that makes a reasoned judgment about things on the basis of empirical observation and logical calculation. And the "eye" referred to is not the eye of sensible apprehension—for Plato, like Heraclitus before him, held that the senses are unreliable witnesses when it comes to discerning what is unchangingly true. The "eye of the mind" is an intuitive faculty of the soul, which permits it to grasp metaphysical and spiritual realities which are not subject to change, as is every reality conditioned in whatever way by time and space. "To bring forth"

time to travel—however short the distance—it is more exact to say that we see what things *have been doing*. This is the way in which we 'see' all material objects, whether 'near' or 'far,' but it is impressed on us in the case of the stars, because we understand that the light of the nearest star—our Sun—takes over eight minutes to reach the Earth, and the light from the Sun's nearest neighbor nearly four years, while the flight of the light from the great majority of stars, it is said, 'is to be reckoned in hundreds of years.' Truly, though we see the star shine, we can hardly say that we see the stars shining (the action of our bodily sight, therefore, is an act of faith—for Faith is 'the evidence of things not seen'). If we see, then, in the material world only what a thing is doing—or has done—but not the thing itself, how may we hope that our Love, or Faith, or Hope will ever discover its objective? Divine Love—which knows all Things—is, and therefore does not depend on time to reach things, or on that which we call 'nearness'—and in the very word confess distance. In the heart of Man there is the shining of all his 'stars'—those 'stars' which he cannot reach, or even see with his bodily eyes—but yet he may be in touch with them—Divine Love in his heart sees the stars for him."

means to grasp and hold with unwavering stability a truth of the mind beyond the world of the senses. It is, as Plato goes on to say, to grasp "a reality" as opposed to "an image" (or representation) of beauty. Plato is pointing out that external appearances, because they are the very fabric of which transient reality is woven, have something illusory or deceptive about them. He is making the distinction between that which possesses true, permanent Being, and things which exist only in the mind as a mental abstraction. So, when he speaks of "bringing forth and nourishing" he is referring to the archetypal truths that enter into one's very being so as to become part of our very identity, rather than truths of a more ephemeral nature that are temporarily registered in the imagination as a transient image. When the contemplator is truly absorbed into these archetypal truths or Ideas, he or she becomes, as Diotima continues, "the friend of God and . . . immortal." That is to say, the contemplator assumes or takes on the identity of the archetypal or of the Divine within, to the extent he or she is able to shed the grosser demands and predilections of the empirical ego.

An early familiarity with the idea that an approach to the Divine entails the sacrifice of one's ego is reflected in the fact that at the age of twenty-five, in 1897, Johnston wrote on a parchment, "The best way to see Divine Light is to put out your own candle" (L79).

Now all this may seem a far cry from the practice of calligraphy, but that it was important to Johnston we cannot doubt. What we must hold clearly in our minds is the truth that this contemplation of, and entering into, objective beauty is the grasping of a reality that is never materially embodied. It is an intuitive, unanalyzable experience that is known directly without the intervention of mediate, mental activity—that is, without any sort of mental calculation that effectively puts a distance between, or distinguishes, the knower and the known. It may be difficult for the modern mind, with its rational and materialist training and bias, to see that such archetypal Ideas are more true and more real than the products of mental calculation on the one hand, or physical realities on the other. But Johnston's belief that this is so becomes evident from a careful reading of the relevant passages of his writings. That he was more a Platonist than a modernist also goes a long way to explain why he was increasingly at odds with the progressive, industrial world that surrounded him.[5]

To help us get an idea of how this archetypal reality might apply to letterforms, we can turn to a passage in Johnston's *Writing and Illuminating, and Lettering*. He says: "The mere taking to pieces, or analyzing, followed by 'putting together,' is only a means of becoming acquainted with the mechanism of construction, and will not reproduce the original beauty of a thing" (Wxix). In other words, that part of the mind that calculates, measures, and co-ordinates what the interaction of the hand, the eye, and the mind must apply in the making of a letterform does not go deep enough in itself to touch upon the "original beauty" of the perfect letterform that is nonetheless sought, whether implicitly or explicitly, in the craftsman's pursuit of the "perfect" letterform. This impalpable, archetypal letter (as we might call it), which lives in the deep recesses of the "eye of the mind," is what actually underpins the perfect unity of that physical and mental action required to shape palpably beautiful letters in whatever substance. When a manifestly beautiful letter is fully realized by the craftsman, then the archetype is, as it were, sounded so that what results is a letterform whose beauty reduces the observer to silence, unable to describe or quantify that in which its perfection consists. And, conversely, I would suggest that whenever we look at a letter that appears insufficient in some way, even though all its elements are "correctly" present, then in that experience of impoverishment we are intuitively sensing the absence of any reverberation of the archetypal "original beauty" which Johnston refers to.

Here, in parenthesis, it is interesting to note that in a "Report on Art Schools" that W.R. Lethaby prepared in 1898, a few months before meeting Johnston, he wrote: "Lettering of all kinds is almost without exception *bad*. Such students as endeavor to apply lettering harmoniously to their designs seem to endeavor to invent new and contorted forms out of their heads. Of all things the form of letters

---

5. It might be noted that Robert Speaight, in his biography of Eric Gill, records Johnston reading Plato aloud to Gill in his workshop when they were close neighbors in Hammersmith.

has been shaped by tradition and in most cases the effort to be orig-inal is an effort to be *bad*" (P12).

Lethaby is surely noting here that such *bad* letterforms arise from the use only of that superficial part of the rational mind (if that!) that takes to pieces, analyzes, and puts together the basic elements of letters on the basis of personal preference. And when he says that the forms of letters have been shaped by tradition—with the impli-cation that such forms are "good" and "beautiful"—it would surely be bad logic to interpret Lethaby as meaning that such forms are arrived at simply on the basis of habits of past precedent. An ugly or bad letterform does not acquire beauty or legitimacy in the process of being copied and repeated, for however long. Beauty is of another order than the mere passage of time.

Johnston himself, early in his career, defined "Beauty" as "obedi-ence made manifest to the Laws of Truth" (P134)—we note the use of capitals on the words Beauty, Laws, and Truth. He did not signifi-cantly change his mind in later life, even though he went on to inves-tigate those laws exactingly, testing them again and again against rigorous thought and assiduous practice. He never lost sight either of the earthly/heavenly axis along which, traditionally, the practice of any craft proceeds. Speaking of the old scribes at their work, he remarked that even more than their skill and the *speed* with which they wrote—as if writing an ordinary letter—and even though they were "engaged on serious work" and were not concerned with "art" as we think of it, "they had in their hearts a kind of dream of divine beauty that they were seeking... [and]... note how much that dream was fulfilled" (P153). Let us look a little closer at this "dream."

All that we know of Johnston presents us with a picture of an entirely practical man. There was nothing "abstract" or "airy-fairy" about him, nothing "arty." Indeed, we might doubt whether there was anything about him that was superficial. "Preoccupied," cer-tainly, as the notice he made for his study door proclaimed, aimed at repelling unwelcome visitors. His daughter Priscilla said of him that "for all his lassitude he was extremely forceful, indeed domi-nant. It was not an active forcefulness of vitality but a kind of latent forcefulness of character" (P125).

But his was no utilitarian practicality. Johnston's vision of his craft begins at the beginning. By this I mean literally the beginning of all things—his testing of his ideas took him that far. Noel Rooke reports of him that "he related his subject to everything in heaven and earth" because he saw it as essentially part of a whole. Even when it came to describing a single element of letter formation— that of contrast—he took the comprehensive view: "Contrast is at the very root of formal penmanship. So is harmony. That is why our work, when well done, is so sparkling. It has that unique possession, the best of both sides; the idea of Heaven and Earth is there, harmony and contrast" (L176).

And Priscilla Johnston relates that her father once spoke to her of his taking a class, "of how he was able to give (the students) the feeling that it really was worth doing and a little of his vision, also, the spirit of it, over and above the technical side. He quoted *Man shall not live by bread alone* and spoke of the excitement of the vision" (P263). Can we not sense in this passage Johnston's desire to communicate the idea that the perfection of work which is the aim of the true craftsman must involve more that the mastery of practical skills, if indeed the craftsman is to become "a friend of God" as the quotation from Plato puts it?

Since man is created in the Divine Image (as Johnston believed), it follows that in the exercise of his vocation, the craftsman, by analogy, shares in the actions of the making of the world by its Creator. Johnston thought of the process of creation as involving three stages: "embodying, animating, and inspiring." The three stages must be understood and actualized in the context of man's origin and place in the fabric of the Creation. "In a book for craftsmen," Johnston wrote, "the primary order is Genesis 2:7: 'And the Lord God formed man of the dust of the ground, and breathed into his nostrils the breath of life; and man became a living soul'" (L47). Also in connection with man's being created in the Divine Image, Johnston asks us to consider Genesis 2:19, where it is related how God formed every beast and bird and how Adam named every living creature. That is to say, the word by which each thing is named establishes the unique and permanent reality of that thing. In the naming, by Adam, of each thing inheres the archetypal essence or Idea of that thing as it exists in the mind of God: as it exists in the

Word, that is, the Logos—the eternal reason of things. The scribe, giving a manifest form to true and beautiful words, recapitulates the Adamic action of giving each thing God's signature. Thus, named things and meanings co-inhere. And in this co-inherence is the very ligature that binds man to Truth itself. Johnston, true to his life-long insistence that the scribe pay attention to the meanings of the words he writes, is reported as having worn out his dictionary.

How Johnston saw Adam's giving of God's signature to each thing as an analogy of the scribe's action is clearly seen in the following passage:

> All his [the craftsman's] works express Idea [note the Platonic capital, denoting a pre-existing, immaterial potentiality] . . . by substance brought to [material] life—like Adam made of Earth. Each of his [man's] works—like every son of Adam—bears a human touch and is seen to be unique. All things are unique, but the craftsman's works show this—each one [each manuscript of ours] is an autograph. (F141)

As each man bears the signature of God in his deiformity, so each work from the hand of the scribe bears the signature of its creator. Thus it is, infallibly and authentically, a thing brought materially to life from a pre-existing idea in the mind. This analogical wisdom is surely what resonates in Johnston's assertion that the proper task of the scribe is "to make letters live . . . that men themselves may have more life" (P88).

In a letter quoted by Priscilla Johnston, Johnston himself spoke of the *final creative act* as one in which God saw that the Creation was Good—"in fact, a thing is not completely created until it has been appreciated . . . I believe it" (P256). Here Johnston is at his most profound, for he is drawing upon the idea that the final justification for the Creation of the world, by God, is in the realization of the necessity that it is completed by being *known*. It is the responsibility of the craftsman's share in the Divine Creation to see that his work is good, that it is true, for it is the Truth, "both immanent and transcendent" (P308) that prevails. And of Truth, Johnston wrote: "its other names are goodness and beauty, the way and the Life, the Light (of the world), the Word, and many more." Which brings us to the question of beauty.

We can only understand Johnston's view of beauty correctly if we keep it in the context in which he himself placed it: Beauty is approached and found indirectly in the search for Truth, through the discipline of a proper utility of human needs. Priscilla Johnston reports her father as holding that "Beauty is an ultimate Grace which will be conferred upon the craftsman's work if it be well done. If Truth . . . has been served, the result will be Beauty" (L48). Can anyone look at the best of Johnston's works and not see that it is beautiful?

However that may be, it perhaps takes a more trained eye to see that the beauty of his forms arises out of their construction. It remained axiomatic for Johnston that "unless the design arises out of the actual construction of a thing it is reduced to the level of extraneous ornamentation. Design is inherent rather than applied" (P285).

In connection with this principle we might incidentally note that Johnston's reluctance to have his work reproduced was precisely because of the resulting inauthenticity. As he pointed out, "nothing is reproduced, something different is produced" (P285).

As with design, so with the "original Beauty" of a thing. It is not something applied to the surface but comes out of workmanship honestly and straightforwardly undertaken. What, then, does such workmanship entail?

Like Gill, Johnston anchors his answer to all questions that have to do with the validity of the craftsman's activity by going back to the nature of the agent doing the work. What is man? Man is a creature, a body—"the flesh is a *sine qua non* for the spirit of man" (P308)—who looks to God for the answers to the primary questions: What, How, and Why. Why should one, why ought one, why must one, make a thing? And by a "thing" Johnston meant both *"what we make* and *what we do"* (F141). Moreover "things are His [God's] will" (P308). By virtue of asking these questions, man is searching for Truth as well as tacitly proposing that an answer can be found. Other names for Truth are Goodness and Beauty. And Truth "is that against which we sin" (P308). (This thought—that the workman can sin in his actions—may go some way to account for Johnston's lassitude.)

159

In making a thing, the scribe "works in substances . . . with special tools and special methods. He also thinks in substances and in things, and in methods . . . , which direct the tools and form the thing out of the substance." The "prime purpose of writing is to be read." "His direct objective is to write well," so that the work produced is useful. In his primary duty to the author "the words are of the first importance," and with this in mind the scribe aims at a presentation that is beautiful. Such beauty for formal penmanship is achieved by "Sharpness, Unity, and Freedom." In this, his *direct* purpose, "the scribe keeps the idea of usefulness constantly before him." "Usefulness in this context, consists in legibility, fitness for purpose, and perfect presentation. The scribe follows after usefulness since, in the final analysis, the ultimate objective of usefulness is beauty" (F141–42).

So, given that the scribe has mastered all the necessary practical skills, this alone will not suffice to achieve the "original beauty" that must be sought by indirect means. "Original beauty" comes intuitively through concentration upon, and contemplation of, the archetypal Ideas that letterforms embody. The fact that Johnston wrote little on the subject of beauty is itself an indication of the fact that, by its very nature, it is a subject all but unteachable in any direct sense. The pursuit of beauty in isolation from its necessary alignment with truth and legitimate human needs has always been recognized by the wisest minds as being liable to lead men astray, into folly and self-indulgence. Nevertheless, something of what is involved in achieving the original beauty of living letters can be glimpsed in words which Johnston addressed to an audience in Dresden in 1912. The passage occurs in a context touched upon earlier, regarding the scribe's aim to "make letters *live*." The relevant words are: "I think I can claim that, poor as they are, the letters on the blackboard are alive: that is not due to myself—I am only a superior kind of motor or engine—it is due to the pen [chalk!] (which brings life to letters)" (P187). It is "not due to myself": this attributing of his achievement in giving life to letters to a higher agency gives a hint, surely, of what is meant in the passage from Plato's *Symposium* by "nourishing true virtue to become a friend of God"?

To come back to Johnston's "dream" and to end with a question.

Priscilla Johnston, in her memoir of her father, quotes him as saying: "I see no successor who will put his life and heart into the work I love. There are plenty of *good* scribes to whom it is an occupation and a profession but apparently not *a preoccupation and a dream*" (P251, our emphasis). His daughter was inclined to dismiss this remark, but given its pointed wording can we be so sure? Does not another interpretation offer itself? To anyone with a deep religious conviction, such as Johnston possessed, the scribe's vocation must be more than an entertaining and diversionary activity. The whole man must be engaged. Could it be that Johnston found no one willing to attempt, through the craft of the pen, that degree of contemplation, beyond the empirical ego, that engages those "realities"—and not their semblances—that enable the craftsman to "bring forth and nourish true virtue"—that interpenetration of being and knowing that is a gazing upon the heavenly beauty face to face, in so far as "mortal man may"?

12

David Jones's View of Art

We already and first of all discern him making this thing other. His
groping syntax, if we attend, already shapes:

ADSCRIPTAM. RATAM. RATIONABILEM . . . and by preapplication
and for them, under modes and patterns altogether theirs, the
holy and vulnerable hands lift up an efficacious sign.

Opening of *The Anathemata*

"Primitive" man knew nothing of a possible divorce of function
and meaning: *all his inventions were applied meaning.*

ANANDA K. COOMARASWAMY

READING through David Jones's occasional writings one is quickly
made aware of the sense of cultural crisis that pervades them: that
the practice of art is fraught with problems that are perhaps unsolv-
able, and that the theory of art is hedged about with perplexing
considerations that we cannot be certain we have firmly grasped. In
his "A Note on Mr Berenson's Views," for instance, Jones points out
the quite radical difficulties that attend the use of even such basic
terms as *real, represent, form, finish, shape, composition,* and the like
(276–77).[1] This crisis becomes at times the subtext, and on occasion
the text as Jones tentatively probes the cultural fabric of the Christian tradition in order to determine what might be the terms on
which twentieth-century art can validly proceed.

The crisis is rarely explicit in the paintings and drawings, where it
has to be construed from the imagery—for instance in the late work

---

1. These bracketed figures refer to page numbers of *Epoch and Artist* (1959).
Other abbreviations are: DG, *The Dying Gaul* (1978); DGC, *Dai Great Coat* (1980);
and SL, *The Sleeping Lord* (1974).

Aphrodite in Aulis, where it becomes apparent from a reading of the juxtaposition of images drawn from widely separated periods of western (cultural) history. Or, in the poetry, in *The Anathemata*, where the comprehensive intricacy of the poet's attempt at an "effective recalling" at times threatens to overwhelm the reader.

Going yet deeper into the occasional writings it soon becomes clear that the cultural preoccupation of Jones's own "groping syntax" is a profound concern for the interactive natures of art and man; in particular, the essays that deal more specifically with this theme—"Art and Sacrament," "Art and Democracy," "Religion and the Muses," "Use and Sign," and "Art in Relation to War." These demonstrate a mind acutely sensitive to the nuances of meaning, association, and consequence that attach to our understanding of precisely *what* human nature can be said to consist in. In taking stock, and "in spite of the dissolutions and disillusions inherent in this present phase of the decline of the West" (274), Jones saw that we must begin to find answers to our problems by starting, not from *where* we are, but from *what* we are.

Although it was axiomatic for Jones that the artist must begin with the materials of one's own time this does not make him a modernist—except in a nominal sense, and then only in the period of the late 1920s and early 1930s, up to his first nervous breakdown in 1932. During this period he was most responsive to the innovative energies of his contemporaries.

Jones did not believe it to be the task of the artist simply to reflect his particular phase of history. For him no lasting veracity could be given to cultural activity on the level of history alone since history—that product peculiar to man—no less than man himself, is by its very nature in need of redemption. The criteria by which the arts of man are to be judged must ultimately come from values and meanings that originate in a domain that transcends history as such.

Jones's whole view of art, like that of Gill,[2] rests firmly upon a body of wisdom that is immemorial—aboriginal with man himself.

---

2. There are obvious temperamental differences between the two men. Having hold of fundamental principles Gill regards himself as one fully-armed and ready for action, to the exclusion of some subtlety in dealing with related matters. Where

To this extent it rests upon objective criteria. His occasional writings are not what one commentator has called Jones's "special theories." It is true they are in part personal. But this is incidental, not for the sake of self-expression, and arises from the sheer diversity of the artist's *materia poetica*. The style of his pictures and of his poetry is resolutely objective, at one and the same time highly—often bafflingly—idiosyncratic, but non-subjective. They have the quality of things made to demonstrate an integral perfection.[3]

The assumption that Jones had "his own special theories" could only come from one unfamiliar with the Scholastic doctrine of art, itself a western formulation of a universally true "normal view of art," as Coomaraswamy has called it. This Scholastic formulation is strongly colored by its sources; the logic of Aristotle's category of the intellectual virtues in which the principle of art is a practical wisdom involving a true course of reasoning. And then by the Scholastics themselves in their attempt to present a thorough, rational analysis of this operational habit or virtue as it resides in the mind as being the informing skill *by* which all works are made. This principle was eventually assimilated (by St. Bonaventure, for instance),

---

Gill is dogmatic Jones is tentative, being more prepared to take account of man's current predicament in the face of the impoverishment of the sacramental in the modern world and what this implies for man-the-artist and his attempt to create a *valid* art form. In Jones's work the terms *valid* and *effective* are heavily loaded with denotative and connotative resonances as we shall see below.

3. A recent commentator asserts that Jones developed his very own individual version of Clive Bell's theory of Significant Form. This is a misleading simplification. It is pointed out that Jones thought it an unreasonable reaction of Eric Gill to respond to the same theory, "significant to what?" But Jones himself wrote in "Art and Sacrament," "a sign then must be significant of something, hence of some 'reality,' so of something 'good,' so of something that is 'sacred.'" Now apart from the pertinence of Gill's question, as well as the fact that Bell's theory can hardly be interpreted as accounting for art as a vehicle for the transmission, via the supra-sensible archetype of the "Good," of a sacred truth, Jones's terms the "real," the "good," and the "sacred" must be understood in the context from which they derive, that of Scholastic metaphysics. This alone can explain the series of "leaps" from "real" to "good" to "sacred" as a movement toward a goal that is in some sense a revelation of the Divine. Jones's words are very close to a passage from Coomaraswamy's essay "Is Art a Superstition?": "If we sometimes make use of such high-sounding expressions as 'significant form' we do so ignoring that nothing can prop-

to the light of the Logos as ultimately a divine manner of under-standing. It need hardly be added that the Scholastic formulation was wholly consistent, both spiritually and practically, with Jones's profound Catholic faith. The self-authenticating intelligibility of the traditional doctrine had an objectivity that appealed to Jones as answering his need to free himself from the subjectivist dilemma posed by modern abstraction, which amounts to an evasion of the question of the relationship of form to content on the one hand, and the diminishments of *signum* in representing natural appear-ances on the other.

From the point of view of Jones's understanding of the relation-ship of form to content, the form of a work of art is determined by the "inner necessity" of a thing that has to be re-presented. The spe-cifically modernist aesthetic is no more than a will to display tech-nique. But technique exists as a result of intention. So what of an intention to display technique? The so-often posed question—What is it?—indicates a cognitive necessity to penetrate beyond the inadequacy of defining a thing in terms of what it does. The mind needs to know what a thing—a work of art—is! Jones's insistence that *signum,* as an order of signs in the domain of art, binds man to the transcendental order exposes the circularity of the modernist, abnormal aesthetic in which a work of art cannot point to anything

erly be called a 'sign' that is not significant of something other than itself." Bell's the-ory is tautological in seeking to establish a "significance" on the basis of a generali-zation extrapolated from individual sensibility. But the generalization inferred does not go beyond the specific realm of aesthetic emotion. It refers to nothing outside of the artistic process itself. Moreover, his theory is based on the notion of "art" as an *external product,* an aesthetic category of things set aside from other works on the supposition of their superior aesthetic content. This subjectivism was exactly what Jones fought to free himself from in following the Scholastic doctrine that "art" is an *interior principle,* "a strategy," "an activity," "a fitting together," "a human skill," whose exercise is nothing other than to perfect the operation of making. Something of Jones's effort to avoid propounding a subjective theory of *poesis* can be seen from his letter to Harman Grisewood (April 13, 1940) in reference to his reading of W. F. Jackson Knight's *Cumean Gates:* "It's *so* hard to find any detachment within oneself." We might also recall his strictures, in his essay "Art and Sacrament," against "self-expression" as well as his welcoming the "objective views" of Maritain's treatise *Art and Scholasticism* as a bulwark against the struggle with "the tide of subjectivism."

beyond itself. What could be more reductive for the spectator than for the artist to innovate for the sake of innovation?

Jones's occasional writings on art in the main came about as a result of his attempt to apprehend the complexities and "show forth" the implications of the Catholic wisdom with regard to the nature of man and his works. That being so his claim that art "does not need to be justified by metaphysical argument" (DG164) is somewhat disingenuous. Justified no. But any art worthy of the name (and certainly art on the terms that Jones would acknowledge) embodies substantial values. And we can hardly doubt that Jones's work, taken as a whole, invites our assent to a credible and substantial thesis that of its nature must be either true or false: and that truth ultimately metaphysical. The present chapter will concentrate on those parts of Jones's exposition that are illuminated by being seen in the light of the metaphysical doctrines they rest on.[4]

The artist has stated clearly his intention to

raise the question of what is involved *for all of us* in the notion of sacrament and the sign-world in its multifarious aspects.

4. For this purpose I have drawn heavily, as with Gill, from Jacques Maritain's *Art and Scholasticism* (1930), many traditional sources, and especially from the writings of Coomaraswamy. We will presumably never know why Jones does not mention the latter's work. The parallels of symbolic and doctrinal understanding are so numerous and mutually illuminating that it seems impossible Jones was not in some degree influenced by the scholar Gill corresponded with and indeed eulogized with the words: "I believe that no other living writer has written the truth in matters of art and life and religion and piety with such wisdom and understanding." Some of these parallels would, of course, be inevitable given the nature and source of the doctrines. But I recall a conversation with René Hague in London in the summer of 1978 in which he told me that David did (at least) read the offprints of articles that Coomaraswamy was in the habit of sending to Gill. It seems more than likely that some subsequent discussion of these would have taken place between such close associates as were Jones and Gill. In a letter to Harman Grisewood (DG 95) Jones eulogized the scholar W. F. Jackson Knight: "If there were one or two more Jackson Knights who combined real slap-up scholarship with a nose for the patterns and eternal correspondences of this with that, it would be jolly nice and helpful." Why did Jones not recognize in Coomaraswamy just such a scholar— par excellence? A critical review of Jackson Knight's *Cumean Gates* (which sparked off the eulogy) by René Guénon is published in his *Fundamental Symbols: The Universal Language of Sacred Science* (1995), chapter 31.

The technocracy in which we live and which conditions us all, tends, in all sorts of contexts and at every level, to draw away from this sign-world. I feel that almost all of us, indeed all of us, duck this issue. People speak of sacraments with a capital "S" without seeming to notice that sign and sacrament with a small "s" are everywhere eroded and in some contexts non–existent. Such dichotomies are not healthy. (12–13)

Everybody has at some time experienced the sense of a restored inner harmony, a re-alignment and balance of the faculties, after successfully undertaking some practical task the end product of which is only incidentally aesthetically pleasing. Such a sense gives us the most direct experience of how the practical intelligence can provide the means to draw upon our deeper resources. In contrast to the modern artist and the modern "worker," the traditional artist-craftsman operates within a metaphysical context that provides the spiritual and practical continuities needed for the experience of his craft to be an effective agent in the realization of these resources. By this means the individual is able to go beyond the limitations of the ego in order to link his entire being to a deeper order of reality. This traditional conception of work as the application and extension of metaphysical principles provides the objective criteria for Jones's assertion that "in the arts 'the best' can only easily and naturally be available to the hierarchic, corporate, symbolic demands of the Church if the epoch itself is characterized by those qualities" (97). The implicit recognition that such "qualities" are not readily accessible to the twentieth-century artist should not escape notice.

The importance of art for any society cannot be over-emphasized and is at all times taken for granted by Jones for whom, as from the traditional standpoint, "the terms 'man' and 'artist' can be said to be interchangeable: Man is the only artist and only artists are men" (94). The product of the artist is not therefore a luxury enjoyed in order to indicate a progressive refinement of individual sensibility, but is the fruit of an analogy that visualizes the creative act of man in terms of the Divine Act of Creation. Among the creatures man occupies a central position—half-divine, half-animal. Man alone carries within himself the possibility of intellectual certitude and spiritual perfection. Man himself is a work of art by virtue of his being an image of God, and an artist by virtue of his ability to imitate the operative manner of the Divine Intellect in producing works ("Art imitates nature in her manner of operation," as St. Thomas Aquinas wrote). This analogy of the artist with the Divine Creative Act is so envisaged since the artist's "first gesture is an interior and contemplative act in which the intellect envisages the thing (to be created) not as the senses know it, nor with respect to its value, but as intelligible form or species; the likeness of which he afterwards proceeds to embody in the material."[5]

The act of the human artist in identifying himself with the intellectual prototype that is the likeness of the thing to be made is in imitation of God, who, from His limitless love, creates the world out of nothing that is exterior to Him to become the object of His own "vision."

The specific achievement of the Renaissance was to dismantle the analogical wisdom of the Scholastic doctrine in order to establish the illusory autonomy of man from the sacred. The three hundred years from 1400 to 1700 were witness to a progressive deprivation of the image of God and the representational forms of the sacred. In the following centuries the metaphysical corollary of this new condition worked its way to the surface in an inevitable and progressive degradation of the image of man. From man as the image of God to God in the image of man and, finally, man in the image of purely physical processes. From the seventeenth century all mediation between man and the sacred has been effectively eroded so that man has become estranged from a nature and history become increasingly profane.

As Jones repeatedly points out, forms in art are of vital importance as an indication of man's own image of his creaturehood. What man represents man becomes. The arts are the final intercessionary instrument between man and God as they represent the external limit of a mutual, sacred partnership outside of which the forces of profane, brute utility begin to engulf man and his works.

It is man's ability to contemplate the infinite that characterizes

---

5. Ananda K. Coomaraswamy, *Figures of Speech or Figures of Thought* (1946), p. 80.

the unique nature of his being and sets him apart from the angels and the animals. But from the point of view of his works it is the sacramental nature of artefacture "that is the very quality by which 'man' is distinguished from 'animal' and from 'angel'" (178). Moreover, if "theology supposes man to be, first and foremost, a sapiential mammal" (147), then this *sapientia* by which man proceeds implies—since "it is axiomatic that the origin of things conditions their ends" (45)—"that this mammal has an end other than that of the other mammals . . . [and] must have a supernatural end. In catechismal terminology this is expressed by asserting that the natural end of man (i.e., the end conformable to man's nature) is eternal felicity" (147–48).

Sacramental works, then, have the specific function of serving as an adjunct to that perfecting of intuition that is the realization of the "eternal felicity" that is man's last end, since by the law whereby extremes meet, the works that man makes are the very manifestation that in turn shapes the mode and manner of his innermost resources. "The more man behaves as artist and the more the artist in man determines the whole shape of his behaviour, so much the more is he man" (86). In this reciprocal relationship we have the true meaning of forms in art—not a mere formalism of shapes but a real science of symbols that translates, according to and in recognition of certain cosmic laws of correspondence, the essentially sacred reality at the heart of all created things. From Jones's standpoint, if art is free to elaborate and extend its technical and expressive means arbitrarily, in ignorance of these laws of correspondence that inform both the objective criteria man's *sapientia* demands and the "supernatural end" to which his nature is conformable, then we are simply conditioned by what is *beneath* our nature and any talk of *signum* becomes meaningless.

If art were indeed inaccessible to any criteria of objective truth, then there would be no grounds for the apprehension that underlies an essay such as "The Utile." It is just such a formalism of shapes, having no correspondence with the spiritual needs of man, that Jones refers to in this essay, and elsewhere. The recognition that the "characteristic forms of our present technology" seek as their highest objective the merely "utile" requires us also to recognize that when "man's works seek utility only they can appear to become 'utilitarian' in a most derogatory sense, that is to say they appear 'sub-human.'" (181). Were we able to suffer this utilitarian imposition entirely without conscience the question of form would be of no importance, and a seeking for more than the utile would be "an aesthete's faddishness." Our misgivings persist for good reason:

> for in the age of technics the tendency is for creativeness to become dehumanised, for contrivance to usurp imagination, for the will toward shape to become almost indistinguishable from a mere will toward power. There is a deflection, a mass-deflection, from the proper "habit of art" toward forms which owe their existence and meaning to what they *effect* rather than to what they *are*. Power-extension and multiplication become the objectives, and the utile is the sole factor determining the forms, and the symbolic loses altogether its central and presiding position. (104)

The problem is further compounded by the fact that the modern "maker" is no longer man the "sacrament-maker," and has grown accustomed to standards of behavior that require the distinction of needs from desires. What he *needs* (that which supports the realization of his last end) is one thing; what he may *desire* (that which merely facilitates his appetites) quite another. For man the "sacrament maker" desires and needs ought to coincide. It is these, man's *real* needs, that for Jones—as for tradition (see Plato's *Republic* 369–70)—are the proper occasion of art. But in the industrial society we have an art that is a formalism of shapes, textures, and colors that offers aesthetic stimulation for its own sake, standing in opposition to sub-human standards of manufacture applied to technical contrivances from which our spiritual needs have been expressly eliminated. The debilitating effects of this dichotomy, the spiritual questions it gives rise to, and the practical problems it poses, run like a leitmotif throughout Jones's critique of our particular cultural phase.

The coincidence of needs and desires in the sense in which they have been used above presupposes that art, as the norm of workmanship, can be the instrument whereby every "maker" can so harmonize inner and outer faculties as to bring about the conformity of his being to an order of reality that goes beyond his individuality.

Such a norm is the ultimate referent of Jones's equating "man" with "artist." "Sign and sacrament are to be predicated not of *some* men and their practices but of *all* men and their practices" (166).

> Unless man is of his essential nature a *poeta*, one who makes things that are signs of something, then the central act of the Christian religion is totally without meaning. How can there be a manual act that makes *anamnesis* unless man is man-the-maker, and thus *poesis* his nature and authentic mode of apperception and in the end his only mode? (13)

One is reminded of Eckhart's "No person can in this life reach the point at which he is excused from outward works"; therefore "work in all things" and "fulfil thy destiny."[6]

Jones made use of Gregory Dix's definition of the meaning of *anamnesis,* which tends to emphasize the temporal connotations of the word. In his preface to *The Anathema* Jones, in a footnote, quotes from Dix's *The Shape of the Liturgy*:

> It (anamnesis) is not quite easy to represent accurately in English, words like "remembrance" or "memorial" having for us a connotation of something *absent* which is only mentally recollected. But in the Scriptures of both the Old and New Testament *anamnesis* and the cognate verb have a sense of "recalling" or "re-presenting" before God an event in the past so that is becomes *here and now operative by its effects.* (126)

Dix has in mind here the celebration of the Mass in which the celebrant is occasioned to "do this in remembrance of me." But this is not fully helpful in understanding the relation of *anamnesis* to the application of the practical intelligence that is art in Jones's thinking. In this context the significance of *anamnesis,* as Guénon and Coomaraswamy have shown, is rather that of *metanoia,* a real "change of heart" involving a "wakening up" of the latent spiritual resources such as man possesses within himself. On this reading

---

6. Quoted by Coomaraswamy, *The Transformation of Nature in Art* (1934), p. 92. Eric Gill, writing to thank the author for the gift of this volume wrote, "I am really overwhelmed by it . . . it seems to me splendid, magnificent, marvellous and altogether excellent." It is almost inconceivable that Jones did not see this volume and read its chapter "Meister Eckhart's View of Art."

homo faber, as *poeta,* is not so much a "rememberer" (141) of past events, as one whose making and doing effectively recall the supra-human criteria on which, ultimately, human nature rests.

Undoubtedly the central motif of David Jones's work was to understand art in relation to the Eucharist: "The crucial question is: Why did the Lord employ art-forms and establish a tradition commanding the continued employment of those forms?" (162). What is here initiated is a ritual action that rests ontologically upon the incarnate Logos in which, through His love of His own creature, God assumes man's nature in the person of Christ. Given that we understand by "form" the sense of *forma,* that is the qualitative imprint of a being or a thing, this may be expressed in symbolic terms as the divine nature of Christ, as the principle of form, giving immanent form to all that is formless. "According to this spiritual view, the participation of the human form of the Christ in His Divine Essence is (as it were) the 'type' of all symbolism: the Incarnation presupposes the ontological link which unites every form with its eternal archetype; at the same time it safeguards that link."[7]

The Eucharist sacrifice, at the center of the liturgy, is thus the means to grace instituted by Christ Himself and so belongs to the order of Divine Art, an art made possible on the basis of the science of symbols, itself based on the qualitative essence of things and which, by a real and effective ontological correspondence, concedes the transparency of the existential world to the transcendental order. This same law permits man to see himself as one eternally begotten in the likeness of His exemplary image in the sense of a prior imitable prototype. "It is in-as-much as God knows his essence as being imitable by this or that creature, that he knows it as the particular reason and idea of that creature."[8]

Christ's statement, "Do this in remembrance of me," represents the institution of a sacrificial rite—a ritual performance that makes sacred or holy. The performance of this rite becomes for Jones the paradigmatic performance of *all* acts of making: "For in the Cenacle the Victim himself did something and said something which no

7. Titus Burckhardt, *Sacred Art in East and West* (1967), p. 70.
8. Coomaraswamy, *Figures of Speech or Figures of Thought* (1946), p. 76.

matter how it is theologically interpreted ... was unmistakeably and undeniably a sign-making and a rite-making and so an act of Ars; moreover an act to be, in some sense, repeated" (168). This rite, therefore, institutes a form of comprehension that, to make use of a passage from Coomaraswamy, "reduces the whole distinction of sacred from profane and the opposition of spirit from matter, a perception of all things at the same time in their temporal and in their eternal significance."[9]

God's sacrifice of Himself in order to generate a world that is "other" than Him as He is in Himself is mirrored in the ritual mimesis of Christ's Passion. But the procession of the Divine Substance from potency to act on the divine plane, on being reflected on to the human plane, is inverted so that man the "sacrament maker" is called to an act of remembrance (*anamnesis*) of that which was his original substance. This necessitates the death or sacrifice of the outer man or ego—the illusion of self-autonomy. By so acting man "re-collects" the deiform prototype or "foretype" of his nativity in his sacrament making. Which is why the poet wrote, in *A. a. a. Domine Deus*, "I have felt for his Wounds in nozzles and containers."

Jones's insistence that *homo faber* must find "His presence" in the actual substance of material artefacts before they can be used as "signs" is guaranteed by the Incarnation. That they can be "valid" signs of man's redeemability is guaranteed by the Resurrection. The incarnate Logos, present in and uniting all things, is the decisive sanction for the artist's task. Such "signs" as the strategy of art "shows forth" can only be "radiant with form and abhorrent of vacua by the action of the Artifex, the Logos, who is known to our tradition as the Pontifex who formed a bridge 'from nothing' and who then, like Brân in the *Mabinogion*, himself became the bridge by the Incarnation and Passion and subsequent Apotheoses" (160).

Jones sees the crisis of our technocratic civilization as one in which the resonances of the Logos—"abhorrent of vacua"—are effectively emptied out of the things we make and do; which things,

---

9. [With a slightly different wording, this sentence can be found in "The Religious Basis of the Forms of Indian Society," *Studies in Comparative Religion* 15, nos. 1–2 (Winter–Spring, 1983): 18. —Ed.]

in a sense, *make us* in that we feel, see, touch, and love through the particularity of things made and done. In this sense also art "knows only the unique." This should prepare us to understand more fully what is involved when Jones writes:

> If in the Cenacle, forms of words were used and manual acts employed involving material substances these things can have been done only by virtue of the doer being a man along with us; more explicitly, by his being man-the-artist along with us. What was done would have been neither necessary nor possible unless man is man-the-artist. (167)

Here we return to the question of forms being able to translate truth according to the hierarchy of cosmic values. The qualitative essence inherent in things at the level of formal manifestation permits the analogous expression of the Divine Essence in man's making, so that Christ, as the incarnate Logos, becomes the first cause of all that is created by the agency of *ars*. The analogy between "Divine Art" and human art operates through this reciprocity of inner essence and outward manifestation. Such a reciprocity is common to all men since the human intellect, in its intuitive ground, is a mirror of the Divine Logos. As the traditional formulation of this doctrine reminds us: the artist is not a special kind of man but every man is a special kind of artist and represents the "normal" (that is, conforming to an inner rule or standard) man. As Maritain puts it in *Art and Scholasticism*, "If Christ willed to be an artisan in an insignificant village, it was because He wanted to assume the common lot of humanity."

Hardly less central to his thinking is Jones's concern with the gratuitousness of art: "It is the intransitivity and gratuitousness of man's art that is the sign of man's uniqueness; not merely that he makes things, nor yet that those things have beauty" (149). Kenelm Foster has complained that Jones does not closely define what he means in using the terms *intransitivity* and *gratuitousness.* However this may be, it is clear that Jones, in using these terms, is consistent with the traditional doctrines of free will and the gratuitousness of the Creation.

In the act of creation God is free from any external determination or imposition, the Creation being none other than the outward realization of a potentiality in the divine plenitude that permits, so to say, the manifestation of those parts of God that are manifestable. This emanation from potency to act is akin to a light giving forth light by the very nature of light itself, illuminating all things yet without diminution of itself. In the same way there is in God a material cause *in principle* that becomes outwardly a material cause as the origin of created things. Wholly consistent within the nature of the instantaneity of this free act of creation, and proceeding from the deiform prototype in which man is created in the image of God, is man's free will—the bestowal of a freedom wholly undetermined and without imposition. This freedom is not so much the granting of a choice to the soul, as it is the gift of a condition of being that permits man to divest himself of the illusion that he has an autonomous nature apart from God: a state of being which, in its perfect realization, wholly unites the will of the individual with the will of God. In other words, the soul is granted the freedom to become what it essentially *is*—in theological terms to *be* what it was before the Fall.

But given man's fallen nature, any such "freedom" to divest oneself of an illusory autonomy, in order to be fully operative, must of necessity involve commitment to a discipline, albeit entered into freely. This is the function of religion. So, as Jones concludes,

> with regard to the etymology of the word *religio* . . . a binding of some sort is indicated. The same root is in "ligament," a binding which supports an organ and assures that organ its freedom of use as part of a body. . . . The binding makes possible the freedom. Cut the ligament and there is atrophy—corpse rather than *corpus*. If this is true, then the word *religio*, no less than the words *prudentia*, *ars* and *signum*, means nothing, makes no sense, unless we presuppose a freedom of some sort. (158)

Were this freedom not present then all man's efforts to attain truth, love, and justice, would be set at naught as governed by a prior command upon his nature. And as we all recognize, love under the yoke of compulsion is impossible.

As with the will of *homo faber*, so with his works. That "art is the sole intransitive activity of man," is indicative of the freedom of man, in perfecting his works, to perfect himself, as "intransitivity and gratuitousness in man's art ... is the sign of man's uniqueness." Moreover, "the animals, lacking choice, are excluded from Prudentia and though they share man's corporeality they are excluded from Ars, again for lack of this power of choice which man alone shares with the incorporeal intelligences" (150). It is true "that works of meticulous perfection and beauty of many kinds are commonly produced by beasts of many kinds" (149). But such works are more the product of a creature "subject to a pure determinism ... e.g., the reflexes of its own instincts" (148). In such "animalic making" there is no "evidence of the gratuitous, nor is there any evidence of 'sign.' This making is wholly functional, these activities are transitive" (149).[10]

This gratuitous character of man's making can be thought of as a kind of play, since "this 'intransitive activity' called art" seeks of its nature to evade the consequences of the "fall" (DG156), in that unity and harmony of inner and outer faculties that results from an act of perfectly realized making. Such intransitive activity "passes over" to another order that is beauty made manifest, a "felicitous quality" (154), shown forth in the work itself by means of that sense of "fun" or "play" that is not the goal of man's making but nonetheless perfects the productive operation. It is the immanent Logos that permits such "showing forth," for "it is Holy Wisdom herself who says *ludo*. ... She was with the Logos when all things were formed, 'playing before him at all times' and as the Knox translation puts it: 'I made play in this world of dust, with the sons of Adam for my playfellows'" (154).

This sense of play is far removed from any notion of "art for art's sake," for, even though "it must be understood that 'art' *as such* is 'heaven,' it has outflanked 'the fall'" (DG164)—as he says earlier in his essay "Art in Relation to War"—"in its operations in the world

---

10. However, this does not rule out the possibility that such "animalic making" might be made subsequently intransitive by man, as this passage from *The Sleeping Lord* indicates: "the tall, tapering, flax-cored candela of pure wax (the natural produce of the creatures labouring in the royal hives but made a true artefact by the best chandlers of the royal *maenol*)" (SL76).

of fact [*ars*] only makes the fall more obvious" (DG156). For the Fall incurs the misalignment and disharmony of our inner and outer faculties in which human making becomes a burden of sin that disrupts the proper ordering of the Logos.

This clarifies what Jones means when he refers to the "disinterestedness" of art: "I understand the theologians to say that God's creation of the cosmos was a gratuitous act: it is interesting therefore that it is that very quality of gratuitousness which we recognize in the creative works of man" (275). Here, we must make a distinction between the practice of art as instrumental cause and the artist as creative agent. It is said of the former that its work is done "disinterestedly" for no other reason than the good that is the integral perfection of the task in hand. However, the artist, as a creative agent, is not similarly "disinterested," for as a rational and moral being he may act to other ends unconnected with the exercise of his art. The work of the Creation was certainly a gratuitous act, but in so acting God had in mind an end which was, in Maritain's words, "of an order superior to the art—the communication of the divine Goodness."

It is instructive to consider Jones's many statements on the gratuitousness of art alongside those of Meister Eckhart collated by Coomaraswamy. As we have seen, and as Jones holds, "Man is either in some sense and to some degree a free agent or he does not exist." Thus it can be said he is "a creature which is not only capable of gratuitous acts but of which it can be said that such acts are this creature's hall-mark and sign-manual" (148). And further, there is a real analogy between such a "showing forth again under forms" (177) and the works of God, for art is alike in man and God, human making being the agent of God's creativity in the sense that, as Eckhart says, "finding thee ready, he is obliged to act, to overflow into thee; just as the sun must needs burst forth when the air is bright, and is unable to contain itself." And, as Coomaraswamy adds,

> the "being ready" is otherwise expressed as matter's being "insatiable for form"; so God "must do willy-nilly," according to his nature, without a why. In man this becomes what has been called the gratuitousness of art: "man ought not to work for any why, not

for God not for his glory nor for anything at all that is outside him, but only for that which is his being, his very life within him."[11]

Such a passage throws into sharper relief Jones's statement that, "man is a creature whose end is extra-mundane and whose nature is to make things and that the things made are not only things of mundane requirement but are of necessity the signs of something other" (150). "At the root of the matter," he argues further,

> Ars knows only a "sacred" activity. I believe this must be so once we grant that the notion of "sign" cannot be separated from this activity of art. Why, granted the sign-making nature of man's art must those signs be "sacred"? Is "sacredness" implicit in "sign"? I think it to be so if we assent to what philosophers say about "being," *esse* . . . for anything to be real it must have esse. (157)

If, as Jones subscribes, man is "understood to be a creature whose informing principle of soul is rational; a creature who is unlike any other corporeal creature in having a measure of freedom of will and hence committed, of its nature, to what is labelled 'faith and morals'" (148), then the gratuitousness of art only makes sense in respect of a freedom to perfect his actions in relation to the demands that pertain to his "extra mundane" and "last end": absolute freedom— "the state of eternal felicity" (148). This is the territory of prudence.

The relation of art to prudence "is a degree of freedom of some sort that causes man to be, of necessity, an artist and the same freedom of sorts commits him of necessity to Prudentia" (150). But we must understand that, "the one is concerned only for our intentions and dispositions, and the other only for the formal dispositions that comprise an artefact. One cares for us and our final condition, the other for the work and *its* final condition" (125). Here Jones is echoing St. Thomas, and Gill, in seeing that the whole of the active life of man comprises a doing governed by prudence and a making governed by art, prudence being the norm of conduct, art the norm of workmanship—and both depending for their correction upon the contemplative life.

---

11. *The Transformation of Nature in Art*, p. 88.

From the standpoint of practical action, Jones continues, "our final condition or last end is not yet, whereas our artefacts have their completion now or never. For which reason, while Prudentia is exercised about our intentions, Ars is concerned with the shape of a finished article. She *cannot*, as the other *must*, wait till the Judgement" (125).

At which Judgment the question of sin becomes relevant, for just as there is a moral sin so there is an artistic sin, the former allowing discernment to be overridden by illusion and wickedness, the latter by an insufficient reason. Sin arises in connection with art when there is, as St. Thomas says, a "departure from the particular end intended by the artist" and in connection with doing when there is a "departure from the general end of human life . . . for the former sin the artist is blamed as an artist; while for the latter he is blamed as a man."[12] So, as Jones observes,

> it emerges that both [Ars and Prudentia] are concerned with the proper integration and perfection of shape, in the one case that of persons and in the other of perishable things. Both then are concerned with what is patient of being "devoted," "laid up from other things," "consecrated to divine use," made anathemata in some sense or other. (125)

If it is art that discerns and applies the means of attaining the "proper integration and perfection of shape" in the good of the work to be done, then as Maritain concludes, it is prudence that "discerns and applies the means of attaining our moral ends, which are themselves subordinate to the ultimate end of all human life-that is to say, God." Implicit in this "perfection of shape" is the perfecting of one's self, for as "man is a maker he, in one sense, makes the shape even of himself" (86).

Here again Jones restates traditional doctrine. The final attainment envisaged in all sapiential wisdom is that vision of man as he is in God—knowledge of the Self. This remains the perennial quest of human life. Art, in the final analysis, must in some way endorse this end if it is to avoid, on the one hand, the mere exercise of sensi-

12. *Summa theologica* I–II, q. 21, a. 2.

bility, and on the other labor undertaken merely for the sake of utility; this later achieving "the vacuity and deprivation apparent in the thousand-and-one utensils and impedimenta of our daily lives, domestic or public" (181). For all progress toward knowledge of "our final condition" it is self-evident that "the workman must be dead to himself while engaged upon the work, otherwise we have that sort of 'self-expression' which is as undesirable in the painter or the writer as in the carpenter, the cantor, the half-back, or the cook" (110). The artist is not "necessarily, a person vastly more aware than his friends and relations of the beauties of nature, but rather he is the person most aware of the nature of an art" (29). In his possession of the "habit of art" he is *moved by the nature of whatever art he practises*" (29); which is his by convention and training from "some artist or some existing art-form," the exercise of which is corrected by that Self of which he makes himself the creature—an inspiration for which he is the "vessel" never the author. And this lest he be, in Blake's words, "seiz'd and giv'n into the hands of his own selfhood"—the empirical ego that is possessed of will but never in possession of free will.

The artist, *"homo faber,"* "sacrament-maker," as Jones variously calls him, is not a self-sufficient "genius intent upon upsetting accepted values and conditions on the basis of personal innovation," but one whose "self-possession" is the unifying principle in the integration of not only his own individuality but also the collective body politic. The immanent order to which art is signally conformable has its life ultimately in a transcendent, supra-human spiritual authority, and so cannot be imposed from outside the act of making by any temporal power: "Any order, new or old, 'ours or theirs,' local or a world-state, which binds the Muses, breaks the totems, and withdraws the people from contemplation, is already dead in the judgement of history, no matter what fanatic vitality shines in its morale, or however reputable its ethic" (100).

Again and again Jones drives home the nature of modern man's crisis as the fundamental breakdown of a vision of man as *homo faber,* a breakdown that, so far as the modern world is concerned, has all the signs of being the death of true humanity. "What shall it profit a community of men if it gain the whole world of political and economic and social rights and equalities and loses the 'habit of art'?" (90).

Considered in relation to the tendency of our age to make something of a religion out of art, Jones's remarks on Wilde's dictum "art for art's sake" remain salutary. "If not *the* truth the dictum at least contains 'a truth,' if properly related to the whole behaviour of Man and not to the behaviour of special sorts of men such as can only exist in the tired and artificial phases of late civilizations" (95). Certainly, as Jones points out, "the 'aesthetic' in man will out," seeing that a need and longing for the beautiful are natural to man. But the beauty man needs is connatural with his intelligence—what the Scholastics termed the "radiance of truth" that inspires a liberating joy. Rightly, as Jones, echoing Gill, acknowledges, "the true aesthetic nature of man . . . must find an unconscious fulfilment." Whenever and wherever art is granted its natural role as the norm of workmanship there is a justice and harmony in man's "sacrament-making" in which the specific aesthetic need of man is taken care of. But, as is the case with what Jones calls "megapolitan man today," the aesthetic as such has become that eccentricity, an end in itself.

> If the art of some men is abnormal it is because most men have been made so *sub*-normal as to have no art to practise . . . only it is well that this deprivation should be understood to be eccentric and not concentric in Man. We may be forced to accept the situation in the world of fact, but to accept it as normal is the final capitulation. (95)

13

Images of the Unknown:
Looking at Cecil Collins

THE CRITICAL RESPONSE to the Cecil Collins retrospective exhibition at the Tate Gallery last year was an adequate demonstration that the premises of modernism have little or nothing to contribute to an assessment of his work. We can only avoid bringing to the work of Collins's visionary imagination irrelevant pre-conceptions of appreciation and judgment if we make some attempt to situate that work in relation to those values and meanings to which he addressed himself in his life and work. And this process might usefully begin by viewing his achievement alongside that of a contemporary and friend who also is best appreciated according to values and meanings that go beyond the specifically modernist aesthetic.

Cecil Collins and David Jones are the two great "outsiders" of modern British painting. To link them together in this way, far from being merely gratuitous, can not only illuminate the imaginative qualities they share—and which isolate them from the mainstream of modern art—but also those modes of expression which are idiosyncratic in each of them. There is a sense in which their respective visions were timely in that they could not have been realized at any other time in history. But there is a dimension inherent in the vision of both men that is never simply of its time. This double perspective moves in parallel throughout their work, constantly informing it and relating it to a level of meaning that transcends art as such.

As near contemporaries, and thus sharing the same historical period, David Jones and Cecil Collins are positioned in relation to one another as two complementary faces of a single focal point which takes in the perspective of both the temporal and the timeless. The substance of Jones's art is largely taken from the history of

European Christendom as it is ordered and transformed according to the ahistorical significance of the Catholic Mass. With Collins, on the other hand, the substance of his imaginative vision is that of the soul's immersion in the world of time, but with the ever-present possibility of its illumination by the Divine. From this shared focal point Jones faces backward and outward; Collins forward and inward. Jones's images are taken, for the most part from cultural history and from the world we observe. He is an Aristotelian and a Scholastic for whom art is, predominantly, the perfection that is integral to work—integrity having here the sense of precision and correctness as well as that of unity. The presiding paradigm of his art is the analogy of the artist as maker who works in a likeness to God as the maker of all things.

Cecil Collins's art, facing forward and inward, is of images of expectation and spiritual progress that are freighted with no historical context at all and which owe little to the appearance of observed reality. His images exist purely to act as the vehicle of a visionary world that is itself the instrument of self-transcendence. Collins is a Neoplatonist for whom the image acts as an interior analog which seeks to orientate and drive the viewer's consciousness inward to the realization of its unawakened possibilities. In their import Collins's images are iconic, and as such their presiding paradigm is the contemplation of the analogy of the human image as fashioned after that of the divine image. David Jones's imaginative disposition is toward envisaging the outer world as charged with the traces of a divine transcendence, while Collins's disposition is toward invoking the inner world of the soul as the theater of our divine immanence. It would, however, be a mistake to see in their respective dispositions any incompatibility, since in the fullness of the reality they both address their imaginative perspectives are conformable at a level beyond artistic and aesthetic values.

There is another important way in which this juxtaposing of Jones and Collins may prove illuminating. It is part of the art of both men that their distinctive visions are realized against the implied background of the sense of loss and alienation which characterizes the spiritual crisis of modern man. A comparison of the manifest signs of this implicit sense of loss and alienation shows each artist keeping faith with his own imaginative experience while at the same time pointing to the profound effect upon the human condition that the historic period in question has engendered. With David Jones the signs are a looking outward to the external effects of the crisis and finding them in the loss of a sense of place in the history and "mythus" of the Christian cultural inheritance. In his pictures and in his poetry Jones collects and concentrates, particularly in his most mature and elaborate works, the cultural history of the West in an effort to stave off the loss of memory and rootedness to spiritual context that accompanies the collapse—the eclipse—of a civilization and its trans-historical values. To this extent his work is a resume, a gathering together in an act of recognition and celebration, of what man has witnessed and embodied in his artefacts; those things he can no longer be and do by means of the same modes of cultural action and assimilation. This effort of recognition necessitates, for Jones, a pictorial structure or poetic narrative of, at times, extreme complexity which might at first sight seem over-elaborate, even excessive, but on closer acquaintance reveals itself as minutely articulated detail possessing that "characteristic evanescence, meeting and mingling of contours and planes of reality which characterise the Celtic genius" (Jones's words).

For Cecil Collins this same crisis is a loss of Paradise, an alienation from the intuition of pure consciousness. His is an art that expresses the need for purification in the face of worldly decay and impoverishment; not an escape into the private and subjective, but certainly a flight from all those modes of reflective consciousness that are determined and conditioned by the dualism of a mentality that pits itself against an external reality, and whose fruits now, historically, threaten to engulf us. Where David Jones evokes cultural pattern Collins invokes a lyrical consciousness that makes use of a simpler, more direct means of pictorial expression, frequently no more than one or two figures against a background of primordial simplicity—often no more than a single head. The cultural dynamic of Jones's imagery is in Collins's work complemented by a static gradation of mood that seeks to embody a given state of being. This inward movement of essentialization carries with it what might be called a metaphysical imperative, and Collins has left an eloquent testimony to his understanding of what is demanded by this imperative. In his essay "Art and Modern Man" he wrote,

> The artist is concerned to personify experience, to reveal the identity, the nuance, the being of things, the presence. He is interested in transforming the thing in the spontaneous creative movement, the unexpected moment of eternity, the moment of freedom; unexpected, because the unexpected moment is the unpossessed moment. This is perhaps one of the deepest insights of the creative experience; whereas in process knowledge intellectual possession is the essential condition prior to analysis. Therefore art is a kind of redemption of consciousness and environment.[1]

Collins's vision of the need for this kind of healing redemption makes him the artist who truly divines the current of life at the end of the historic cycle that is the modern age—a current in which a certain "metaphysical depreciation" is inevitable: the artist who perhaps most fully appreciates that even at the eleventh hour, when negative impulses seem to prevail over positive, there are compensatory possibilities of renewal at work in the deepest intuitions of imaginative consciousness. In their looking forward—not assuredly in terms of a passage through time but in the expectation of the individual soul's orientation toward the sacred—Collins's images bathe us in the true source of transformation of being. His Fools, Sibyls, and Angels resonate with the presence of what is inviolate at the roots of our consciousness. They are auguries of that joy and innocence from the world's processes that tire and soil us, and which cast the inevitable shadow of insufficiency upon every form of worldly effort and distraction. In the presence of these images we are called to witness the final inadequacy of those processes to our full being, that unknown that continually relieves and freshens the burden of the known.

It is just this lack of the dimension of transformation and renewal that precludes the art of Francis Bacon, for instance—who might be considered artistically to be the polar opposite of Collins—from

---

1. [This essay and other statements by Collins in the current chapter are collected in *The Vision of the Fool and Other Writings,* edited by Brian Keeble (2002). —Ed.]

expressing the real nature of the human condition. In their depiction of the unattractive and the repellent, Bacon's images place us passively at the surface of things, for the shadow pre-supposes the light. Hell is the absence of that higher realm without which Hell itself would have no substance and therefore no meaning. Satan, we should not forget, is a fallen angel and not a power equal and opposite to God. An artist has perhaps earned the right to show us into Hell when he can also show us the way out. The proper condition of man has always been and remains that of relating to his essence—a question of self-identity, which identity Collins's imagery serves by withdrawing the viewer from the world of objects and sensations and reactions to them. So it is on the level of the soul that the human drama is played out, and Collins has called his art a "theatre of the soul." Those by whom it is peopled have as their task to "search out and prefigure the mysterious unity of all life," without which nothing is comprehensible, and life is reduced to a meaningless stream of sensations.

Cecil Collins's art is supremely the art of the imaginative, symbolic image. Both in his rejection of abstraction on the one hand and of naturalism on the other, Collins refuses, in effect, to repudiate the abiding and intimate connection between form and mind. If the aspiration toward the spiritual (in distinction from the simply immaterial) by means of images is to be effective then it follows that images must have a content. An image does not exist of itself. It is the appearance of something, it affirms something. An image is also a call to some form of action. A television commercial exhorts us to act outwardly; a Byzantine icon should move us to act inwardly.

When the images of art become self-regarding to the point where their sole obligation is to claim that they are no more or no less than what they are (as is the case with so-called "pure abstraction") then they are shut off from the seamless matrix of values and meanings which gives them life. So they diminish their claim upon us and, ultimately, negate the very conditions for their own survival. They have to pretend that it is not the condition of human communication to involve intelligence, perception, convention, memory, and so on. That is to say an image is not some sort of quasi-absolute, but carries a burden of meaning and so must, of necessity, stand in some relationship to truth. This relationship ultimately questions the ontological status of the imagination.

At its simplest the imagination is nothing more than the image-making faculty of the mind. But images are a likeness of a reality, and what concerns us with Cecil Collins's imaginative linages is whether the reality in question leads us merely to the private psychology of the artist or toward the source of the Real itself. Artistic images are drawn from the whole world of apprehended appearances, whether they are made to imitate the appearance of external nature, or whether they borrow elements of that nature in order to serve what Collins has called "the vested interests of the ego." In such cases the artist himself is the subject of the image. And this is no less true of naturalistic images—nature seen with not through the eye—than it is of abstract images where the image is unique, and so by definition has "no like." But in the images of art that are inherently symbolic the artist's personality is transcended. Such images mirror the unmanifest truth that is the source of the Real itself. They embody, in other words, the correspondence between manifest existence and the hidden divine immanence that gives it life. In Collins's own words, in his "attempt to manifest the Face of the God of life" the artist "sets free an instant of vision, things seen in their archetypal essence in the sacrament of image and colour."

Thus, as Collins has stated, art is a "metaphysical activity." That is why the viewer who sees in his world of the Fool, the Angel, the Pilgrim, the Sibyl, the Eternal Bride, his trees, clouds, birds, and rivers, nothing more than the expression of a private fantasy, has failed to grasp that these images arise from an intensity of vision that drives the viewer beyond the picture itself to the very source of conscious life. Yet even as they reject empirical observation as the arbiter of pictorial truth, as an imaginative language these images accord with the recognizable in so far as they envisage the unmanifest according to the modes of human perception. Such images exist concretely. They do not make use of existing things to represent other things. They exist to enhance our apprehension of those spiritual energies that are the life-giving property of the unknown. "The Reality of life is incomprehensible and the Artist creates an incomprehensible image of it." In this way Collins's images enact a mystery where an interiorizing vision is served by the language of analogy and invocation and where, conversely, ambiguity and obscurity are consumed in the clarity of primal vision. So there must always remain an irreducible hermetic essence in Collins's pictures which cannot fully disclose itself until we as viewers are transformed as participants in them.

"Painting is a metaphysical activity." Nor is this to be understood as meaning that painting is an attempt to indulge the creative process as if it were a quasi-mystical experience. At its most mature and articulate, when it is informed by his most profound insight Collins's imaginative language emerges from and surmounts the creative process to exist objectively. It has a dialectic. It is the instrument of a level of experience that is communicable in terms that relate to the knowledge and wisdom of the saint and the mystic. By way of reservation it might be said that in his "matrix" pictures something of the artist's personality remains caught up in the creative process so that the images remain nascent and inchoate— perhaps the rather less than fortunate influence of abstract expressionism. There are those who admire most the energy and the brilliance of these "matrix" paintings, and it is through such works that his art is most likely to seem assimilable to modernist presuppositions, since it is in such works he is most like a number of his contemporaries. Nevertheless, Collins's mastery is undoubtedly at its quintessentially characteristic in the fully realized formal perfection of the iconic image. This is his unique contribution to the art of his time (and most likely will confirm the measure of his significance beyond it), for in such works he may truly be said to be incomparable.

"Painting is a metaphysical activity" since each work is a "place" where the life of the soul is enacted, each "place" being a momentary pre-figuration of the hidden unity of life. Such places cannot be "located" since we only see them in a moment of initiation in that imaginative space where we are already projected beyond the confines of our fragmentary, habitual world. Such imaginative moments must be lived on the plane at which they are realized— that is, "where" they are. The Angel's sensuous beauty, the clothing of its presence in painterly attire, parades before us an intimation of what we have yet to become. It is the "space" of the Angel that we must inhabit. Angel, Fool, Sibyl, Anima, each by its presence utters some pulsation of that hidden reality.

This is why the artist makes his most audacious claim, "There are no objects in my paintings," so that we should not attempt to correlate the content of his pictures with the created world that comprises an indefinite number of discrete entities, the world of opposites and differentia where one thing is seen and known never to be another. The world inhabited by Collins's Angels, Fools, Pilgrims, trees, rivers, birds, and so on is never conditioned by this law of separated existence. Here we have to reverse the habits of outward perception to recognize that one thing has the possibility to become another. For these images are a series of evocative, resonant, correspondences of the unmanifest unity of existence experienced as states of the soul. Collins's "scenery" is the soul's impalpable habitat as Fool, Angel, Pilgrim, and so on, are its figurative guises. All these figures and scenes are the instruments of a gnosis of association and relationship of the seamless continuity and connectedness that is the unity of life. Thus in many of the works what appears to be a structural device, the visual rhyme, has a further significance: the texture of a tree trunk is that of a river also, hair is like water, the foliage of a tree is the shape of a wing, an angel's wing is a leaf, grasses are flames or waves of the sea, tree trunks shoot up like volcanoes to burst into cloud-like foliage. A fool holds a butterfly that returns his gaze as from a "human" face—an emblematic moment of the friendliness of all living things. Collins has described the initiatory moment that led him to find the pictorial analogy for the intuition of the primordial unity. "One April afternoon, there'd been a shower . . . and the sun was just sinking behind the wood, and the light was shining on this bush . . . it had drops of rain on the leaves and the light was shining through them. They were like diamonds. And on top was a thrush singing. I suddenly saw that this bush was the shape of the song of the bird."

Collins's rejection of the "puritanism" of abstraction is precisely on the grounds that it posits a world of mental forms torn away from the inclusive and indivisible abiding unity of life. The eloquence of this unity is, for this artist, no less present in an insect's wing, a bird, a mountain as they are contemplated in the soul, than it is in the spectrum of colors refracted into the modes of poetic consciousness. Because "imagination is the organ of the interior nature" the artist discovers in these modes of poetic consciousness, as they are realized in the particularity of their image, the beauty that is proper to the human. Plotinus states the doctrine: "We ourselves possess Beauty when we are true to our own being, ugliness is going over to another order; knowing ourselves, we are beautiful, in self-ignorance we are ugly."[2]

With Collins's artistic language we must accustom our eyes to a world whose expression bears little or no resemblance to that of any other artist. To be sure he did not "invent" the Angel, any more than the Eternal Bride. But at his touch they are infallibly of his vision. To play the game of source hunting and cross-checking of influences with other artists is already to defer to a slack, unfocused perception. Such is the nature of the iconic image that it demands all our attention or nothing, not as an idolatrous object, but because it discloses its inviolate substance only to our utmost response. In the totality of our absorption there must be no space to be occupied by those familiar forms and outlines we are accustomed to transpose either from nature or from the work of other artists. Given the recurrent figure of the Fool, whether caressing a bird, at prayer, or dancing the naked joy of his innocence, we should have no interval to clothe him with our pre-suppositions. In his gesture is the fecundity of the Spirit; at his touch the flower breathes forth its perfume; by his sight the bird discovers the color of its plumage; by his kneeling the landscape is sanctified. His is no physical form. Clothed in the "fantastic garments of love," beneath which there is no muscle or bone, there is nothing that could deceive us into imagining that his presence suffers the weight of corporeality, the obligations of a physical exertion. But we discern, nonetheless, qualities that inform the human: movement, rhythm, tenderness, elegance, gaiety. Such qualities transform the pen or brush stroke into a living reality. The Fool, no less than his companions in other works, is a "station of transmission." That is to say each pictorial image is the nodal point

2. [*Fifth Ennead*, eighth tractate.—Ed.]

at which multiple levels of meaning cohere in the nuance of line, color, and shape. By this configuration on the picture surface they have their life and are perceived as transforming agents of consciousness. In the bending of the Fool to touch the flower is the moment of benediction in which we apprehend the grace that is bestowed by the unity of inner and outer natures. The specific beauty of the painted image is the occasion of our recognition that the division of subject from object is already the tool of a reductive consciousness; as if through that beauty unity of being was able to fulfill itself.

Often we are given only the head of the Fool in whose implacable gaze is condensed the mystery of our birth into consciousness—our coming into being. His melancholy and openness are never wholly revealed in any one painting. His impersonal life is partly lived in all the other pictures in which he is present, each appearance implied in every other in an almost sequential inter-relatedness of images from picture to picture. This characteristic is shared by the whole of Collins's work. Each Angel is one of a community of Angels; each Pilgrim journeys part of the way that is only fully undertaken in the cumulative journey of each and every Pilgrim; each Sibyl utters her prophecy as the fragment of an omniscience known only to all Sibyls together. Each painting and drawing is a window onto a continually unfolding vision, inexhaustible in its nature.

All of which seems to suggest that the pictures themselves might be effete, sapped of the reality proper to them as works rendered in paint or pencil, like rarified ghosts of the artist's consciousness. But Cecil Collins has complete technical mastery of every medium he works with. Each picture, whether in ink, paint, pencil, or whatever, portrays ample evidence of the artist's proper concern and delight in the properties of his chosen medium. How could it be otherwise? No artist could adequately express such a depth of resonance as is here were he not able to take it for granted that no privation or hindrance would be imposed upon him by his own technical insufficiency. Collins's mastery has the effect of each picture living only in the medium in which it is created. You could not transpose a drawing, for instance, to the medium of paint without destroying the specific life of the image that is drawn, so indissoluble is the bond between applied technique and the realization of the image. Recessed beyond layer after layer of pigment and varnish, can we say that this head—Fool or Anima—is other than the physical substance of its rendering? Is the image given birth from the medium; has the artist been taken unawares to see the worked substance congeal into a living presence? Or, in the dry austerity of tempera, could it be that the tree, the bird, and the woman were already alive under the surface leaving the painter with only the task of brushing away the covering that concealed their presence? In the final analysis, moment of vision and rendered image, like the dancer and the dance, have no life apart from one another, each painted and drawn image intuits the miraculous gift of incarnation.

Collins's compelling technical mastery, both as colorist and as draughtsman, is never deployed for its own sake. He has spoken of such vacuity as producing "visual confectionery." For him technique has its own meditative content. How else are we to understand that an art devoted to invoking the spontaneity of intuitive consciousness should proceed by means of techniques that are as often as not deliberately slow and painstaking in their execution? In his composition Collins puts aside the more customary architectonic devices for ordering the picture plane. Instead, an almost musical notation comes into play so that we find a picture is formally organized through the counterpoint of visual rhymes, motivic repetitions, and carefully modulated tonal ranges of color with harmonic complements and discordant clashes.

In *Hymn to Night* (1951), a typical example, the depth and benevolence of ultramarine and cobalt collects and interiorizes our gaze, taking it inward to a landscape in the foreground of which a feminine figure is poised by a tree. The one articulated rhythm of life's energy is echoed throughout, flowing down the hair, then up the tree trunk, then spread abundantly in the leaves no less than in the river that flows in the middle distance. The seeming mirror image of the woman's crossed hands is echoed repeatedly, as if from a pivotal point, in the dual image of the tree's foliage, an angel's wings, the raised wings of several swans, and in the branches of the trees that cover a distant hill. Within the narrow spectrum of color woman and landscape are possessed of a single tonal being. In

Daybreak (1971). 75 x 85 cm. Mixed media on board.

Hymn to the Night (1951). 90 x 120 cm. Oil on canvas.

The Wounded Angel (1967). 75 x 90 cm. Mixed media on board.

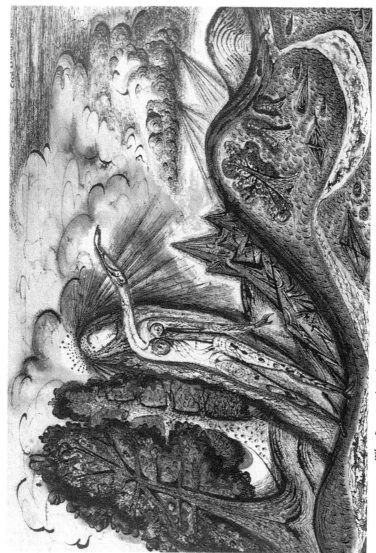

The Invocation (1944). 38 x 56 cm. Ink and watercolor on paper.

Paradise (1976). 46 x 42 cm. Pencil on paper.

The Angel of the Flowing Light (1968). 122 x 106 cm. Oil on board.

Daybreak (1971) is the burden of hope that is present in green. Beyond the turbulent energy of generative waves, already receding before the onlooker, three feminine figures emerge from a placid sea. They proffer a token of new birth in the shape of a flowering plant whose blooms are already vivified with the chrome of the rising sun. A bird, emblem of the soul, held by one of the figures, has its sight fixed resolutely on the horizon, its breast, like that of the three faces, kindled by the sun's light. In *Wounded Angel* (1967) the harmonic interval from orange to violet offers its sanctuary to an Angel which, in the lightness of its being, has returned to rest on the floor of Paradise, exhausted from the effort of witnessing the self-disfiguration of man's forgetfulness of the Divine. In the drawings, often the dynamism and energy of the theme is paradoxically enhanced by means of techniques that on examination, are evidently laborious and exact, the result of a meticulous application of thousands of single strokes of the pen or pencil.

Cecil Collins's iconic perceptions have engendered a comparatively limited range of pictorial ideas which have nonetheless been explored with considerable penetration, not only in the pictures themselves, but in the artist's writings, poems, and recorded statements. These texts, because they are integrally a part of the same visionary language, form a perfect complement to the visually executed works. The pictures do not illustrate the thesis of these texts any more than the texts are a commentary upon the pictures.

The principal images in which Collins's vision is focused and participated are the trinity of Fool, Angel, and feminine Anima. About the Fool the artist has himself spoken in detail in his manifesto "The Vision of the Fool" (1947 and 1981).[3] The Fool affirms that purity of consciousness in which knowledge absolute, premodal, unqualified plenitude, resides. Simple, innocent, vulnerable, the Fool bequeaths to us the ultimate freedom of our identity and destiny. His joy and essence are that charity of the heart that in love and beauty redeems the politics of time.

---

3. [Also collected in *The Vision of the Fool.* —Ed.]

The winged Angel, agent of transformation and the divine wisdom, an intermediary of Truth, seeks only to awaken our assent. Ever watchful, guardian, guide, judge, the Angel, as companion to the Fool, is always about some action—its presence always purposeful—its role to pierce with the divine brightness the darkening substance that is the desolation of this world.

The Anima, Eternal Bride, often only a head, has a complex role. By contrast unmoving, rejecting nothing, vigilant, uncensorious, she reflects in her wise compassion an absorbed, unfathomable passivity. She is the subjective pole of the moment of intuitive imagination, the masculine pole of which is performed by the process of visualization which is the act of making these visionary images as objects. In virtue of the complementarity of these two poles the whole realm of Collins's art comes into existence. This situation is analogous to the traditional symbolism of the *animus,* masculine spirit, and *anima,* feminine soul, who, in their inter-relationship generate the world in so far as it is objectively knowable. Priestess and guardian, unmaternal, nonetheless from Collins's eternal feminine all actions flow and to her enduring benediction they return. In her is mirrored the mysterious depth of the human universe as an image of contemplation.

Cecil Collins's isolation as an artist is due, not only to the unexpected nature of his visual language, but also to the fact that an imaginative vision such as his is without protection in the cultural consensus of modernism to which it is a rebuke. As if in answer to some inevitable summons, some objectifying instinct, and against the resistance of a malaise and a blindness, these images have been conjured into existence to pose the metaphysical imperative to an age mesmerized by the surface of things. Yet planted within them are the seeds of what must take their place, to lift the malaise, to restore sight, and affirm their opposite. Collins's imaginative vision, which has no concern for the substance of history, by a supreme paradox has about it the air of historical necessity. For the beauty and the serenity of these images comprehend the true measure of our cultural exhaustion. In them we are finally given some purchase against the successive depredations of the secular, self-disfiguring patterns of our culture. In them we witness emblems of our true humanity as it is renewed and refreshed in the sacred unknown.

14

Michael Cardew:
The Potter as Primordial Maker

> A vessel is hollowed by molding clay, but the empty space where nothing exists makes the pot effective.... Therefore, whereas the tangible [the existent] serves for the possession, it is the intangible [the non-existent] that makes it effective.
>
> Adapted from the *Tao Te Ching*

As WE have seen in the preceding chapters, those who have radically questioned the prevailing status of industrial production have recognized that the ultimate value of work is as much related to the needs of the soul as to the needs of the body. They have sought to re-awaken in the modern mind the idea that it is essential to human well-being so to arrange the production of necessary things that the spiritual aspiration that is at the heart of work is defended as its guiding principle. In attempting to locate and arrest the progressive dehumanization of man, those voices have been raised not out of some misplaced nostalgia for the past, but out of a fundamental conviction that the industrial method is deeply flawed and represents a distortion, a curtailment, of what it means to be human. It is hardly surprising that the defense of manual skills as a repository of human values has been made, in many cases, by practitioners of the crafts.

To the practical and polemical challenge of those who have already been mentioned must certainly be added the name of Michael Cardew. To turn to his example as a demonstration of the organic unity of manual skill, material substance, and productive method is possible because the art of the potter represents the condition of human work in its most primordial mode. For the potter brings man into the closest possible contact with material substance as such. Not only does he utilize the four elements—fire, air, earth, and water—but for the most part not even a rudimentary tool intervenes between the worker and the substance that he works. In foregoing the usual intermediary of an instrumental technique the potter makes of himself the tool needed to effect his purposes. He, above all others, most directly experiences the demands placed upon his inner resources as a workman.

The true potter establishes his workshop where nature provides a plentiful supply of clay. He digs the substance of his trade himself from the immediate environment. The raw clay must be made ready for his work, a process that is demanding of his physical effort. This bodily effort of blending and de-airing the clay allows the potter to establish a rapport with his material, feeling for its possibilities, testing its readiness to receive the imprint of its final shape. For the possibilities of clay belong to clay as to no other substance. Its potentiality for form is unique to itself. The pulse of its life is different from that of wood or stone or metal. This pulse the potter feels and absorbs in the preparation of his material. What might seem to the outsider to be a physical drudgery that could be dispensed with by the use of a machine, once the tension of aching muscles and the stubborn matter of the clay are fused, becomes a subtle process of physical transformation whereby the resistance of the body is resolved and energized and the demands of the ego are stilled. The soul of the potter and the soul of the clay must, after all, become one if there is to be harmony between the worker and his work. In this necessary transmutation the ego has no place.

The potter works on the clay as if on himself. Intuitively he is possessed by the "not-self" of the clay's substance, drawing it into his own being. What the clay comes to express is nothing other than the potter's being, at the same time as it expresses what it is its own nature to be. The inner form of the worked clay becomes the substance of the potter, as the soul of the potter is made malleable by the outward, physical effort of preparing the clay. The prepared clay becomes the receptacle of the potter's intention as the potter's skill becomes the vehicle for the realization of the clay's final outward shape. By means of this interchange the potter and the pot are drawn toward that perfect formation that is their mutual fullest potentiality for being. The qualitative imprint of the pot is within the potter in so far as it is renewed endlessly through the potter's skill in exploring the clay's very plasticity. The perfect form of the operative action resides in the clay in so far as the clay variously provides the occasion for its embodiment. This intuitive reciprocity of maker and made, physical and mental, inner and outer, form and substance, imposition and receptivity, is brought about by that self-denying discipline that is the informing principle of consummate skill.

By developing the habit of prolonged concentration upon his repetitive tasks the potter induces in himself a state of physical and mental integration, a state of receptivity whereby the conscious effort of actually forming his material becomes effortless and unconscious. This state permits his inspiration to flow unheeded and for the resulting work to embody those hidden possibilities of formal beauty that reside, as it were, objectively in the clay. For the artefact that is true to its archetype must be free from the idiosyncrasies of the personality of its maker. It must eschew innovative contrivance for its own sake, and all painstaking effort must evaporate in a beauty and creative joy that are at one with the nature of the materials in question.

In working "objectively" upon the outer product of his skill, so the potter must equally concentrate "subjectively" upon the inner substance of his being. For the potter, inner and outer are literally two faces of the same reality while his hands manipulate the clay. In his exploration of space he works continually with the sphere—the most perfect symbol of unity—as the guiding yet unmanifest paradigm that informs his every move as he brings given centrifugal force and applied physical pressure into creative interplay. For the potter the "face" of reality is the complementarity of convex and concave. The convex surface radiating outward is complemented by the concave surface that concentrates inward. The concave nurtures the inner potentiality of the form's coming into being—the seed of fertility and growth hidden in the darkness of what is unseen. The convex presents an outward, light-reflecting surface—applied knowledge drawing out and imposing limitations of being upon material substance. Nothing intervenes between the creative agent and the character of the material that is in the process of being formed. The challenge upon the potter's inner resources is due to the fact that clay, in its working state, is formless and yet is receptive to all forms. As Cardew notes, all the discipline to form must come from the potter, who has to overcome the paradoxical fact that because clay will easily respond to any treatment it is most difficult to control.

It was from the Japanese potter Shoji Hamada that Cardew first learned that "technical accomplishment counts for little beside inner life."[1] In learning, during his apprentice years with Hamada and Bernard Leach, that there is more to pottery than being merely an efficient producer, Cardew also learned that "whatever you made would have its own indelible character, good or bad; and this character was the most important part of the pot, and necessarily came straight out of 'the real you.'" This does not mean that "moral beauty necessarily produces artistic beauty—it obviously doesn't," but that an operative and harmonious balance between technical mastery, aesthetic beauty, and "ethical rightness" is only achieved by maintaining a standard of utility in repetitive, practical work: "You must make pots unceasingly even if they betray—as they almost certainly will—the worst as well as the best in you." This repetitive work, an essential part of the potter's craft, has a fundamentally important function. Cardew claimed that a man who gets bored making the same pot over and over again was not fit to be a potter at all. But more than this the very act of repetition imparts a sort of non-conscious condition into the creative act itself. The self-conscious, contriving part of the mind is stilled sufficiently for the clay to respond immediately to disciplined bodily action, so that the potter will "find himself making pots as naturally as a tree makes leaves or fruits," as he put it in his essay "The Fatal Impact."

There is considerable significance in the fact that in inducing this

1. The quotations from Cardew's writings for which no sources are given are taken from his posthumously published autobiography, *Michael Cardew: Pioneer Potter* (1988), and "Michael Cardew at 75," compiled by Len Dutton, *Ceramics Review*, no. 40 (July–August 1976): 4–10. A bibliography of his uncollected writings can be found in *Michael Cardew: A Collection of Essays*, Crafts Advisory Committee (1976).

state of "no-mind," as we may call it, Cardew rejected the "fallacy in the gospel of labour-saving devices." It was doing the "donkey work" with his own hands and muscles that brought him into a deeper rapport with his materials, as well as polarizing his mind in preparation for the task in hand—the rhythm and tempo of kneading the raw clay, drawing the potter's being into the pre-formal essence of the pot soon to come to life at his fingertips. From this process it emerges, as with all the elementary crafts, that "every touch by the potter is *physiognomic*—that is, it is an infallible guide to his real character, to the state of his mind (or his soul)." Moreover, "the more you enter into a long campaign of exploring the inner character of even a simple form, the more completely and excitingly it reveals itself with each new realisation on the wheel." As Cardew himself put it in his essay "Stoneware Pottery," the revelation of form is a living reciprocity of inner and outer worlds, of "technique and inspiration . . . as much one as the inner and outer faces of a crystal surface." The potter

> starts by thinking he wants to express something in clay, but after a time (if he is any good) the clay takes charge and expresses something through him . . . it is a right and proper state of affairs—the technical processes and materials are not a category distinct and separate from the expression the artist makes from them. On the contrary, they are themselves part and parcel of the meaning which he can only express by endlessly studying their structure and the minutest subtleties of their behaviour: finding out what the material wants to say is the only way to say anything through the material. A good potter loves clay disinterestedly, for its own character, not because it is an obedient mirror for his own personal ideas, however interesting they may be.

If, at the start, the potter senses there is something missing from his work, it is likely that he will feel an impulse to put something there by means of a "deliberate willed injection of personality." In "Potters and Amateur Pottery," Cardew warned against this:

> It's a mistake because the something which is missing—call it character or personality or originality or whatever you prefer—is in fact a very mysterious and elusive thing, which cannot be

pinned down and captured by a direct assault. The only chance of catching it is by stalking and taking it by surprise; you have to approach the mystery by an indirect road. This indirect road is skill, or craftsmanship—not only manual control, dexterity, efficiency, and all those things, but also expertise, learning how to overcome all sorts of technical difficulties and all the various obstacles which nature puts in the way of art . . . skill is the channel along which your creative juices can flow.

Skill, he wrote elsewhere, "like any other regimen or course of training, is not an end in itself but a means to something beyond it." In other words the workman does not work to express his "skill" for its own sake, or a "style" for its own sake, or work merely for the sake of work alone, for all these "accidents" of his activity will inevitably express what little of his "personality" needs to be present in the finished work.

Not only is it obvious that by the industrial method it is the machine that overcomes the "technical difficulties and obstacles which nature puts in the way of art," but also that the channel of skill is by the same method circumvented and so forecloses on the exercise of art. The notion of difficulty implies that by which it is overcome. The good workman values difficulty in his work, not for its own sake, but in so far as it challenges his powers of invention and accomplishment. This points to the presence in work of something more than the efficient and routine manipulation of matter. Difficulty is a form of self-revelation through conquest, by the human person, over the brute nature of matter. It is a momentary conquest of those exterior circumstances that impose themselves upon us and which obscure or distort the mirror of our self-knowing. These contingencies deflect us one way or another away from the simple and direct experience of that timeless self-absorption in which we are at one with ourselves and our actions but without which, paradoxically, we so rarely achieve that self-absorption. That is surely the heart of true work, true art. And is that not the reason why we are reluctant to give our heartfelt assent to work easily done, work that has not passed through the refining fire of discipline to emerge its triumphant master?

The "willed injection of personality" is an attempt to introduce from outside the process of making something of a self-conscious aesthetic element that does not arise integrally from its production. It does not conduce to the realization of the work's first cause, the bringing to perfection of what is first conceived in the mind's eye— the revelation of the maker's art. For just as the soul is the form of the body, so the art in the artist is the form of the work. No less false than this intrusion of self-consciousness into the proper integral order of workmanship is the ruthlessly imposed industrial idea of functional efficiency. In his essay "Design" Cardew spoke of the effect such an imposition would have, of the pain and destruction it could cause, if the delicately balanced polarity of man's sensual and intellectual involvement in the making process is denied. He thought that the deprivation and frustration would eventually drive people mad, and noted that it "seems to some people to be exactly the way we are going at the present moment."

Cardew's life and work have always been associated with the epithet "pioneer," and it is necessary to an understanding of his achievement to remember on what this association rests. Cardew joined Shoji Hamada and Bernard Leach at the latter's St. Ives pottery in the early 1920s. This was the beginning of the studio pottery movement in England, which was itself the revival of pottery making on the handicraft basis. It was also a challenge to the deadening and sterile methods of the factory system which had instituted a productive process on the basis of a division of responsibility between the designer and the producer of pottery ware. In other words, as Gill never tired of pointing out, the workman is by this method only responsible for doing what he is told and has no "responsibility for the form or quality, the intellectual quality, of what he takes part in making." It was this division, made necessary by the tyranny of economic opportunism, that the studio pottery movement sought to heal. Cardew's belief was that the living root ("art," as he defined it, the unconscious wellspring that animates the will to create) of craftsmanship would gradually emerge to "repudiate the false ideal of servile obedience," as he hopefully announced in 1942 in "Industry and the Studio Potter."

Even if he rejected this "false ideal" Cardew was never prepared to go to the same lengths as Gill in condemning the factory system.

Late in his life he acknowledged that the first machines "degraded and dehumanised the work of the skilled craftsman and turned him into a machine minder." In the light of this it is difficult to see what evidence he might have brought to his claim that "in retrospect we can see that the nineteenth century factory system carried within itself the means of curing its own faults and shortcomings."

However, he had to acknowledge that the very efficiency of the industrial system inevitably

> did violence to the character of the material itself: something of its potential beauty has to be sacrificed in order to obtain the necessary efficiency combined with economy. Whether it is hand-made or machine-made, pottery needs another element in addition to form, colour and decoration. This more vital something is what potters call quality, or warmth or depth. The penurious and cold quality of industrial earthenware is due to the technique itself which for anyone trained in the Oriental school amounts to killing the body before you glaze it.

In "Industry and the Studio Potter" of 1942 (which Katherine Pleydell Bouverie called his "fighting manifesto"), Cardew is still optimistic that there could be a fruitful collaboration between the studio potter and industry. However, in that same essay he also outlined what he thought were the criteria for good design in pottery; criteria obviously inimical to the factory system.

> Good design in pottery is the product of tension or "dialectic" between the demands of pure utility and those of pure beauty, and only long experience and continual struggle enable you to achieve a successful fusion of the two.... You only get good designs for pottery from potters [rather than industrial pottery operatives!], because they are the only people who understand art by experience and with their whole personality.

Wherever the human norm of manufacture through personal skill is allowed to operate naturally—as in the case of Cardew's work— the idea of beauty is "only achieved by a balance and a synthesis of use and beauty." Beauty in manufacture is not achieved automatically, as the factory system falsely supposes, by attending to the demands of "consumer appeal": "You cannot, by making use of

Design impose beauty on the objects of utility. It is their birthright. If they are not born right, nothing can help them," he wrote in "Stoneware Pottery."

If the factory system had achieved some excellence of beauty in the past—the seventeenth- and eighteenth-century Staffordshire industry for instance—that was because individual potters were still able to work on a handicraft basis. And their designs were "a synthesis of traditional thrower's shapes, inherited from the Middle Ages, with the idea of convenience and refinement acquired in the eighteenth century." But the factory system is "based on a foundation that does not exist . . . the assumption that there is no such thing as 'pure craftsmanship' into which no element of originality ['art'] enters." Therefore, Cardew finally concludes, "the factory system is based on the existence of the operative as opposed to the true workman."

The rejection of the factory system and of the self-consciously aesthetic (this "Narcissus-dream, which ought to be just a temporary phase in the evolution of a craftsman seems [today] to have become a fixation, elevated into an idea or an orthodoxy") approach to the making of pots was, then, for Cardew the necessary rejection of complementary aspects of the same falsehood. He could not have been more categorical in his repudiation of it than when in his later judgment (in his essay "Stoneware Pottery"), he came to reject the idea that the studio potter could be a designer for industry—the "Art in Industry fallacy," as he called it.

> The fallacy is, that there is a "department" or category called Utility, and another called Art. Utility is for Utensils, Art is for Delectation—"a kind of noble play" and all that talk.
>
> Those who think this fill both their departments with objects of horror. They fill the world with Well-Designed Utilities, but the essential meaning of works of art will always (though they will never know it) elude them.

So the stream of true creative work is unstopped in a state of "no–mind"; a state that from the depths of the workman's being releases the hidden potentiality toward the creation of outward shapes. Along the pure channel of skill, unvitiated by aesthetic sentiment and unhindered by mechanical intervention, flows the profound rapport between the mystery of the "person" and the unconscious sources of "art": that "person" whose paradoxical nature it is both to localize the subjectivity of the creative act yet whose identity is never the occasion for what is created.

But who is this "self" that the workman knows himself to be? Firstly,

> you know nothing about it, it's the mysterious inside of you which you cannot know any more than you can know what you look like by looking in a looking glass. Secondly, it's something that's not self that you are dealing with. When concentrating on the form of something you are unaware of being yourself, yet you are nourishing yourself, and the form that you do produce is yourself. No power on earth can prevent it from being yourself.... It comes out absolutely naturally and inevitably when expressed in the majesty of form.

> There's a very significant thing about shapes. Some shapes are perfectly correct and don't say anything; other shapes seem very odd but pack a great deal of significance, definitely say something, are expressive.... Significant of what? The simple answer is we don't know, it's too big a question.

So we are led full circle to the primordial wisdom for whom the workman, artist, craftsman (ultimately these are, at worst, confusing, at best, illogical distinctions) is one whose productive method is in keeping with the natural rhythms and substance of nature—a nature of which the workman is himself a part. What began as a discovery of the doctrines of Zen Buddhism with Hamada and Leach in the 1920s—not gainsaying a temporary reaction against the notion that "Oriental peoples are always right and western man is always wrong"—Cardew later found to be true from his own experience. This reaction was no doubt set in motion by an early discovery of the "great impetus which Catholic Neo-Thomists brought to all the old arguments of John Ruskin and William Morris in favour of craftsmanship and against the industrial system."

A quotation from Aristotle was axiomatic for Cardew: *Ars imitatur naturam in sua operatione.*

> A fatal idea but properly interpreted it means that art imitates nature in her operations, or as Eric Gill translated it, "art imitates nature by working as nature works." That's a very illuminating

remark. The art referred to by Aristotle was the art of medicine—you tried to cure people by imitating the methods which nature uses—and it's absolutely splendid as applied to what we call art, which includes pottery.

A great maxim from the Middle Ages—translated as "The essence and existence of everything on earth is derived from the beauty of God" ["The Beauty of God is the cause of the being of all that is": St. Dionysius the Areopagite]—sums up the absolutely irrational [a-rational] feelings of confidence that a long regime of working on art engenders in you.

In "The Fatal Impact," and as a result of his experiences in Africa, Cardew was moved to challenge the argument against the incursions of materialist progress. Whatever the extent of the "lost potential for happiness," he wrote, "the family lives, ethnic traditions and ancestral arts of the slaves—their descendants achieved a great moral power . . . of more value than any art or craft or even than happiness itself." This argument is in effect the argument in favor of the advantage of material progress come what may the disadvantages. But the argument will not bear much examination since it is founded on the pretense that material progress is guided in its encroachments by a vision of the final good. But such progress has blind impetus as its master. That it is also the expression of all that is contrary to human nature is no less true, if far less obvious. On the level of its operation such progress does not present society with any option, only an all-encompassing imperative whose obligations and persuasions have no properly human counter-balance. As Cardew noted, it is an argument "human beings . . . are not entitled to use not being competent to judge the balance of loss or gain in such tremendous matters; we do not possess the scales in which to weigh them."

There are, nonetheless, things we are obliged to judge because of our nature:

> these are the data of ethics, and of aesthetics. Ethics is about our duties to our neighbor; but aesthetics is about our duties to all the things and creatures of the world we belong to. Our aesthetic conscience is therefore just as tender and just as imperious as the ethical conscience. Anyone who has felt the value—that is, *the*

meaning—of primitive arts feels also that we must try to do something to defend them, because they are necessities, not just academic curiosities. We need them, not as dead specimens, but as things which have the power to make us grow and change and to nourish us in the future.

In other words the crafts are, in his judicious phrase, "a depository of the soul."

The proper significance of progress, as he finally saw, is a question of "where to" and on what terms. Its value is essential not consequential. As he confessed in his autobiography: "Progress is both necessary and supremely desirable to man, because all real progress is a progress of the soul."

15

Samuel Palmer's Vision of Nature

I have beheld as in the spirit, such nooks, caught such glimpses of the perfumed and enchanted twilight—of natural mid-summer, as well as, at some other times of day, other scenes, as passed thro' the intense purifying separating transmuting heat of the soul's infabulous alchymy.

SAMUEL PALMER, November 14, 1827

AT SOME TIME during 1824 and 1825 Samuel Palmer painted an unusual picture now known as *The Rest on the Flight into Egypt,* or *The Repose of the Holy Family.* It was begun in the painter's nineteenth year. The picture, painted in oil and tempera, is curious for two reasons. First, there had not been anything quite like it in the history of English painting. It is stylistically almost without precedent. Second, the picture is an odd mixture of not quite resolved pictorial features. It shows the Holy Family in what appears to be an English landscape. But, incongruously, to the right, is a large palm-like tree. In the middle distance is a richly autumnal wooded landscape typical of the Kentish hills around Shoreham with which Palmer was already familiar and with which, in the following decade, he was to become intimately associated. In the picture, this wooded landscape gives way, toward the skyline, to another sort of landscape more reminiscent of the Alps than anything one might see in England. To the left of the picture is a steeply banked field which reveals, rather too precipitously, a cottage with a smoking chimney. In the right foreground the Holy Family is at rest. It is not quite clear on what they are resting owing to the ambiguity of the ground plane beneath them. For this reason it looks the most unlikely place to rest with, presumably, the hill falling away just behind them. There is considerable distortion in the figure of Mary; and Joseph makes a somewhat token appearance just behind her.

All this would not matter were it not for the fact that the picture is painted in a style that is, in its detail, representative of natural appearances. Any prolonged contemplation of the picture is likely to leave the viewer with the impression that the representation is not sufficiently removed from naturalism for its incongruities to be resolved. It is a beautiful picture, richly worked, and yet it has something of the appearance of a transitional work, as important for what it heralds as for what it accomplishes. And what it heralds is a style of painting that immediately after was to result in the six masterpieces of the year 1825. These are the six sepia wash drawings that are among Palmer's greatest works.

These six pictures are painted in a style that manages a fruitful and balanced tension of naturalistic and abstract elements. They present a convincing and homogeneous pictorial reality that in varying degrees only partially corresponds to the reality of physical appearances yet nonetheless in such a way that any visual incongruities we might find in the pictorial reality seem to be acceptable and do not disturb the mind's eye. In *Early Morning*, for instance, it does not strike us as incongruous that it is not clear where the source of the light is. Does it come, as perhaps it should, from the large mushroom-shaped tree, or does it come from a source beyond the left side of the picture? The three slender tree trunks to the right seem to indicate this, but then their shadows are not angled consistently.

In *A Rustic Scene*, the spatial depth from the head of the front ox to the thatch of the cottage is foreshortened to the point of having no extent at all. Again, the ground plane is ambiguous so that it is not certain on quite what the back ox is standing. The ears of corn in the middle distance are of a size that would, in natural fact, make them the size of small trees. (Such corn is also a feature of *The Valley Thick with Corn* and *Late Twilight*.) In front of the cottage to the left of the picture there are four wooden palings of a fence that seems stout beyond its function as such. And what is the fringed triangle of leaves that cuts across the bottom left-hand corner of the picture?

In *The Valley Thick with Corn* multiple perspectives seem to operate so that one part of the scene is inconsistent with another from the unifying point of view of the observer's eye. It is as if the painter wants us to look closely and to absorb areas of the picture to the exclusion from our field of vision of other areas, so that a series of minutely articulated scenes "join up" at their edges to cohere pictorially as we draw away and take in the whole picture at a glance. By means of this sectioning of the picture plane we are made to inhabit imaginative space which itself replaces physical space. This lack of physical depth is registered in several instances: by the two birds to the right of the trunk of the mushroom-shaped tree in *Early Morning*, for instance, and those to the left of the central tree; as well as the shepherd and his sheep on the escarpment in the top right-hand corner of *The Skirts of a Wood*. The birds in flight in the center of *The Valley Thick with Corn*, and the three fruits in the top left-hand corner of *A Rustic Scene* are all devices that in conventional pictorial language would be used to measure distance. But here they do not quite succeed in that function.

More generally, but with the possible exception of *The Valley with a Bright Cloud*, which is redolent of an after-storm calm, we note that in all these pictures there is no climatic atmosphere. No mist has ever formed, no wind blown through, no rain fallen upon these landscapes. In their ecstatic ripeness they are aloof from the transitory vicissitudes of weather and of the seasons. These, and any other ambiguities and incongruities we might find, seem rather to be beside the point in the context of the stylistic means that Palmer deploys, and which is entirely consistent with its own imaginative intention. The stylistic balance of naturalism and abstraction, depicting as it does a rapt stillness that honors the theophanic miracle of the observable creation, he seldom again brought to such a pitch of concentration as here in these six works.

We cannot say how our overall view of Palmer's Shoreham period would be altered were the works destroyed by his son restored to us. But in only a few other pictures does this stylistic synthesis of naturalism and abstraction form such an integral part of the pictorial reality. These are *A Hilly Scene*, of 1826 (which is a masterly summation of the 1825 sepia works); *A Shepherd and His Flock under the Moon and Stars*, of 1827; *Ruth Returning from the Gleaning*, of 1828–29; *Coming from Evening Church*; and perhaps *The Magic Apple Tree*, both of 1830. All of Palmer's other paintings, including the typically "Shoreham" works, show scenes that are plausible in terms of naturalistic representation. In the six sepia works of 1825 such representation does not seem to be in question. They stand apart, so much so that we must conclude that here something different was intended.

The maturity of the conception and the mastery of the execution of these works are, to say the least, surprising in a painter of only twenty years of age. The possible iconographic sources of their pictorial and stylistic richness have been well researched and identified. But useful as such studies are, they reveal almost nothing of the motivation, the creative impulse, behind the making of these pictures. Apart from the literary sources (no less important in this case than the pictorial), the only visual precedents for them that we have from Palmer's own hand are to be found in his sketchbook of 1824. Here, in embryo, along with intensely detailed studies of natural forms, are those radiant scenes of magical intimacy; here is the landscape forming itself into unlikely extra-geological configurations; here trees and plants no longer quite answer to strict botanical categorization. In these pages the elements of a pictorial style are being tried and tested for their imaginative significance no less than for their pictorial value.

Something of Palmer's mental state can be inferred from an entry in another notebook described by his son A. H. Palmer as covering the period November 1823 to July 1824: "I . . . shall try to work with a child's simple feeling and with the industry of humility." Nothing could be further removed from simplicity than the painter's work of this period, unless we understand him to mean innocence of vision—the direct imaginative apprehension of the child. Indeed, in another entry in the same notebook Palmer refers to his "very early years, in which I distinctly remember that I felt the finest scenery and the country in general with a very strong and pure feeling." Yet another entry for January 2, 1825, gives us an insight into his then somewhat febrile mental condition with its highly strung spiritual pre-disposition:

> Now is begun a new year. Here I pause to look back on the time
> between this and about the 15th of last July. Then I laid by the

[Holy] Family in much distress, anxiety and fear; which had plunged me into despair but for God's mercy. . . . I then sought Christ's help, the giver of all good talents whether acknowledged or not. . . . I improved more since I resolved to depend on Him till now . . . and have felt much more assistance and consolation. For very soon after my deep humblement and distress, I resumed and finished my *Twilight,* and quickly took up my *Joseph's Dream,* and sketched in my new sketchbook . . . knowing my own stupidness. . . . I gave back the praise to God who kindly sent it, and had granted to me desponding, that at eventide it should be light.

At the time of writing this passage Palmer had known the painter John Linnell (later to become his father-in-law) some fifteen months. The older man had encouraged Palmer a good deal and of this fateful friendship he was to write, "it pleased God to send Mr Linnell as a good angel from Heaven to pluck me from the pit of modern art; and after struggling to get out for the space of a year and a half, I have just enough cleared my eyes from the slime of the pit to see what a miserable state I am now in." During 1824 Linnell also introduced Palmer—in "fear and trembling"—to William Blake.

It is difficult to ascribe the greater degree of importance either to Blake's personality or to his work in so far as they were to influence Palmer. But of one thing we can be certain, the incalculable influence on him of Blake's half-visionary, half-pastoral woodcuts executed for Dr. Thornton's Virgil in 1821. The impact of these small pictures on Palmer was immeasurable: his own testimony being well known. He described them as

visions of little dells, and nooks, and corners of Paradise; models of the exquisitest pitch of intense poetry. . . . There is in all such a mystic and dreamy glimmer as penetrates and kindles the inmost soul, and gives complete and unreserved delight, unlike the gaudy daylight of this world. They are, like all that wonderful artist's works, the drawing aside of the fleshly curtain, and the glimpse which all the most holy, studious saints and sages have enjoyed, of that rest which remaineth to the people of God.

What emerges from this confluence of training, of influences and inspirations is that Palmer, whose first recorded drawing had been executed at the age of seven, and who had sold a picture at the Royal

Academy at the age of fourteen, had reached what he considered an artistic impasse at the age of seventeen. This impasse—the "pit of modern art"—was clearly the more or less unquestioned assumption of the age that the art of painting was the art of naturalistic representation. Yet within three years, at the age of twenty, with the help of Linnell and Blake, Palmer had painted six masterpieces in a style that had little in common with either of his mentors' work. Blake was understood by very few of his contemporaries because there was no widespread convention at the time to grasp the meaning of his images. The same fate befell Palmer's works of the Shoreham years, for they remained mostly unsold. A baffled critic, commenting in the *European Magazine* of August 1825, wrote of two of them that they are "so amazing that we feel the most intense curiosity to see what manner of man it was who produced such performances." We forget how recent appreciation of these pictures is, and for reasons that are not always helpful for an understanding of them, as we shall see.

In order to grasp more fully Palmer's achievement in these six pictures we must recall that neither Blake nor Linnell painted in a style such as we now associate with Palmer's Shoreham years. It seems likely that Linnell had re-focused Palmer's sense of pictorial value by directing him to certain "very ancient Italian and German masters." His recent friendship with Blake no doubt reinforced his incipient awareness of the significance of imaginative vision—of the supremacy of the soul's cognition over the sensory apprehension of the world of appearances. With his newly clarified vision Palmer felt sufficiently confident to dismiss his contemporaries' attempts at naturalistic representation, saying he "wondered what the moderns could mean by what they called their 'effects.'" That is, seeing nature as a series of retinal impressions. And a memorandum of the period, "guard against bleakness and Grandeur," demonstrates his early resolve to resist the eighteenth-century artistic ideal of the sublime.

It must be assumed that it was Blake's friendship that gave Palmer's naturally Platonic bent just the support and encouragement it needed, seeing that, with the exception of the Virgil woodcuts, the human dynamic of Blake's figurative compositions has little in common with Palmer's empathic pastoralism. Whereas Blake transcribed what he saw inwardly, Palmer alchemized what he saw outwardly. But what is meant by speaking of Palmer's "Platonic bent"? Here we must examine more closely Palmer's own record of his intentions. In this we are fortunate since the painter was hardly less able to describe in words his intentions than he was able to execute them by pictorial means.

When Palmer wrote, in a letter to George and Juliet Richmond dated June 1836, and quoting from Milton's *Comus,* "every little self denial and agonizing brings after it 'a sacred and home-felt delight,' so, on the large scale, our whole earthly existence ought to be a short agony to secure eternal blessedness," we might be forgiven for thinking that he was prey to a degree of morbidness. But we cannot gainsay the other-worldly direction of the sentiment, one which remained with him throughout his life. Moreover, it is obvious from much that he wrote that the painter had at times a pressing acquaintance with the powers of evil. An entry for August 31, 1826, in his notebook reads:

> After dinner I was helped against the enemy so that I thought one good thought. I immediately drew on my cartoon much quicker and better. . . . Satan tries violently to make me leave reading the Bible and praying. . . . O artful enemy, to keep me, who devote myself entirely to poetic things . . . I will endeavour, God helping, to begin the day by dwelling on some short piece of scripture, and praying for the Holy Ghost thro' the day to inspire my art.

A few years later he wrote again to the painter Richmond (September 21, 1832): "If only people knew how deeply the whole world lieth in wickedness, and how totally it is estranged and set in opposition to God." Obviously Palmer shared with Blake a keen sense of the fulcrum of good and evil at the point of inspiration for human motivation and action.

Yet Palmer was far from seeing man's position in this world as being one of sin and hopelessness. In the same letter he refers to man's pre-fallen image as "the similitude of a divine parentage." And in a letter to John Giles's family dated October 1838 he advised his brother Albert to go on drawing, continue to study from the divine, eternal, naked form of man.... The devout and holy study of the naked form purifies the imagination and affections, and makes us less pervious to evil temptation.... In eternity that human form is, as it were, the body and symbol of goodness and truth.... It existed from eternity in the Divine Idea.

This "archetypal perspective," as one might call it, remained with Palmer throughout his life. Writing from Italy in 1838 to the Giles family he ranged the "old Platonic philosophy" against the materialistic, pragmatic "Useful Knowledge Society" of his day, remarking "money and beef are not, as people imagine, the solid things of the *mind*; but as unreal and unsatisfying to the immortal part, as a lecture on metaphysics could be to a hungry belly."

Palmer must have read Plato in the translation by Thomas Taylor, whose *Works of Plato* was published in 1804, which would have familiarized the painter with the idea that the human soul, while in its earthly body, is in exile from its true state in the divine realm. If we add to this what Palmer would, as a Christian, have understood of the Creation as the artifice of God, a manifestation of His goodness and beauty, then we have the essential sources for nearly every one of Palmer's reflections on the human condition in relation to his vocation as a painter of appearances. But the reality beyond created appearances is consistently the focal point of Palmer's art and thought. On the evidence of his writings the Platonic myth of the cave was a leitmotif of his thinking from first to last. From the time of his adolescence to his old age it was natural for him to think of the world of nature in terms of its insubstantiality, its ephemerality. In his "Observations on the Country and on Rural Poetry," written in his more philosophical old age (in fact the last year of his life) and published in 1883 as a preface to his *Eclogues of Virgil*, he rejected the "Facts and Mutton" vision of the universe habitual to the modern intelligence, but doubted whether he could warn such as were possessed by it of the unreality of what they saw: "We must not tell him that perhaps his back is to the light, like those men in Plato's Cavern; and that though his eyes are wide open, he may be watching shadows."

Palmer never makes the assumption of the naive materialist that reality is what we observe. For him appearances are the shadows, the language, even, of the world we should strive to see. To this extent art, for Palmer, has a moral obligation, as well as a spiritual import. There is on the one hand the perfect form of man, the immortal soul, divine in its essence, and on the other hand there is the insufficiency of the natural world acknowledged by our senses. The resolution of this duality that is the very condition of man's earthly existence is for Palmer the task of art. Nature, as he wrote to Linnell in December 1828, "does yet leave a space for the soul to climb above her steepest summits: as, in her own dominion she swells from the herring to leviathan; from the hodmandod to the Elephant, so divine Art piles mountains on her hills, and continents upon those mountains." The nature we see is not another reality "opposed," as it were, to the Divine: it is rather as if what we see is the "wrong side of the tapestry." (The six sepia works do indeed have something of the texture of a tapestry in the way they are closely worked with interwoven shapes over their entire surface.) It is not for the eyes of flesh to penetrate to the right side, for only the cognitive vision of the soul, imagination proper—"intellectual eyes" as he called it—can fathom the true reality. Palmer used this phrase in a letter to George Richmond in September of the same year, where he complained of the danger to students of having their "intellectual eyes jaundiced" by merely copying natural appearances.

This duality suggests if not an opposition between art and nature at least a distinction in their purpose. And so there is. Writing to his patron Leonard Rowe Valpy in May 1815 Palmer notes: "Nature knowledge and art knowledge ought to be in harmony, but they are two distinct things." That this harmony is not brought about in the attempt to represent natural appearances becomes obvious from much that Palmer wrote in an effort to explain his intentions. For instance, in a letter to Philip Gilbert Hamerton in February 1874, long after his Shoreham years, he concluded,

> As for the last thirty years we have been working backwards, not toward nature but naturalism.
>
> The Philosophers, who are by no means too imaginative, can set us right. Lord Bacon says it is the office of poetry to suit the show

of things to the desires of the mind. We seem to aim at suiting the desires of the mind to the show of things. Does not the former imply a much more profound and inclusive study of the "show of things"—"nature," as we call it, itself?

Unlike Blake, Palmer had little to say on the subject of imagination. But clearly it was for him the faculty or transmuting agent that joins sensible perceptions of beauty to their paradigms in the Divine. Writing in his *In Memoriam* for Oliver Finch in 1863 he observed: "He had imagination, that inner sense which receives impressions of beauty as simply and surely as we smell the sweetness of the rose and the woodbine." And later, in his "Observations" of 1883, he elaborated: "A bird deprived of her wings is not more incomplete than the human mind without imagination, a faculty distinct from the spiritual and rational, yet having a common language; for the language of imagination is poetry, and it is in poetry that both sacred aspiration and secular wisdom have found their noblest utterance."

From such passages we may deduce that for Palmer the function of imagination is to resolve the opposing tensions that exist between the demands the outward world makes upon the senses and the inward aspiration that beauty inspires in the soul. The symbol of the bird is aptly chosen, for does not the bird's wing presuppose the possibility of upward flight? Such imaginative resolution must surely be what Palmer was referring to when he wrote, in a letter to Linnell on December 21, 1828, "creation sometimes pours into the spiritual eye the radiance of Heaven," so that the effects of natural beauty "not only thrill the optic nerve, but shed a mild, a grateful, an unearthly luster into the inmost Spirits and seem the unchanging twilight of that peaceful country, where there is no sorrow and no night." In other words, the resolution of opposites that is the "rest which remaineth to the people of God," is an act of imaginative perception: the greatest art, as he wrote to Valpy in May 1875, addresses "not the perception chiefly, but the imagination, and here is the hinge and essence of this whole matter."

But how is this resolution between the generated creation and the Divine Reality, and between nature and art, effected? For the depiction of what is beyond the "fleshly curtain" by means of some

A Rustic Scene (1825). 20 x 24 cm. Mixed media.

The Valley with a Bright Cloud (1825). 18 x 28 cm. Mixed media.

Early Morning (1825). 19 x 23 cm. Mixed media.

Late Twilight (1825). 18 x 24 cm. Mixed media.

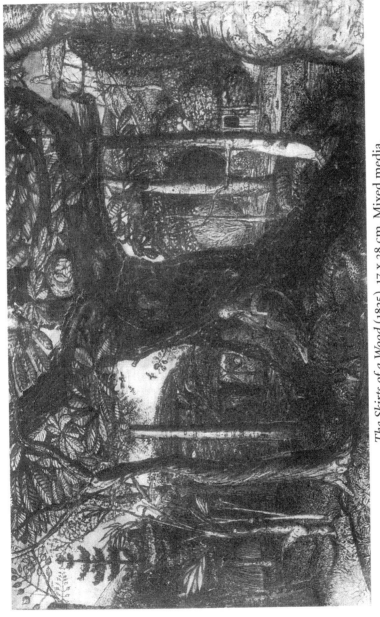

The Skirts of a Wood (1825). 17 x 28 cm. Mixed media.

The Valley Thick with Corn (1825). 18 x 28 cm. Mixed media.

semblance of created appearances must surely have inherent in it the danger either of idolatry to those appearances, thus increasing the possibility of our being attached to sensible beauties rather than to the truth of their unmanifest source, or of some form of pantheism that obscures the distinction between the Creator and the Creation? The dilemma Palmer, in effect, posed in the letter to Linnell in December 1828:

> I have . . . no doubt but the drawing of choice positions and aspects of external objects is one of the varieties of study requisite to build up an artist, who should be a magnet to all kinds of knowledge; though, at the same time I can't help seeing that the general characteristics of Nature's beauty not only differ from, but are, in some respects, opposed to those of Imaginative Art.

But does not the very existence of the incarnation imply the sacramental nature of material things? In which case the Creation is best seen as a vehicle of grace where the minute study of its manifest forms—"Temporal Creation, whose beauties are, in their kind, perfect" (as he called it in the same letter)—leads to contemplation of its hidden prototypes, "those abstracted, essential, fiery, and eternal conceptions known by few in any age" (letter to George Richmond, September 1828). It is precisely this intimate correspondence between the revealed manifestation and the veiled essence that permits the "material tablet" to "receive the perfect tracings of celestial beauty" (notebook 1824).

The "material tablet" is not, after all, some vague, amorphous entity but a theophanic array of living minute particulars. For the artist the study of nature is not so much the imitation of how those particulars appear to the ocular sense as the use of them to dismask appearances, to reveal the "right side of the tapestry"; nature used as the language of forms to convey the very sacredness of the Creation. Martin Budin, in his edition of the 1824 notebook, has pointed out how the power of Palmer's drawing is related to a heightened vision of direct perception of natural forms and how this power diminishes in so far as it draws upon the imagination; meaning, in this case, personal fantasy.

This being so, it is noticeable how during the Shoreham years Palmer had an almost obsessive concern to balance an intense study of natural detail with his spiritual preoccupations. Both the written and drawn entries to the 1824 sketchbook show his absorption in physical details, but on page 81 we find:

> It is not enough on coming home to make recollections in which shall be united the scattered parts about those sweet fields into a sentimental and Dulwich looking whole. No. But considering Dulwich as the gate into the world of vision one must try behind the hills to bring up a mystic glimmer like that which lights our dreams. And those same hills, (hard task) should give us promise that the country beyond them is Paradise.

To suppose that the "abstract" element of Palmer's style during the Shoreham years reveals a desire to experiment with the shapes of natural forms obscures the point: it suggests that the painter's intentions were more or less exclusively aesthetic and artistic whereas he was obviously and equally concerned to make a faithful rendering of his spiritual discoveries.

It seems likely that Palmer's spiritual ardor was at its most intense during the time of his early acquaintance with Linnell and his introduction to Blake; the years 1823 and 1825. And if Linnell's influence led him to the minute study of natural forms, then the influence of Blake was no doubt instrumental in showing Palmer how the observational and inspirational impulses could be creatively joined. Blake's advice to the young painter was to "draw anything you want to master a hundred times from nature till you have learned it from heart." Such advice could only mean to receive the image of a thing into one's very soul so that it can be freed from the incidental qualities of its material existence and recognized from an interior, visionary state of concentration. This assimilation of the knower into the known throws light on another entry in Palmer's 1824 sketchbook: "Nature is not at all the standard of art, but art is the standard of nature. The visions of the soul, being perfect, are the only true standard by which nature must be tried." Some years later, in 1845, Palmer was still referring to this process of inner purification as one of the essentials of artistic practice: "It is almost impossible to do rightly or wisely. That conceit, self-complacency, and indolence, should be incessantly hunted out of the inner man."

Blake further advised Palmer: "you have only to work up imagination to the state of vision and the thing is done." A.H. Palmer spoke of his father's "vivid intensity of mental 'vision' that preceded the actual working of a design." This faculty Palmer evidently shared with Blake. Indeed, the "ripeness" of the things of nature's garment that is such a telling characteristic of the 1825 sepia works seems in itself to be mysteriously consistent with the intensity of the painter's absorption in the imagery of nature. It is as if the sheer abundance of the latent spiritual possibilities that might exist between observer and observed, between man and nature, is suddenly unlocked and realized in a unity that is greater than their simple addition. This would explain the profound "interior" stillness of these works, their lack of that climatic atmosphere which is the life-blood of a Constable or a Turner landscape.

A.H. Palmer wrote in his *Life* of his father,

> Judging by the hundreds of other examples I have of my father's work, executed before and since he became acquainted with Mr Linnell—judging by the most characteristic works of any period, it is possible to maintain that what made him "singular among his fellows" ... was not borrowed from anybody but was essentially his own. Further, that his art is particularly remarkable for belonging to no school; and that his "pictorial genealogy" cannot easily be traced through any other artist.

This judgment remains largely true. The efforts of commentators have only marginally traced his stylistic antecedents. Artistic sources alone could never adequately account for the sudden flowering of the six sepia works. There is nothing transitional about them; their style is as fully accomplished as their appearance is dramatic. The fact is that in his journals, notebooks, and letters Palmer is nearly always speaking, in effect, of his attempt to visualize nature internally. Here was an artist, barely out of adolescence, yet already his own master, who had been granted a direct inspiration to record a hermetic vision of nature.

Palmer's stylistic achievement seems all the more audacious when we realize that it was also a challenge to the whole ethos of the modern intelligence with its bias in favor of granting a higher ontological status to the material than to the spiritual. The young Palmer was, by implication, striving to repair the rupture between man himself and the agnostic, nominalist view of nature as simply a mechanistic, external process devoid of any spiritual significance. Palmer has been described as a medievalist, and this is so to the degree it is understood that his contemplative approach to nature harks back to that of the gnostic for whom nature is an intermediary between the human soul and the Divine Presence. To label him an "idealist" is also true but only to the extent that his aspirations are seen to be meaningful in the latter context.

At least in these Shoreham works Palmer was a gnostic in that he looked to nature as the channel of grace which mitigates man's fallen condition and so narrows the gap between God and His creature. If art differs from nature it is precisely because of the need to bridge this gap, for the very multiplicity of nature, by turns ensnaring and dissipating the senses, divides us from the Divine Unity in which multiplicity itself participates. But in those arts in which the imaginative act is allowed its proper function, as Palmer understood it, unity is sought and recovered, not by abandoning the immanent beauties of nature, but through the convivial stimulation they afford as energizing the aspiration to reach their transcendent source: as he wrote to Linnell, December 21, 1828:

> Terrestrial Spring showers blossoms and odours in profusion, which at some moments "Breathe on earth the air of Paradise"; indeed sometimes, when the spirits are in Heav'n, earth itself, as in emulation, blooms again into Eden.... Still the perfection of nature is not the perfection of severest art: they are two things: the former we may liken to an easy charming colloquy of intellectual friends; the latter is "Imperial Tragedy." *That*, is graceful humanity: *This*, is Plato's Vision; who, somewhere in untracked regions, primigeneous Unity, above all things, holds his head, and bears his forehead among the stars, tremendous to the Gods!

Palmer's endeavor, especially during the Shoreham years, was analogous to that of the mystic who seeks truth *through* the world of appearances. The fact that mastery of the ego-bound self is not lastingly attained by artistic means should not disguise from us the significance of that spiritual nostalgia that floods both his writings and his pictures during this period. It leaves us with no option but to see Palmer's work in this analogous light. For Palmer art is a form of the pursuit of wisdom, and the attainment of Truth comes via the soul whose own pre-fallen essence is of the same substance as the energies that spread the "fleshly curtain" of the world before our eyes.

Palmer's pre-occupation with light, for instance—"to bring up a mystic glimmer like that which lights our dreams"—is as much a concern with those consonances between the soul's faculties and their proper object, the self-illuminating interiority of things, the sacredness of their being, as it is with the "material light" which must in some mode engage the painter. In an entry to his 1824 sketchbook written at nine o'clock in the evening on July 15 he spoke of just such an "inherent light" as seemed to make a thing "luminous in itself" in his description of a tower observed in the summer twilight. Whereas natural objects merely reflect "the gaudy day light of this world." To penetrate beyond "brute matter" to this interior illumination of things is to perceive "a subdued solemn light which seems their own and not reflected, send out a lustre into the heart of him who looks—a mystical and spiritual more than a material light."

To this painter's eye mass, line, and extension are the harbingers of a qualitative mode of discourse. The "abstraction" of Palmer's style in the sepia works is an attempt to deploy empathic symbols, imbued with the sentiment of personal emotion and the mystical overtones of a visionary intuition. Such symbols as would allow him to reveal the eternal face of things: "After all, I doubt not but there must be the study of this creation, as well as art and vision; tho' I cannot think it other than the veil of heaven, through which her divine features are dimly smiling" (letter to Linnell, December 21, 1828).

No truly symbolic language was available to Palmer, who was thereby obliged to adopt something of the naturalistic conventions of the art of his time. In practice this meant using, so to say, *natura naturata* to give a countenance to *natura naturans*—the ever-becoming forms of generated nature to show forth the eternally fecund source that gives birth to them, original nature. But little by little, and with the loss of the contemplative leisure the Shoreham years afforded him, the painter's eye was drawn more and more exclusively into an intensive study of natural detail to become, eventually, the observation of appearances. That is to say, visionary contemplation became absorbed imitation as the painter's eye became ensnared, woven into the living texture of the phenomena under observation. As we have seen, during the period of the 1824 sketch-book and the sepia works of 1825, in aspiring to render the spiritual essence of nature Palmer was confronting his own spiritual self. For as men envisage themselves so they envisage nature. There is no such thing as a spiritually enlightened soul that looks upon nature as part of a profane, mechanistic universe.

All this is borne out by Palmer's writings as well as the pictures themselves. In the years that succeeded his Kentish sojourn he gradually became solely pre-occupied with the rendering of observed effects as the spiritual ardor of his imaginative vision declined. And here indeed we do find "transitional" works. In the Shoreham pictures that share something of the stylistic features of the six sepia works we notice a growing dependence upon naturalistic representation. By 1828 we have the Lullingstone Park tree studies that are almost wholly based upon observation, as well as such works as *Sepham Barn* and *Barn with a Mossy Roof*. By the time he painted *Pastoral with a Horse-Chestnut* in 1831–32 the abstract element of the sepia works is all but absent, and is totally so by 1833 in a work such as *The Gleaning Field*. In *The White Cloud* of 1833–34 and *The Bright Cloud* of the following year climatic atmosphere becomes a constituent of the landscape; and in *A Pastoral Scene* of 1835 something of the "sublime" manner of Turner makes an entry.

By 1835, and away from Shoreham, in a work such as *Pistyll Mawddach, North Wales*, we see not only a total pre-occupation with depicting observed detail (even if recollected in tranquility) but Palmer's mastery of it as well. His correspondence at this time shows him searching for "views" to paint as he travels through

Devon and Wales. Such mastery of "realism" was to earn the painter Ruskin's approbation; he wrote (in the third edition of *Modern Painters*), "A less known artist, S. Palmer . . . is deserving of the very highest place among faithful followers of nature. His studies of foreign foliage especially are beyond all praise for care and fullness. I have never seen a stone pine or a cypress drawn except by him." And this of a man who had written to Linnell in 1828, "I will, God help me, never be a naturalist by profession." Palmer's memoranda and journals of 1839–45 are full of notes of physical effects he had observed and prescriptive of how they might be rendered.

In the light of this development it is revealing to compare the vocabulary of his notebook entries. For instance, writing at Princes Risborough in 1845, after noting the inherent limitation of art to imitate natural effects, he concludes of his efforts that they "should perhaps only be considered as the *corpse* which is to be animated." By contrast, an entry in his 1824 sketchbook, after speaking of possible subjects for pictures he might with the help of Christ's inspiration undertake, he writes, "But smaller studies of separate *glories of Heaven* might be tried."

In his *Catalogue Raisonné* of Palmer's work Raymond Lister draws attention to the fact that among the painter's favorite books was John Flavell's *Husbandry Spiritualized* (1669). The preface to this book contains the alchemical formula, "That the world below, is a Glass to discover the World above." The spiritual import of the formula Palmer would certainly have understood. But for the western artist the pursuit of nature in and through the imitation of her outward effects has always been problematic. Another Hermetic formula is "Nature loves to hide."

In other words, what constitutes the essential reality of a thing is not obvious to sensory perception. For nature is a kind of generative "play," a form of cosmic magic so sustained in attunement to the senses that it produces the illusion of being permanent—of being a fixed reality. But the history of the idea that art should *imitare la natura* has over and over again demonstrated the illusiveness of nature's identity. The Renaissance re-discovery and application of perspective and the representation of physical space did not make the imitation of the reality we perceive any the less illusive. The development of pictorial styles from the sixteenth to the twentieth century illustrates nothing if not that sensible perception is never free from presumptive conventions in the rendering of physical appearances. Even with the advent of the humanist ideal of verisimilitude it took a long time for artists to really look at natural appearances.

Turner thought he saw nature at its closest in her moods of grandeur and sublimity. Constable sought to capture nature in the mutability of her habitat as providing the background to man's life on earth. Artists were still searching for nature at the time of the Impressionists. Monet thought he could capture her very impermanence and took the logical step, in his paintings of the façade of Rouen Cathedral, of trying to record her movement through the passage of time. For Seurat the true imitation of sensory perception required the atomization of the spectrum, and hence of the artist's palette. With the Cubists nature was absorbed into the psychology of the cognitive act: form is what you *know* is there and not what you see. It is obviously one thing to decide that art should imitate nature but quite another to determine quite what nature is. The history of post-Renaissance European painting can be seen as a series of attempts to answer this question.

It ended in the breakdown of the idea altogether; in abstraction. Finally, shape, color, and line are released from the necessity to represent anything but themselves and so become the arbitrary tokens of emotional volition. Had not nature, in keeping with its immemorial designation as illusive "play" (*maya*), proved to be a chimera after all? And is not *natura naturata* precisely the "fantasy" of *natura naturans*? Nature, true to its nature, proved as illusive as ever and in abstraction disappeared! It was then but a short step to concluding that abstraction is the appropriate manner of expression for the ineffable content of spiritual perception because it seems to accord so intimately with subjectivity. Here nature is redundant after all and our senses hopelessly deceptive in being unable to provide any sort of language appropriate to spiritual discourse. But if there is no possible analogy between the natural world we perceive and the veiled, spiritual reality we seek—between, that is, creature and Creator—then why at least in our creaturehood are we so evidently fitted through our senses for a world that turns out to be unnecessary? Why seek to be transformed by a supra-human reality if all that is needed is an act of psychological volition? In natureless abstraction the mind acts as if reality is given out from the human subject. But intelligence is nothing if it is not meant to *take in* reality. All this Palmer, at the height of his visionary powers, implicitly challenged and rejected. In so far as he has left a visual and written record of his struggle against the materialist bias of his time, so we understand that for him the Real is "hidden" in the very forms that pre-determine the mode and manner of its actualization. That is to say, nature, the theophany of the Creation, is nothing more and nothing less than a series of epiphanic moments prepared for the senses, like divine gifts to be transmitted in the interiority of the soul.

It has been necessary to rehearse something of the logic of the development of the imitation of nature in western art if only to clarify an area of misunderstanding with regard to Palmer's visionary style. This concerns the view that Palmer's Shoreham works, and especially the six sepia works of 1825, look forward to the twentieth century. One must suppose that this is because several modern painters who have confessed to an admiration and an indebtedness to Palmer's work, have deployed a semi-representative, semi-abstract style. However, the stylistic "abstraction" in the works of such painters as Sutherland, Nash, Minton, Vaughan, Reynolds, and others can hardly be said to spring from the same source as the spiritual imperative of Palmer's attempt to express the hidden essence of natural forms. In the case of these painters the element of abstraction is the legacy of the breakdown of the notion of representation in western art so as to become merely a feature of their personal style. As such it is never anything more than of aesthetic significance and does not refer to anything beyond the intrinsic considerations of twentieth-century pictorial innovation. Palmer's visionary style is inexplicable in terms of such a self-referring limitation that would in any case make nonsense of all he ever wrote concerning his intentions. Palmer's style was, so to say, forced upon

him and in defiance of any contemporary convention and precedent of picture making.

Moreover, it should be obvious that to speak (as has been done)
of Palmer's landscapes as having an "idealized content," or of their
being in any way "escapist" is to misconstrue both his intention and
his achievement. In this case Palmer's "abstraction" is taken to
imply that his visionary style must be interpreted as accepting natural forms as a starting point for a development that becomes more
expressive of personal emotion as it moves away from sensory perception. Such a misreading of his work could only arise from a one-
dimensional view of perception not shared by Palmer himself.
Palmer's abstraction does not seek to impose a surrogate "reality"
onto perception but to locate the Real *in and through* the particularity of the cognitive act itself. The "escapist" is one who will not face
the fact that the manifest world—"this outward perishable creation," as Blake called it—is the fleeting image, the shadow of an
unmanifest and permanent Reality, what Palmer himself referred to
in a letter to Leonard Rowe Valpy dated September 1864:

> that mystery which cannot be commanded, that immaterial and
> *therefore* real image, that seed of all true beauty in picture or poem
> falls into earthly soil and becomes subject in a great measure to the
> conditions of matter, and fails or fares as the soil permits—the
> desert sand; the ploughed field; the rich garden mould. To say that
> the seed does everything is fanaticism.

In the final analysis the imagery of Palmer's Shoreham works,
and especially the six sepia works, is iconographic rather than
abstract, their latent import hieratic rather than ideal. His inability
to sustain the implications of this were as much due to the age and
its artistic conventions as to any personal failure. His vision
demanded an art impossible on the terms of his age. But he never
lost sight of the vision he wished to attain even though he had not,
in the end, been able to throw off the yoke of the "naturalism" he so
abhorred. He caught a glimpse of that far-off goal to which his
visionary propensities had earlier driven him when he wrote to
Leonard Valpy in 1875,

Earth hath not many things to show more fair than the west front of Wells Cathedral. It shows what Christian art might have become in this country, had not abuses brought it down with a crash, and left us, after three centuries, with a national preference of domesticated beasts and their portraits, before all other kinds of art whatsoever.

16

Time's Glass Breaks:
On the Poetry of Vernon Watkins

Man, though fallen, has this strong *Sensibility* and reaching *Desire* after all the *Beauties* that can be picked up in fallen Nature. Had not this been the Case, had not *Beauty* and Light, and the *Glory* of Brightness been his *first State* by *Creation,* he would now no more want the Beauty of Objects, than the *Ox* wants to have his Pasture enclosed with beautiful Walls, and painted Gates.

WILLIAM LAW

I am entirely concerned with metaphysical truth.

VERNON WATKINS

HERE, the reader had best respect the poet's confession, for the poetry of Vernon Watkins, like that of his mentors Dante, Blake, Shelley, Hölderlin, and Yeats among them, is best understood in the context of that analogical wisdom which has always conceived the nature and destiny of man as recapitulating within his being the unity of material and spiritual worlds. Watkins's ability to visualize what from the viewpoint of common experience is paradoxical but to intuitive perception becomes transparently clear, stems directly from the "revolution of sensibility" he underwent as a young man. The change was irreversible and he found himself unable ever again to write from the perspective of time. From the viewpoint of his altered sensibility, the poet gives an unequivocal acknowledgment of the transient nature of knowledge derived from sensory experience alone. These are poems whose central theme is the metaphysics of vision.

From the outset we must acknowledge that the world of temporal duration and of sensible appearances is, in terms of Watkins's poetry, to be "conquered," if we are to understand the nature of the poet's constantly implied assertion that the natural world is not the ultimate reality. This does not mean that the poetry reduces the objects of sensory experience to mere epiphenomena. What is in question here is clearly the ontological significance of the materially real. Watkins's view presupposes that the apprehension of reality possesses a degree less certitude to the extent that it is removed from ultimate reality itself The "material shell" (the spectrum or "music of colours") is the extreme reflexive limit of that which is only perceived in the direct immediacy of imaginative intuition.

To move in apprehension from sensory experience toward increasingly immaterial levels of reality, perception itself must be appropriate to the level of reality so perceived. Watkins's use of the symbolism of light, stream, fire, fountain, and music implicitly claims the ontological act of poetic imagination as the means by which man is able to perceive the interpenetration of levels of reality, and presupposes that the qualitative essences of things may be expressed in a language of analogy based on images of nature. There is no real ambivalence involved in Watkins's view that all transience is an "illusion," for while it has being in a moment of time, it is, as a manifestation of the Divine Principle, never lost to the eternal order of things. Aspects of this perspective are tacitly present in nearly all of the poems from first to last. The late sonnet "Candle Constant" perfectly concentrates the theme into a single poem:

> This man perceived that time could never catch
> The candle, where it flickered and declined.
> Each flying thought a second thought would snatch,
> Leaving the outline of the first behind;
> A certain aura from a blown-out match
> Was lost, then re-established in the mind.
> What, then, was constant? Still, beyond all doubt,
> All flames were gathered where the last burnt out.
>
> True for him also, certain notes would stay,
> The meaning of their own supreme desire
> Established perfect where they died away.

> Such music, not unlike that constant fire,
> Made Earth, as though a fountain were to play,
> Fresh for a thousand seasons, night and day.

Here, the permanence of the Eternal is glimpsed in and through the fluid web of individual impressions registered by the discursive mind, the continuity of whose apprehensions remains paradoxical since, considered analytically, that continuity is subject to the dying and renewal of each moment of time. Thus the relation between perceiver and perceived, at the level of discursive cognition, can never be immutable. Watkins is employing here the law of analogy that sees reflected in the most transient of objects the very archetype of Beauty itself. The poet explores the motif of flux embodying "constancy" in "The Replica," where the waterfall, as a symbol of ontological renewal, creates

> a perpetual music, and gives light
> In fading always from the measuring mind.

In "Candle Constant," however, the symbol of renewal is only tacitly present. The act of poetic vision itself is the intuitive agent of that immanent and inexhaustible spirit of being "established perfect" in the seeming continuity of those individual, fleeting impressions. Only in the intuitive act of imagination is the consubstantiality of "candle light" and archetypal fire ("all flames") guaranteed, for there it is the constant witness of every perception despite all igneous flames having been extinguished. The recurrent symbol of fire—it is the informing principle elsewhere, for instance, in "Earth and Fire" and "Unity of the Stream"—in relation to the notion of intuitive perception is important, being central to Watkins's vision where, as traditionally, it is indicative of the one substance that is alike the soul's intelligence and the intellect of divine origin that is cosmic activity. The poet's "constant fire" is none other than the immediate "fiery Breath of the Total Presence within us" (Coomaraswamy).

As is so often the case there is a cosmological principle involved in a central belief of the poet's that nothing of the generated world is created in vain. The Infinite Essence, in the process of its manifestation from essence to substance, could not give rise to anything superfluous, since its progressive exteriorization of Itself is none other than a "descent" from principial perfection. Since the material world is the extreme limit of this process, its phenomena represent the objective reflection of the Essence, while the underlying coherence of phenomena is the immediate symbol of the Divine Principle. That which explains Plato's view of the world as the fairest of creations also explains the profound reverence accorded to the minute particulars in Watkins's vision. If in their negative aspect the transient nature of appearances makes them illusory, then in their positive aspect—the permanence of their essence—they are the divine "art." The abiding reality of appearances is not at their surface but in their interior depth so that they function as symbols when considered from the viewpoint of their qualitative essences. For Watkins, the natural law of decay and regeneration in nature becomes, on the level of intuitive perception, the mirror-image of eternal renewal itself. The poet conveys a sense of the beauties of a natural scene as the magical "play" of Cosmic Power, all the more tellingly perhaps for its being informed by his belief in the power of art itself, to hold sway over the soul as mediator of the Eternal.

To illustrate both these aspects of his vision one might turn to his poem "The Immortal in Nature." The creative tension engendered by the shining of the transcendent in and through the mundane levels of reality is further elaborated in the fourth stanza with the motif of the office of kingship, which, we recall, is the *perpetual* source of temporal power reflecting spiritual authority regardless of the individual human occupant of the office:

> I must forget these things, and yet lose none.
> Music is light, and shadows all are they.
> White is the fountain that begot the sun.
> Light on the petal falls; then falls the may.
>
> Sometimes the vulture sees his carrion
> A speck on Ganges. White on Himalay
> The snows ascend above the light of dawn.
> Though distance calls us like a clarion,
> How ancient is the voice our souls obey.

I tell my soul: Although they be withdrawn,
Meditate on those lovers. Think of Donne
Who could contract all ages to one day,
Knowing they were but copies of that one:
The first being true, then none can pass away.

Where time is not, all nature is undone,
For nature grows in grandeur of decay.
These royal colours that the leaves put on
Mark the year living in its kingly way;
Yet, when he dies, not he but time is gone.

Beethoven's music nature could not stun.
Light rushed from Milton.
                              See the Sistine ray.
There burns the form eternally begun.
That soul whose very hand made marble pray,
The untempted, mightiest master, holds in sway
The wrestling sinews death had seemed to own
And might have owned, but that they were not clay.

In "Muse, Poet and Fountain" Watkins suggests that the poet himself, in the act of imaginative perception, is capable of overcoming the destructive, sorrowing experience of the Creation's passing and decay in his ability to reconcile the discordancies and the contrarieties through the abiding focal point of Eternity:

Though time still falls from future into past,
Nothing is gone my hand may not restore.
Mine is the pulse that makes your pulse beat fast,
Harmonious joy with stillness at the core.

Again, in "Demands of the Muse" we find these lines:

Born into time of love's perceptions, he
Is not of time. The acts of time to him
Are marginal. From the first hour he knows me
Until the last, he shall divine my words.
In his solitude he hears another.

which reiterate the same motif but in terms approaching Blake's "Eternity is in love with the productions of time." The poet speaks from the perspective of imaginative intuition in the guise of the poet's Muse who possesses the knowledge that enables Her to see all time in its simultaneity, in a single act of cognitive apprehension, for "Vision makes wise at once."

This viewpoint of the transcendent "witness of consciousness" it is the labor of the poet's craft to embody; labors which, as the related poem, "Demands of the Poet," tells us

> bring the authentic tears
> Which recognise the moment without age.

If man did not possess in the incorruptible core of his soul that for which he continually thirsts, a faculty that permits him, in moments of visionary perception, to see beyond the limits of his individual consciousness to a domain of greater permanence and certainty, then the loss and suffering, the degeneracy that is so indissolubly a part of "time's wrong" could never be redeemed. Indeed, even life and death in such circumstances would lose their meaning since only by that which transcends time can time be measured: only by that which remains unaffected by "living" can the meaning of life be fathomed. To such a viewpoint the poems often signal their commitment, as in this middle section of "Green Names, Green Moss":

> Swing, life-leaping bell;
> Strike, in the mourning trees.
> No ravisher can tell
> Their secret histories;
> Not one can you reclaim,
> But side-track their loss
> Until the last, loved name
> Is covered with moss,
> Yet every moment must,
> Each turn of head or hand,
> Though disfigured by dust,
> Incorruptibly stand;
> If they are nothing now
> Then they were nothing then.

Blinded with thirst I know,
Beneath my foot lie men
Each laid in his own caul
Too intricately still
In the rock of his soul
Where the pure fountains fill,
Too sacred to be touched
By memory or bell.

The inescapability of our sensory involvement in generated existence necessarily directs our perceptions toward that which by its very nature is limited and contingent. But these very limitations are, as it were, the stage on which the interplay between the eternal and the actual worlds is enacted. In Watkins's view the specific function of the poetic vocation is to effect a redemption of this divisive and incomplete mode of perception. The subtle, all-pervasive presence of this theme is present in many of the poems. One such is "Poets, in Whom Truth Lives," where it becomes the polarizing core of a lyricism of exceptional delicacy, illustrated here by these, the first and last two stanzas.

Poets, in whom truth lives
Until you say you know,
Gone are the birds; the leaves
Drop, drift away, and snow
Surrounds you where you sing,
A silent ring.

. . .

The abounding river stops.
Time in a flash grows less
True than these glittering drops
Caught on a thread of glass
Two frosty branches bear
In trance-like air.

Stoop; for the hollow ground
Integrity yet keeps
True as a viol's sound
Though the musician sleeps.

> Strong is your trust; then wait:
> Your King comes late.

Here, moreover, we find a further extension to a belief of Watkins's poetic faith that the intricate craft of poetry alone gives the true measure to ecstatic vision.[1] The most recurrent motifs that elaborate this theme are those of light and time, whose symbolic ramifications most directly impinge upon the metaphysics of his poetic vision. An exploration of these will clarify by association much else in the poetry.

Light and time only reveal the richness of their full meaning when they are considered as referring to the "indefinite" extension of space as a symbol of the "infinite" nature of Being. Height and depth take on a spiritual and metaphysical significance once it is realized that they are symbolic references to the hierarchical structure of Being. Light is synonymous with the source or center of cosmic manifestation. Being at the highest level qualitatively, it "falls" by degrees into the existential world of the creature where it is recognized as the condition of corporeal vision. Time, likewise, is the "fall" of Eternity and is the very condition of the creature's experience of phenomenal reality. Spiritually, both light and time are modes of the descent of the Spirit into the world of nature. In metaphysical terms they represent the manifestation of the Divine Principle reverberating at the material limit of its power and influence. This limit, seen in terms of a sphere, is at the circumference and is thus furthest from the center or point of origin in Unity and Oneness. It is the plane of utmost differentiation and multiplicity, the natural habitat of, in Watkins's words, man who is "made of clay." In the poems, time is co-extensive with and interdependent upon its apprehension by what the poet terms the "shadow" of individualized consciousness. Manifest light is the image of that immanent Spirit whose illumination is eclipsed by "shadow." Light, the "white light" of the poems, is at the heart of all particular things as a manifestation of their impalpable, eternal essence. It is the "shadow" of

---

1. This theme is explored in greater detail in the author's *Vernon Watkins: Inspiration as Poetry, Poetry as Inspiration* (2002).

sensory perception that veils the divine radiance and transparency of things. In the series of "Music of Colours" poems we can most easily recognize the embodiment and poetic elaboration of these analogical terms of reference.

And yet simply to equate Watkins's symbol of light with Divine Intelligence would do less than justice to the contextual variety of the symbolism in the poems themselves. The appearance of the motifs of "music," "white," "lightning," and "fountain," for instance, represent various modes of the actualization of the primal essence of light prior to its refraction into the colors of particularity. Nonetheless, such an equation does provide a definition which satisfies the basic metaphysical significance underlying its imaginative form.

Just how consistent Watkins's use of the light symbol is in this respect, we can discover by turning first to its earliest use in "Prime Colours," where it appears in conjunction with the fountain motif. Here, Light, being in its origin and potentiality free ("innocent") of any determination, emanates (jets forth) from the primal source, and, like the waters (the inexhaustible potentiality of cosmic possibility) of the Fountain, breaks from a single transparent column into the multiplicity of the colors of the spectrum. The very nature of these qualitative essences, by their brilliance and variegation, "replicate" the beauty of the Divine Love for its Creation. There is an additional symbolic resonance in the poem that invokes those doctrines that speak of the Creation itself as the primordial act of the Divine Mercy that wanted its Perfection to be known as a reverberation in the imperfection of transient life. The immediately relevant lines of the poem "Prime Colours" form the poem's final stanza:

> Born of that mud, innocent light he sees,
> The cornerstone in crumbling masonries.
> His washed eyes, marvelling, resurrect the mountain
> Where love's five colours leap into light's fountain.

If we turn to the much later sonnet "The Measure Moves," light, both inner and outer, is presented through the figure of the blind Samson. In the first stanza the connotations of the symbol are those of the "immediate fiery breath"—the condition of all apprehension to which mere "sight" is blind unless "redeemed" by the vision that acknowledges the celestial origin of every perception. The crucial line is: "Light is redeemed through eyes which cannot see." In the last stanza, Samson, time-conscious, blind and bound to the material darkness, invites physical death as a release from his constriction. In so doing, he invokes God to make of his body a receptacle through which may flow, like innumerable arteries of light, the supreme cosmic power and strength—the "light of life." The poem ends:

> Pour light through me, God, through the rivers of my sinew,
> And stay me to gather the columns, alive and dead.

A study of the various contexts in which the symbolism of light appears reveals that Watkins envisaged the substance of life as the "field of manifestation" of the incarnate Spirit. And while nature in particular is the indirect object of its projection, man, in that love and identity with all things which is his theomorphic and primordial perfection, is intrinsically its direct embodiment. In this connection it can be observed that the connotations of the light symbolism tend to polarize into those of spiritual truth, sometimes with Christian, sometimes with pagan and mythic overtones, and those of spiritual beauty, possessing usually Platonic or Neoplatonic overtones. This polarization reveals the imaginative locus of the poet's sympathies, provided its terms are not pursued to the point of mutual exclusiveness.

For instance, the poem "Serena" reveals the presence of a "light of truth" akin to that of the Fourth Gospel. Here, the context of the symbol could hardly fail to remind us of the Gospel's "light that lighteth every man that cometh into the world." An infant's birth is envisaged in terms that express its soul as the embodiment of the celestial light of the Divine Intellect or "First Cause." The soul ("fallen from light," as the poet wrote in the similar context of "The Mother and Child," whose terms we can utilize, so consistent are they, to gloss the later poem) is buried in the sensuous darkness of the body ("tomb of each breath") that knows only the corporeal world ("of light in eclipse") where the celestial radiance is lost from immediate view. Traherne spoke of "The first Light which shined in my Infancy in its primitive and innocent clarity" being "totally eclipsed" by sensuous knowledge. Here are the first two and the last two stanzas of "Serena":

> The cradle stirs.
> There life, there innocence, there the miracle shines.
> Old, he is old:
> Life's earliest word, the first. Light has created him
> Out of inscrutable deeps.
>
> And the light breathes;
> It breathes in darkness, trembles, trembles and wakes.
> There is no help,
> There is no help in this room. The divining deluge
> Thunders. Time is at hand.
>
> . . .
>
> He will be calm
> In the first calm that glittered before knowledge.
> Nothing shall change
> The Primum Mobile's effectual music
> Planted within the breast.
>
> He will be calm,
> Not through a reason known to man, nor favour,
> But through that gift
> The First Cause left, printing upon his forehead
> The word "Serena."

(The ominous note of the phrase "time is at hand" is surely the inevitable "eclipse" by the "shadow" of individual consciousness that apprehends and is coexistent with temporal duration.) The appearance of the light symbol in terms that suggest Platonic connotations inevitably recalls the myth of the cave as well as the Platonic doctrine of a veiled, divine order of reality against which the world of generated forms seems but a shadowy replica. Here one could point to such poems as "Foal," "The Immortal in Nature," "The Replica," "Bishopston Stream," the first section of "Revisited Waters," and, perhaps more characteristically, "Music of Colours—Dragonfoil and the Furnace of Colours." In this last poem we find an important allusion to that most central of Platonic doctrines: that the hidden order of reality requires for its apprehension a faculty in comparison with which the state of sensory perception can be likened to a blindness—or partial sleep—the Platonic *anamnesis*.

In the natural world pure Being, symbolized in Watkins's "white light" or "fire," the fontal raying of the Divine Principle, is nowhere explicitly evident. Its essence is fragmented into a myriad of contingent aspects known mediately as "patterns of a lost world" in the objects of sense. Each of these "shadows of a different order" is a qualitative essence that is connatural with the supra-mental faculty that perceives them. So, analogously, natural light, "born of white light," is connatural with retinal perception to which light always appears mediately as color. The metaphysical significance of Watkins's "white light" symbolism, then, provides the focal ambience for an aspect of the poet's imaginative thought that could otherwise be mistakenly interpreted as a somewhat pantheistic view of nature. In "Music of Colours—Dragonfoil and the Furnace of Colours," the most substantial of the "Music of Colours" poems, those symbols we have discussed above are interwoven as the very warp and woof of the poem, as these, the last two stanzas, demonstrate:

> Waking entranced, we cannot see that other
> Order of colours moving in the white light.
> Time is for us transfigured into colours
> Known and remembered from an earlier summer,
> Or into breakers.

> Falling on gold sand, bringing all to nothing.
> Fire of the struck brand hides beneath the white spray.
> All life begins there, scattered by the rainbow;
> Yes, and the field flowers, these deceptive blossoms,
> Break from the furnace.

The epiphanic translucence of Watkins's handling of these themes could easily by interpreted in terms of Neoplatonic metaphysical doctrine, provided we guard against the claim that he was a "Neoplatonic poet" (Plotinus *was* one of the poet's sources). That being said there are certain passages in Plotinus where the ultimate meaning of Watkins's motifs is articulated in a mystical, rather than a poetic context. There is no essential conflict, for instance, between the poet's use of light symbolism as the informing essence of the material world and this passage from the *First Ennead* (sixth tractate)—so adequately does it prepare the imaginative ground for the poet's usage:

> The beauty of colour ... derives ... from the conquest of the darkness inherent in Matter by the pouring-in of light, the unembodied, which is a Rational-Principle and an Ideal-Form.
>
> Hence it is that Fire itself is splendid beyond all material bodies, holding the rank of Ideal-Principle to the other elements, making ever upwards, the subtlest ... of all bodies, as very near to the unembodied; itself alone admitting no other, all the others penetrated by it: ... it has colour primally; they receive the Form of colour from it: hence the splendour of its light, the splendour that belongs to the Idea. And all that has resisted and is but uncertainly held by its light remains outside of beauty, as not having absorbed the plenitude of the Form of colour.[2]

The idea that the light of the corporeal world is the most pleasing and most beautiful of bodies is by no means limited to Greek thought—the universality of the symbol points to its presence as integral to the primordial cosmogonic genesis. Having allowed for the time and place of Watkins's use of this inexhaustible motif, we can see it to be in imaginative consonance with the view of Robert Grosseteste—that perception of light is the greatest of all pleasures since sight is but the harmonious meeting of two types of light, that of the physical world and that of consciousness itself. Boethius held that knowledge of the qualitative essences of things is by their "form," which is like a light by which we know what things are *distinctively*. Were it thought that such a consonance did not exist between the poetic vision and the "unspoken" metaphysics, it would be necessary to claim either that the meaning of the following two stanzas (chosen by way of illustration from "Music of Colours: The Blossom Scattered") lay in some elaborate and wholly abstract descriptiveness, or that they are devoid of any intelligible content altogether.

> So the green Earth if first no colour and then green.
> Spirits who walk, who know

2. Plotinus, *The Enneads,* translated by Stephen Mackenna (1962), pp. 58–59.

All is untouchable, and, knowing this, touch so,
Who know the music by which white is seen,
See the world's colours in flashes come and go.
The marguerite's petal is white, and then is white again
Not from time's course, but from the living spring,
Miraculous whiteness, a petal, a wing,
Like light, like lightning, soft thunder, white as jet,
Ageing on ageless breaths. The ages are not yet.

Is there a tree, a bud, that knows not this:
White breaks from darkness, breaks from such a kiss
No mind can measure? Locked in the branching knot,
Conception shudders; that interior shade
Makes light in darkness, light where light was not;
Then the white petal, of whitest darkness made,
Breaks, and is silent. Immaculate they break,
Consuming vision, blinding eyes awake,
Dazzling the eyes with music, light's unspoken sound,
White born of bride and bridegroom, when they take
Love's path through Hades, engendered of dark ground.

The symbolism of light in Watkins's poetry is best understood in terms of the realization that non-spatial, non-temporal intuition remains the condition for any interpretation of the terrestrial world. It follows from this that for those "on whom time's burden falls," the immutably Real is withheld or hidden from common consciousness. Just as the operation rather than the essential nature of retinal perception is by reference to things seen, so we grasp Reality itself only *indirectly* by means of its manifest properties. A discursive knowledge of any *thing* can only be of its existential nature. Thus, reflected in all created things, as the poet writes in "The Replica," is "the image of our life"—that world known to the senses which "lives by being consumed" and whose

> countless changes
> Accumulate to nothing but itself.

But when the organ of perception, that "greatest light" of intuitive vision, purged of all reference to accidents and properties having an anticipated future or remembered past, perceives the "interval of glory," then all division, particularity, and mutability is conquered;

then, as the poet put it in "Great Nights Returning," "the soul knows the fire that first composed it."

Here is the theme as it appears at the close of "The Replica":

> Yet to man alone,
> Moving in time, birth gives a timeless movement,
> To taste the secret of the honeycomb
> And pluck from night that blessing which outweighs
> All the calamities and griefs of time.
> There shines the one scene worthy of his tears,
> For in that dark the greatest light was born
> Which, if man sees, then time is overthrown,
> And afterwards all acts are qualified
> By knowledge of that interval of glory:
> Music from heaven, the incomparable gift
> Of God to man, in every infant's eyes
> That vision which is ichor to the soul
> Transmitted there by lightning majesty,
> The replica, reborn, of Christian love.

This "incomparable gift" is part of man's theomorphic nature, so that Eternity is not "distant" from us though in commonplace experience we are "far" from It. What needs to be shattered is the illusory "permanence" that is created by the continuity of the unending series of transient projections which our psycho-physical existence throws upon the screen of consciousness. When "time's glass breaks," a new reality is not substituted for the familiar one which then becomes somehow impoverished and degraded, but the "breaking" reveals the transparency of phenomena itself to its luminous source beyond the formal and particular nature of its reflective surface.

Watkins's imagination at all times rests upon this analogical correspondences between, at one level, the eternal world and the spiritual essence of man, and at another, between the external-phenomenal world and man's empirical self. The poet's exploration of these correspondences can be illuminated by reference to the symbolic resonances of metaphysical truth. The symbol of "Buried Light," for instance, clearly derives its imaginative power from this source. In just the following few lines alone, the ultimate meaning of honor, sublimity, closed eyes, prayer, nobility, sacrifice, and mockery would be inexplicable but for the tacit presence of an analogical wisdom capable of seeing the external forms of nature in terms of inner spiritual conditions.

> Come, buried light, and honour time
> With your dear gift, your constancy
> That the known world be made sublime
> Through visions that closed eyelids see.
>
> Come, breath, instruct this angry wind
> To listen here where men have prayed,
> That the bold landscape of the mind
> Fly nobler from its wrist of shade.
>
> Sons of true sacrifice are there.
> Rivers and hills are in their hands.
> The lightest petal the winds bear
> Has mocked the Serpent's swaddling-bands.

This should leave us in no doubt that such correspondences are the integral condition of poetic vision itself.

There is a radical discontinuity between the sensual and sentimental observation of nature and spiritual experience only in so far as our perceptions are confined to the natural order as if it harbored the totality of the Real. And were it not for this discontinuity the natural world would appear to our everyday perceptions as an unending theophany. Watkins gives expression to this dichotomy in the octave of the sonnet "Two Sources of Life." The imaginative context of the poem is the flowing river of time beside which stands the Tree of Life. From its branches a man stares at the reflecting surface of the water and is dazzled by the brilliance and vitality of its ever-changing pattern. Yet he is conscious of a deep longing for the need to penetrate beyond this mirrored configuration of the temporal world that so holds him in thrall:

> The time we measure and the time we know
> Move in the branches drinking life, the giver.
> Being young, we bathed here, and shook off the river,
> Then stood above the stream and watched it flow.
> An image in the water shone below,

Armed with a secret we could not deliver.
Those beams were like the arrows in a quiver
For which our expectation was the bow.

The fact that no common measure exists between nature and the
Spirit—a fact implicitly acknowledged in the deep thirst man has
for an absolute certitude—has its corollary in the doctrine that man
must die to his psycho-physical self in order to be reborn in the
Spirit. Only in this way can he begin to realize in his soul those possibilities of his nature that are more directly the manifestation of the
luminous source of his being and the being of all things. Watkins
expresses in the sestet of this sonnet the conjunction of the doctrine
of correspondence and the doctrine of self-annihilation. The man,
once so impassioned by the strength of his natural perceptions, in
maturity suffers a sense of loss of unity and completeness at the
experience of death, a suffering that itself enlarges his perceptions
and situates them in the perspective of the eternal order which corresponds to that of his soul:

But ask: when was it that the current took us
So deeply into life that time forsook us,
Leaving us nothing but the need to give?
We were transfigured by the deaths of others.
That was the spring, when first we knew our brothers
And died into the truth which made us live.

This deep thirst, then, which is the unresolved accompaniment of
all psycho-physical experience, is never at that level alone, satisfied,
for if it were, the world of common consciousness would provide
every solace and resolve every disequilibrium man ever felt the
world had placed upon him. In these lines, from "The Return of
Spring," Watkins can be interpreted as signaling an imaginative
empathy with such abiding truths:

And marvellously the sundering, receding seawaves
Pound the resounding sands; they knock at the hour-glass.
Thunder compels no man, yet a thought compels him,
Lost, neglected, yet tender.

Why in the wood, where already the new leaves mending
Winter's wild net, cast fragile, immature shadows,

Do I tread pure darkness, resisting that green dominion?
What is the thing more sacred?

. . .

Once, once only it breaks. If you plunge your fingers
In the stream, all secrets under the Earth grow articulate
In a moment, and for you only.

Diamonds of light, emeralds of leaves, green jewels:
For me the unnoticed, death-touching script is more passionate.
Cover the tome with dust; there dwells the redeemer,
Deathlessly known by the voice-fall.

Only by means of a wisdom that moves "against time's flow" is the inexorable cycle of death and regeneration redeemed. Beyond the "partial vision" of time-bound consciousness there is a "dying" that opens the door onto truth: for then perception brings to its aid a faculty of the Divine—as we see in "The Betrothal":

I must die first, to look into those eyes,
And yet no lover ever found his bride
But with that look. Brave children were denied
Until I saw the grave where faith must rise
Out of this dust.

Here, in the "intervals of time" where, paradoxical to common sense, one sees with "closed eyelids" and listens to "tongues that are silent," is the condition of man's ultimate freedom. Here to quote again from Coomaraswamy, "It is not by the means of this All that he knows himself, but by this knowledge of himself that he becomes All."[3]

Clearly Watkins's life and work were those of a Christian. It is central to his vision that time, in its anthropomorphic significance, is envisaged in terms of the mercy of the Divine Love as the completion of knowledge and the redemption of man's natural estate. This

3. ["The Hindu Tradition: Theology and Autology," in *The Essential Ananda K. Coomaraswamy* (2004), p. 279.—Ed.]

theme, if not the explicit subject of any one poem, often forms the submerged point of imaginative coherence, at once the genesis and goal of a poem: for instance, of "The Healing of the Leper," "Touch with Your Fingers," "Earth and Fire," "The Instant," and "*Quem Quaeritis?*" in which the "narrow dwelling" of Him who has over-come the tomb"—the temporal death that embraces the infinite life-provides man with the "greatest room." Again, paradoxically, it becomes true that to the extent man is bound by the utmost com-mitment to perception of that "stubborn and ornate" order of par-ticular things by which he is surrounded and rejecting abstraction, the more he becomes free. For the poet, the coterminous nature of humility and free will are the precondition of the creative act itself:

> Verse tests the very marrow in the bone,
> Yet man, being once engaged by song, is freed:
> The act itself is prayer, deliberate in its speed.

He wrote that in "The Interval," and he knew it from many years of meticulous and exacting craftsmanship.

In "Unity of the Stream" the image of the poet's inspiration being "like water from a fount" cannot fail to recall Plato's description that the inspired poet is "like a fountain which gives free course to the rush of its waters" (*Laws* 719c). It ought to be a rehearsal of the obvious to point out that the bulk of Watkins's verse exemplifies the Platonic and traditional view that art is a mode of visionary percep-tion in so far as contemplative experience provides the context of its inspiration—an intuitive power that is prior to any form of reflexive thought, as these lines from "The Coin" affirm:

> Vision, where the fountain fell,
> Masters more than time can tell.
>
> Not by reason or by sense
> Alone, can words be made intense,
>
> But by this, alive and dead,
> Breaking from the fountain-head.

17

Whose Is This Horrifying Face?
Reading David Gascoyne's *Miserere*

And the Word was made flesh, and dwelt among us.

JOHN 1:14

Behold, thou desirest truth in the inward parts: and in the hidden part thou shalt make me to know wisdom.

PSALM 51:6

IN HER ESSAY on the poet, Kathleen Raine speaks of "the noble 'Miserere' sequence" as David Gascoyne's "enduring gift to the world."[1] *Miserere* is clearly an allusion to the penitential Psalm 51, and the additional petitionary tone of the Psalm can also be traced throughout the sequence.

The epigraph above suggests the possibility of a distinction between the truth that is personal spiritual experience within and the yet higher interiority of a knowledge inviolate and incorruptible, the abiding truth of the unmanifest "beyond" that is the domain of the Divine Principle itself. Yet, in order to articulate all that is integral to its infinity, the Principle must, as is its nature, make possible something "other": it becomes, in the context of the Christian mystery, the "Eternal Christ." The spiritual dynamic of the *Miserere* sequence depends entirely upon the awareness that the Principle, in becoming something "other" permits, in the human realm, the possibility of the denial of God. Kathleen Raine goes on,

> The eight poems of this series are in praise of the "Eternal Christ"; the poet speaks from these depths into which the divine Presence

---

1. Kathleen Raine, *Defending Ancient Springs* (1967), pp. 35–65; p. 58.

has descended in order to redeem our fallen world, in a voice of sustained eloquence ... in the name of the divine principle itself, continually betrayed yet ever present in and to mankind, to the end of the world. [The poet] has given expression to that world-long crucifixion to which the "god within" has at all times been subjected.

The spiritual center of gravity of the sequence is placed in the shared ground of existential nihilistic despair and the *via negativa* of the saint. The poems speak in the language of contemporary man who stares fixedly into a void he has himself created out of his determination to make a godless world do his bidding. It is as if the poet, as prophet, is under commission from a visionary imagination to address a society sleepwalking in the emptiness of its existence in order to show that modern man, who "has become above all the most indefatigable mimic of all the ways of being man that have ever been thought striking,"[2] must now relinquish the dream that he amounts to something by virtue of what he has accomplished over two thousand years of Christian culture.

In his later *Night Thoughts* of 1955, it is the modern city, that triumph of "civilization," that becomes the theater of man's nihilistic imprisonment in that both fictively and practically it is the embodiment of man's imaginative volition, subsequently and erroneously consulted as the paradigm of his earthly ambition. This self-regarding has imprisoned man within his own productions. In *Night Thoughts* the "brick cliff" walls and giant smoke stacks of Battersea power station stand

> like symbols for the worship of our age:
> The pillars of a temple raised to man-made Power and Light.

In *Miserere*, in so far as modern man is present and complicit in the event at Calvary, he is a citizen of such a city. Stripped of his illusory

---

2. This quotation from Gascoyne, as well as several others from a variety of sources, some not easily accessible, is taken from Dr. Roger Scott, "David Gascoyne: From Darkness into Light: A Study of His Poetry, 1932–1950" (Ph.D. diss., 2002, Northumbria University), p. 145. I am indebted to Dr. Scott for allowing me to draw upon his work.

status he is now forced to comprehend that his only authentic being is in the recovery of the kernel of the Divine Presence within. The oppressive weight and drag of contemporary events is precisely the burden of having given birth to "the hollowness of a world without a spiritual dimension." As the *Miserere* sequence makes clear, the mask has finally been removed. The horror of the Crucifixion and the inhuman cruelty of world war signal the end of man's hope that he will triumph by living out the mere passage of time; that he will be redeemed by the momentum of an historical progress calculated to deliver him from the burden of his failings. The so long dreamed-of, so long meticulously planned apotheosis of his endeavors has brought man face to face with the blank stare of his own vacuity.

In these terms the *Miserere* poems hold in balance the personal and the universal, the immediacy of the facts of contemporary history with the stark intimation of their final outcome. The eschatological shadow falls across many of David Gascoyne's poems but especially on this sequence, where the observation of things to hand is joined with a sense of their ultimate place in the eventual redemption of time itself.

This sense of things to hand as being a harbinger of things beyond is the theme of one of Gascoyne's most regarded poems, "The Gravel-Pit Field." Written around the same time as *Miserere*, its long, circuitous, unfolding lines, so delicately controlled, steer their inevitable course toward the last stanza, effectively "the far edge of being." Having detailed with meticulous observation, in the preceding stanzas, the features of a piece of waste ground, the poet, in a flash of inspirational insight, beholds

> the field's
> Apotheosis: No-man's-land
> Between this world and the beyond,
> Remote from men and yet more real
> Than any human dwelling place:

Thus the landscape is a *temenos,* a sacred precinct, "more real" since the poet's intuition penetrates beyond anything comprehended by the rational senses. Here the poet finds the "hidden part" of the Psalm that shall "know wisdom":

A tabernacle where one stands
As though within the empty space
Round which revolves the Sage's Wheel.

It is the prerogative of the poet's intuitive knowledge to know beyond the subjective experience of the individual.

David Gascoyne has always been associated with the French surrealist movement: later in life, he felt that this had hampered an understanding of his work. Though not entirely without warrant, this association has in fact tended to obscure the Christian mystical influences that have helped shape his imaginative experience.

Gascoyne's readings in the Bible and the influences of Eckhart, Boehme, and Kierkegaard among others are there to balance his extensive reading in central European and Russian philosophies of the twentieth century; not to mention Hölderlin, and a host of writers, poets, and painters whom he knew personally. But in all this, as he inferred in his essay on Carlyle, he had always been aware of a need "to bear witness to the Divine nature of the true man."

The sometimes explicit sometimes implicit leitmotiv of all his work is the ever-present awareness of "the intolerable nature of human reality when devoid of all spiritual, metaphysical dimensions"; which is to say "the curse of inexistence," as he wrote in "Elsewhere," a poem related to the *Miserere* sequence.

In the years leading up to the Second World War when he was working on the sequence, the poet went through a period of intense speculation on the nature of individual existence. The *nihil* of the existentialists no doubt touched a chord of the English poet's vulnerable sensibility, possibly forcing him to confront a despair to which he nonetheless never succumbed. For Gascoyne it was not a matter of facing a godless world so much as acknowledging a "God-ignoring world," since "God does not ever withdraw."

It is a question of learning to suffer life: *not* in the sense of *passively* suffering it to happen to one, but in the sense that suffering (pain) is one's most *active* experience, since it forces itself upon one's consciousness more definitely and inescapably than any other state.

Such thoughts are a type of the *via negativa*; a conscious penetration of illusory reassurances and a casting off of false consolations, a stripping bare of the soul in the face of a conscious realization (at a time of war) of individual and collective evil and its attendant guilt. What results from the tension between recognizing the divine and evil as simultaneously present in man's nature certainly pulses in the ebb and flow of the moral traction that underscores the *Miserere* sequence. This is apparent just as surely as it is evident that the nihilistic coloring of the poems is mixed with a redemptive tone.

It seems likely that the poet's religious faith could only find its natural depth of expression in a poetic vision and language (as with Blake, Hölderlin, and others) outside the boundaries of a more canonical adherence to his Christian faith. It certainly allowed him to reject any notion that there is an *evident* absence of God in the world, however that world be riven by evil: "we don't find Truth, but the Truth takes possession of us." In a letter written in 1937 he wrote "I have come to believe, to *know*, that one must not only live *from within, outwards*, but also, simultaneously, *from without, inwards*." Truth, then, in so far as it "takes possession of us," is the absolute coincidence of being and knowing, a state to be realized rather than a conception to be imposed. In that "to be" there shines the illumination of a possible redemption. In his *A Kind of Declaration* (1980), the poet wrote "I . . . still . . . believe in fortunately still recurrent moments of certain conviction, in the unprecedented occurrence of the Incarnation and in the meaning of the term Resurrection."

In this *Declaration* Gascoyne speaks of how the poet might still be of some use to the world by preserving "the 'prophetic' function of poetry." In his own poetry, and particularly in the *Miserere* poems, this function was to be that of holding before us a representation of the *nihil* as a passage of transition. Kathleen Raine, in her obituary of the poet, speaks of this when she writes, he "saw the darkness of the period as that of Christ entombed, awaiting Resurrection. The Russian vision of apokatastasis—the restoration of all things—was very real to him." And the poet himself wrote in *The Sun at Midnight* (1970), "Nietzsche's 'God is dead' means man is also dead, devoid of spirit. The early and mid-twentieth century is the time of the Open Tomb."

Gascoyne's call to "Revolution and to Poetry" is a call to establish "the Kingdom of Heaven" on earth. That is the function of the Person of Christ, whose Second Coming confirms, as the poet confessed in his *Declaration*, that "Truth is a Person." Poetry might be said to be propaganda but, as he states in the closing words of his prose poem "The Second Coming," "all propaganda that is not true Christian revolutionary propaganda is sickness and falsehood."

As the title suggests, the *Miserere* sequence is a plea for mercy to a God who is absent from the event that is the death of the Son of God. But it is also a petition, both personal and—since the poet as prophet speaks for his people—collective. Yet another subtle coloring of the sequence is the hidden but present sense that this event takes place at a point in the unfolding of the cosmic process—the Kali Yuga no less—when three-quarters of reality has been withdrawn from human cognizance. We are living the end of the historic cycle when the lowest possibilities necessarily manifest themselves.

The implications and resonances of the sequence are immense, not least in the twelve lines that are the first poem, "Tenebrae." Beginning with the resonant and seminal words of Christ from the Fourth Gospel (19:30), at the very outset we are plunged into the final end of all things. This is the most bleak of these bleak poems. "It is finished": Christ, Son of God, the incarnate Logos, reason, intellect, speech, that by which all is defined as subsisting in the Real, is slaughtered by man. There is no appeal, no escape, no relief: the calamity must be faced without flinching. It is even the case that we must accept the event as having its inevitable place in the eternal order of things for, as Olivier Clément has written, "Creation is in the shadow of the cross. The Lamb of God, according to the Book of Revelation, is slain from the foundations of the world."

"Thus may it be: and worse." Only in the final three lines is there the merest chink of light: the suggestion that by accepting the fact of Christ's execution we descend with Him into Hell in order to "know thy perfect darkness." Read in isolation the poem leaves the reader in some doubt as to the final significance of the *nihil* that falls like a darkening shadow over the center of this poem. However, it should not escape notice that two thousand years of Christian civilization and culture have not prevailed against the brutal drama of the nailing of Christ upon the World Tree. This event stands as the ultimate evidence that man is unable to erect from human resources alone a lasting bulwark against the hope of faith that evil may be conquered. In the final analysis, only the presence in the soul of the Eternal Christ can break the "inhuman pattern" of those actions undertaken in denial and ignorance of that Presence.

"Tenebrae" is possibly the most accomplished of all Gascoyne's poems. Form and content are perfectly dovetailed, diction and cadence intimately balanced and nuanced. The austerity of the language mirrors the poem's bleak pronouncements with heightened directness, being pared back to an elemental clarity to give a polished-mirror reflection of this most central of apocalyptic events.

The words of "Tenebrae" are spoken by the voice of the poet-prophet observing the scene. "Pietà," the second poem of the sequence, shifts to the grief-stricken viewpoint of the Virgin's suffering. The poem's telling unfolds in two intricate, unraveling sentences whose forward momentum is checked and shaped by way of involving suspensions and kept from going astray by a gradual accumulation of images of mounting intensity and relevance to the horror of the occasion. The starkness of the cosmic vision of "Tenebrae" is here moderated, befittingly, to something more intimate and personal.

At the heart of the poem, the Virgin Mother, her face contorted, "grief-scrawled," holds her "dead Son's dear head /. . . like a precious blood-encrusted stone." Her all too human suffering is evident as a comprehensible sign to be "read" to the end of history. The Tree of Life itself "unburdened" by the deposition, He whom "God has forsaken" is held to her "unfathomable breast": the Virgin's inviolable conception, through inscrutable mystery, bore and suckled the human Christ. Thus the Eternal Christ, the "word made flesh," must now be understood by way of the purgation that is the sacrifice of history. This is the mystery of Christ's two natures: if Christ were not human how could He reach from beyond to be the effective instrument of man's redemption? If He were not divine in the name of what would He possess the power to redeem? The death of Christ at the hands of the flesh of man points to the incompleteness of the merely human. Only in the realization of the Eternal Christ is man completed, is his redemption made real.

"Out of these depths" emerges the single sentence that is the fifteen lines of "De Profundis," the third poem of the sequence. Another change of location: we are plunged in hell where the poet takes stock of the depths of human despair at the improvidence of its action. The poet offers the petition that the scales of unbelief be removed from human vision; the eyes of flesh now struck blind by despair subsequent to the drama of Christ's execution, in punishment for which the collective soul of men "wander[s] in the marsh of death." The one sentence of the poem is broken by four caesuras, four line spaces and an ellipsis. These accentuate the sense of alienation and loss of direction of the wandering souls. The death of the incarnate Word has spread confusion among the words of men whose now "confounded tongue" is no longer able to conceive (speak of) the ultimately divine ground of the meaning integral to the spoken word. The only source of illumination in this lightless domain is "death's marsh-light"; the only hope, seeing that "the rock of grief" is unbreakable, becomes the possibility of moving deeper still beyond the obstacle that is grief. Some vision of the Eternal may be recovered seeing that the extremities of hell may bring its inhabitants face to face, beyond the edifice of despair, with ultimate realities. This possibility, as hope, is carried forward to the next poem.

"Kyrie," the fourth of the sequence, is a formal sonnet, but without full rhymes. We notice how the mastery of the poet's linguistic style—that so befittingly matches on the one hand, the bleakness of his subject, and on the other, the profundity of its spiritual evocation—here conveys the imaginative mood of the sequence without the least modification of its overall stylistic contours.

The poem presents a plea for mercy, once again, in the face of the many iniquities of man's baser nature that prompt the poem's opening question: "Is man's destructive lust insatiable?" In whatever direction man thinks and acts he meets: "The black catastrophe that can lay waste our worlds." This would seem to undermine any hope that innocence might prevail. If not, then our predetermined guilt is "fatal," our "complicated anguish" nothing less than inevitable.

Man is ruled by an undermining malevolent power whereby his pleasures, "even in the bride's embrace," are immersed in death; he must wear his habitual fears as an immovable "mask" in order to face the world; his guilt at this inevitability can find no solace in any consolation time and place may offer. A central question posed by the poem is not actually stated as such. It is to ask whether these manifestations of sinfulness are—cruelest of ironies—"unconsciously desired"? If so, what possible redemption can there be for man if his creator has predetermined that sin should be his lot? The "tottering ancestral house" that is the cumulative wisdom of past ages, a wisdom traditionally ascribed to the voice of the Divine Presence within, speaks in "anger" and "prophecy" (after the facts of the drama) of another possible outcome. The poet petitions the Presence, appealing for the illumination of the "extraordinary grace" of the "hidden" Eternal Christ that is "dark in us and deep"; deep beyond all the machinations of false identity that are the root cause of man's capacity for transgression and offense; so deep that any appeal to its illumination, on behalf of the partial and incomplete vision of the merely human, must seem like fathoming the very Person who dreams the dream of the life of innocence we misconstrue from base, egotistical motives. This amounts to a profundity Gascoyne recorded in a much later poem, "On Re-reading Jacob Boehme's *Aurora*": "we must die" to mortal vision "before our eyes can see."

Something of the burden of man's realization at his capacity for evil that pervades "Kyrie" is carried over to the next poem of the sequence. In "Lachrymae" the poet speaks to Christ directly, or more specifically addresses the "weight" of significance borne by Christ's tears seeing that they have, in the ensuing years, never ceased. Christ's tears thus have a cosmic significance for they are shed by the slain God in the foreknowing of their cause and role in shaping the path of man's earthly destiny to the end of time. At which point, when "Unity is filled" (the "perfect prescience / Of the Becoming of the Whole," as we might gloss it with words from "Requiem," a poem related to the *Miserere* sequence), their shedding, drop by drop ("like hourglass sand") having "burnt the years away" is revealed to be one of consummation: "Thy tears were all."

The last five lines of "Lachrymae," the fifth poem, submerge us in the deepest depths of the sequence.

> And when our secret face
> Is blind because of the mysterious
> Surging of tears wrung by our most profound
> Presentiment of evil in man's fate, our cruelest wounds
> Become Thy stigmata. They are Thy tears which fall.

In these lines the expectations of conventional understanding are inverted. The "secret face" of conscience, whose eyes look inward (to the "hidden part" of the Psalm), to discover the deep-seated motivation for the events that took place "on the skull-shaped hill" (as it was aptly described in "Pietà"), experience a blinding by tears of their interior vision at the realization that God is complicit in the fact of evil. Which is to say, the integral infinity of the Divine Principle includes the possibility of its own denial. Such foreboding of his fate is man's "cruelest wound" and becomes, according to the law of reciprocal participation in existent being of Christ and man,[3] Christ's stigmata. The suffering that is the never to be effaced earthly grief of man is at root the Eternal Christ's unstaunchable tears.

"Ex Nihilo" is, in effect, a gloss on the words of Christ, spoken in the Garden at Gethsemane but here transposed to the context of the events portrayed in the sequence. "Father, all things are possible unto Thee; take away this cup from me: nevertheless not what I will, but what Thou wilt" (Mark 14:36).

The Son of God addresses the Father, "Lord Light." The no-thingness of the Word by which all things are sustained must have to yield the meaning of the apocalyptic event at Calvary. All time is annihilated, since the Crucifixion was conducted at the place where was found the skull of the first man, Adam, whose dying prophecy foretold the event at the place of his own burial. Christ speaks out of the darkness that accompanies the rending of the veil (Matthew 27:51), in recognition that the event of His giving up the ghost speaks of His fate. That is to say, He must grant it is the will of the Father that out of

---

3. "For He became human in order for us to be made divine" (Athanasius, *On the Incarnation of the Word*, 54).

"the debris of all certainties" the incarnate Son "must learn / The revelation of despair." The no-thingness of the Word is, through Christ, mirrored in the experience of human despair; precisely the "debris" of all earthly illusion and consolations. If all falsely ascribed realities are now destroyed, on what can rest any recognition of the Eternal? The poem leaves the question unanswered, but we might seek the inherent burden, left undisclosed, by reference to the following lines from "Elsewhere." Beyond the *nihil* that is the "curse of inexistence" (a world without spiritual and metaphysical meaning) is found

> Negation's further shore, the yonder side
> Of sleep and absence, dazzling is the sheer
> Rockface set like an ice-barred gate
> Beneath that nether tableland's pure height:
> Whose sky is the negation of our sky,
> Where all earth's ruins are rebuilt
> Of stone that sings, and cold fire burns
> The scentless incense of the air:
> Where time and number are once more atoned
> And to its true existence the Unnamed returns.

That is, the one and only true existent, the Holy Spirit, the prefigurement of the Eternal Christ.

In the penultimate poem of the sequence there is a change of language, which is explained by its largely interpretative content, contrasting with what elsewhere has been mostly the case, the imagery of things seen and experienced.

The title, "Sanctus," suggests the thrice holy "Lord of Hosts: the whole earth is full of His Glory" (Isaiah 6:3). The whole of the Biblical chapter resonates in the poem, speaking as it does in the voice of Christ addressing the Father—"O Master"—of the cleansing and transfiguration of vision. Central to the poem is the theme that the "blind eyes" that are the prison of the body of flesh should, in the face of despair, "see no more" in order that, in going beyond despair (the *nihil* of the sequence) they "may see at last."

"Sanctus" is in two parts, the first beginning with the word "incomprehensible," the second with "uncomprehending": thereby signaling, in cryptic fashion, a transition. If the mystery of what is incomprehensible to him who has yet to recover his true identity; if he is to have revealed to him the "long promised / Revelation"—the "spirit's force" at the "dense core / Of this existence"—then the "blind eyes" of the natural man of flesh must be acknowledged as being uncomprehending. This aligns the possibility that the inner eye of spiritual vision may be opened to embrace the sanctity of all it sees —that which is the fullness of "his Glory." The "fate and mystery / And message" of Christ's death on Calvary is thus the transfiguration of man's mortality in order that it should embrace the Eternal Christ. That is the redemption of the despair, the "withering blight," "long desperation, war," and "confusion" sown by evil.

In the final poem, "Ecce Homo," the starkness of the language plunges us one last time into the horror of Calvary.

> Whose is this horrifying face,
> This putrid flesh, discoloured, flayed,
> Fed on by flies, scorched by the sun?
> Whose are these hollow red-filmed eyes
> And thorn-spiked head and spear-stuck side?
> Behold the Man: He is Man's Son.

The use of intermittent rhyme through the twelve six-line stanzas conveys the sense, especially when heard being read aloud, of the poem's form alternately relaxing and tightening as the reader moves from being an "onlooker at the crime" to being a participant in the moral and spiritual repercussions of this "slow torture of God."

What in the first stanza is on one level the poet recalling the figure of Christ as depicted on the Eisenheim Altarpiece by Grünewald, is on another level a scathing indictment of man's complicity in the murder of the Son of Man. "Behold the Man," who, in so far as He is the earthly Christ, and thus able to be killed as any mortal may, becomes "Man's Son" in virtue of being the issue of man's evil action.

By the second stanza the poem's prophetic tone becomes dominant as the distance of years between the Crucifixion and the Second World War is collapsed: both events, seen as contemporaneous, being catastrophes of a kind. Only when the veil of "legend" and decency, woven to mitigate man's guilt, has been torn aside will the candor of the truth be faced for what it is: Christ's wounds are forever made new.

Thus the Roman centurion and the Nazi soldier (and, as stanzas 5 and 6 go on to imply, all men) are alike brothers at the murder of the Earthly Christ. However, from the depths of the compassion that is His prerogative as being also the Eternal Christ, He once again judges man to be ignorant of the nature of his crime: that is to live and act as if there was a justice exclusive to the earthly kingdom, meted out according to the expediencies of political and social demands.

The poignancy of the eighth stanza intensifies the poem's drama by pointing to the other-worldly dimension of the event: Christ's self-knowledge, not only of the appalling agony of His execution, but also His full knowledge—"as He foretold"—that the agony would be extended across the whole of history.

> He who wept for Jerusalem
> Now sees His prophecy extend
> Across the greatest cities of the world,
> A guilty panic reason cannot stem
> Rising to raze them all as He foretold;
> And He must watch this drama to the end.

Through the last four stanzas the poem moves toward the "beyond despair" that is the sought-for terminus of the poet's vision. In contrast to the Christ whose "kingdom is not of this world"—the very Christ who possesses prophecy and foreknowledge and who is "unknown" to the "dark kingdom" that is the world of men—each man must bear the weight of his complicit guilt to go "blindfolded to his fate."

The last three stanzas are a call for the intervention of the "Christ of Revolution and of Poetry." Faced with the horror of man's unprecedented action, here, the poet ventures, must be the "turning point of history," in which the shed Blood of the dying Christ is transfigured to become the instrument of Resurrection. Again norms are inverted in order that, at last, even the dispossessed and least among men might "become / Agents of the divine." Theirs too shall be possession of true poetic vision of the Divine Presence.

The final lines of the poem propose that man's long journey through the night of "human pain"—from Calvary to World War—

has brought him to the ultimate pitch of despair against which two thousand years of subscription to dogma, ceremony, and symbol have not won through. Now, only by an unconditional surrender in and through the *nihil*, to the Eternal Christ, will the life of man prove not to have been in vain.

In his *Miserere* sequence David Gascoyne expresses a vision both personal and collective: personal in that it gives us the private reactions of a vulnerable psychological temperament possessed of an unflinching eye, collective in that it conveys a more widespread sense of the anguish of a society witnessing its own destruction. The poet does this with a visionary directness and an imaginative power that go far beyond the supposed objectivity of the merely self-effacing. Now that the events of the period have become the inexhaustible resource of historians world-wide, and Europe has settled into a different sort of sleep-walking—the moral anesthesia of consumer excess—we are invited to consider whether the substance of the events that led Gascoyne to see this period as "the time of the Open Tomb" has shifted its ground. In our own time the growing complexities of human existence are often described as having left all the doors to heaven and hell wide open. We live now in the age of the convergence of religions in which is implied a more universal perspective that moves beyond the specific context of the Christian redemption the poet wrestled with. Now, what seems more pressing, when each of the diverse religions makes a claim to exclusive possession of Truth, is the question of where Truth is to be located.

Explanation is not the role of poetry, which is to cultivate and sustain our intuitive participation in the numinous. The poems of *Miserere*, surely, still possess the power to effect this. Perhaps one of their most lasting resonances is that they convey a compelling sense of meaning without attempting to circumscribe the mystery they portray with the reductive implements of interpretation. As *we* stare into the abyss what we discover there will depend upon what we bring to the experience.

18

Kathleen Raine:
Poetic Imagination and the
Vision of Reality

No ONE can doubt that the advent of modernist poetry introduced hitherto unexplored areas of creative expression. The sweep of its innovations allowed for an expansion of poetic vocabulary. New rhythmic possibilities were explored, and there was a move toward a diction that was closer to the cadences and usage of everyday living speech. But this ground was won at some cost. Beauty was certainly off the agenda. And the soul was more or less banished—made obsolete as a faculty of perception as materialist ideologies tightened their grip on all areas of intellectual inquiry.

As a result perhaps the greatest loss was in a narrowing of the sphere of imagination, the soul's natural habitat. So effective was this curtailment of the soul's function that contemporary poetry has adopted as something of a norm the habit of assuming that it can do no more than speak from a presumption of reality that is limited to the outer world of sensory perception and its objects on the one hand, and on the other, as it were facing it, the inner world of personal emotion. These two domains, the one seemingly concrete and objective, the other a type of private "fantasy," the contemporary poet seeks to join through straightforward description of phenomenal reality or some form of subjective invention. Yet each remains cut off from the other by a gulf it cannot bridge.

And why not? it might be objected. These domains, after all, represent the world we inhabit and form the basis on which we communicate our experiences to each another. It is to speak of "a" reality shared in common, without which communication would break down altogether. However, the limitations of such a view begin to be felt when we can grant that man possesses a soul whose organ of perception, imagination, is an intuitive sense that there lies beyond the world of sensory experience an order of reality—ineffable, ultimately inexpressible—that is nonetheless the source of the incarnate world in all its reassuring solidity. This metaphysical intuition, native to our very being, when given a degree of realization, can never accept that the world of sensory experience represents any sort of absolute reality. Even more: this intuition by its nature demands that we recognize that the essential condition of our worldly experience is illusory.

Historically, the poet, brother to the mystic, has an honored place among those who have helped us to hold on to this vision of reality. It is the primary nature of poetry to offer us an imaginative re-creation of those interlocking orders of reality—the impalpable and the sensory—by which we come to understand the illusory nature of the sensory world. As the Vedantic doctrine of *maya* teaches, it is not that the world is inexplicable, but that it is not self-explanatory. Quintessentially, the gift that is true poetic imagination is the ability to embody, as if seen from afar, what the mystic has experienced in a state of realization. The primordial poetic utterance is one that offers us a vision of the world as an order of events that is ultimately indefinable. Which is nothing more nor less than to say that poetry reveals, by the use of symbols and in terms of imaginative experience, the structure of illusion. This is the paradox of poetic experience. It is what determines whether or not the poet is concerned with the revelation of truth.

The poet Kathleen Raine began early. She has recorded that, even before she could write, and seated on her mother's lap, she would speak her poems so that her mother could write them down. Notwithstanding a later qualification, that something of this poetry was first put into her head by her mother, what might we give to hear those poems now?

In the foreword to her final *Collected Poems* (compiled in her ninety-first year), the poet wrote "that a writer's early work often contains the essence of the work that follows, a sort of map of that special vision." We might expect, then, as we certainly find, that Kathleen Raine is a poet of continuities. Something of this is the subject of our present exploration.

Despite this early beginning the poet did not publish her first volume, *Stone and Flower,* until her thirty-fifth year in 1943. These, and the poems of her next three collections, have remained among her most cherished and well known. The distinctive qualities of these "early" poems were recognized and praised from the outset.

Their purity of diction using a relatively simple vocabulary; their often ambiguous, floating syntax; their powers of evocation over and above the descriptive; their absence of passive sentiment in ego-less vision in response to worldly experience; and, allied to this vision, an objective precision in the observation of natural objects (reflecting her early training as a botanist in the natural sciences). The poet's ability to invoke the cosmic dimension of love, self, and nature was evident from the beginning, as was the way they "hold" personal emotion in the natural object, thereby "fixing" the eternal in the transient. To these animating continuities she returned again and again. It is perhaps not so easy for us now to measure the impact such a vision made on her contemporaries, marking her out as an unprecedented, refreshing, poetic voice.

In later life, when the poet came to reject many of these early poems, we can see that she was, by so condensing them, attempting to purge them of religiosity and emotional dross, the better to concentrate the authentic substance that was to be the lasting nourishment of her poetic vision.

In the very first poem of her first collection, "Lyric," which remained the first poem of her final, chosen canon, we find incarnate that interpenetration of human and cosmic, spiritual and created universes that stamped her vision from first to last.

> A bird sings on a matin tree
> "Once such a bird was I."
>
> The sky's gaze says
> "Remember your mother."

Seas, trees and voices cry
"Nature is your nature."

I reply
"I am what is not what it was."
Seas, trees, and bird, alas!
Sea, tree, and bird was I.

Here, the natural object *is* the type of that instant of spiritual vision that gives rise to the poem. There is no hiatus of reflective consciousness to give admixture to the experience. In the last section of one her last poems it is no different.

Joy, bird with no place of alighting, fly
Through my sky's
Infinite spaces, boundless
Realms of delight,
At rest in flight.

In the instantaneity of the imaginative experience the warp and woof of opposites that is the cosmic fabric are miraculously woven together in the light of pure wonder.

Only rarely do any of these early poems extend beyond a single page. This is in keeping with the poet's practice at the time, of building a poem around just such a moment of spiritual identity, in which there is no "expanse" to allow a narrative theme to unfold. But this succinctness of expression amounts to more than simply a moment of identity. A characteristic of nearly all of her poetry is that it is centered on the immediacy of the moment of perception as an experience, in part, of the whole of reality. The fragment possesses the nature of the whole. In this moment of interaction in which the whole makes its presence felt is the token of the unity of experience with the Divine—the promise of our undivided life in the primacy of the Spirit. It is so in the early poem "In the Beck."

There is a fish, that quivers in the pool,
Itself a shadow, but its shadow, clear.
Catch it again and again, it still is there.

Against the flowing stream, its life keeps pace
With death—the impulse and the flash of grace
Hiding in its stillness, moves, to be motionless.

> No net will hold it—always it will return
> When the ripples settle, and the sand—
> It lives unmoved, equated with the stream,
> As flowers are fit for air, man for his dream.

It is so, still, in the late "At the Back End of Time."

> At the back end of time
> Leaf-fall of lives, dwindling of the great tree
> To the acorn of forests, returning
> To nothing of all that is,
> The seasons, the leaves, the loves,
> Song to its source, soul to its star—
> Winter's recollection of worlds to be.

The continuity of underlying themes from first to last need not deflect us from recognizing the differences in quality in the early and later poetry. We might note how, in the early lyrics, the implied motif of undivided, omnipresent presence is, as it were, more particularly incarnate in the succession of images. It is as if what was the emotional experience for these early poems is still a living impulse in the image. In the later poems it is more often the case that the lived experience has been reflected and recorded. This observation may be to make no judgment as to merit, but merely to acknowledge the difference of perspective as between formative poetic vision and the more nuanced apprehensions of mature perception. There is certainly no question that each of these different perspectives is meant to serve the ineffable wonder that is a recollection of the seamless unity of the Creation, however evanescent the instant of its embodiment. This is not to say the moment was "unreal," for the moment *was*! Here, it is recorded—haiku-like—with the cosmic and the particular as one, in one of the late "Short Poems":

> World:
> Image in water, waves
> Break and it is gone, yet
> It was.

Which is perhaps, incidentally and in passing, a tribute to Rilke, whom she admired, who speaks of the reality of this moment in these lines, toward the beginning of his penultimate *Elegy:*

>   Just *once*,
>   everything, only for *once. Once* and no more. And we, too,
>   *once*. And never again. But this
>   having been *once*, though only *once*,
>   having been *once* on earth—can it ever be cancelled?[1]

On what, we might ask, is the record of this present moment inscribed that it should be so inerasable? It is surely the living presence of that cosmic dream of the Divine Principle that weaves and unweaves worlds according to the laws of manifestation integral to the outward realization of Itself through love.

This is the theme of that great poem "Amo Ergo Sum" where the very formation of things coming into being so as to be discernible as objects of knowledge—through the human eye, itself miraculously part of the process—is celebrated as the beauty of natural events. Here is the latter part of the poem.

>   Because I love
>   The iridescent shells upon the sand
>   Take forms as fine and intricate as thought.
>
>   Because I love
>   There is an invisible way across the sky,
>   Birds travel by that way, the sun and moon
>   And all the stars travel that path by night.
>
>   Because I love
>   There is a river flowing all night long.
>
>   Because I love
>   All night the river flows into my sleep,
>   Ten thousand living things are sleeping in my arms,
>   And sleeping wake, and flowing are at rest.

By means of its lyric intensity the poem fuses the domains of the natural and the supra-natural, making it impossible to distinguish between the nature of the observer and the thing observed. Each is subsumed in the being that is at once the particularity of the one who observes and the immanent presence of the Divine Person who

---

1. From the Leishman-Spender translation, which Kathleen Raine had on her shelves.

is the cause of the epiphanic moment of what is observed—the "ecstasy-producing dance," as an earlier line of the poem has it.

The poem's refusal to identify the observer as an empirical ego greatly enlarges the field of possible vision. The restrictions of a private response to the experience of reality being removed, the intuition of belonging to the wider panoply of wonders that is the Divine Nature's inexhaustible fertility is given its proper estate. The radical boundary between mind and matter is dissolved in a recognition that both mind and matter are no more than inseparable modes of consciousness, a consciousness that is singular whatever its mode. The source is never possessed as if it were an instrument of the thinking, perceiving "I." Rather it is the modes that collectively possess the "I" who, creating nature through the eyes of love, sees in the beauty of natural things the very essence of the ineffable reality that cannot be contained exclusively by manifest reality.

In the unassuming "Afternoon Sunlight Plays" the moment of wonder is caught without blemish.

> Afternoon sunlight plays
> Through trailing leaves I cannot see,
> Stirred by a little wind that mixes light and leaf
> To filter their quiet pattern on my floor.
> Not real, Plato said, the shadowy dancers,
> Imponderable
> Somewhere beyond, the light; but I am old,
> Content with these shadows of shadows that visit me,
> Present unsummoned, gone without stir.
>
> So angels, it may be.

Going from late to early we note once more the continuity of poetic vision between the lines above and these from the early poem beginning "Not upon earth . . ."

> Not upon earth, as you suppose
> Tower these rocks that turn the wind,
> For on their summits angels stand.
>
> Nor from the earth these waters rise—
> To quench not thirst, but ecstasy
> The waterfall leaps from the sky.

Those nameless clouds that storm and swirl
About the mountain are the veil
That from these sightless eyes shall fall

When senses faint into the ground,
And time and place go down the wind.

If in the early poems "ego-less vision" is something of a confident assertion, in this later poem (as in others) it is an article of faith and experience that underpins the familiar responses of many years of pondered experience. Yet it remains, on every occasion, a momentary realization of an archetypal order of reality.

For all that, we are left with the paradox that the experience happens to a "self"—the poet—a paradox that is solved only when we realize that this "self" is itself a reflected moment of the all-enveloping indefinite number of localizations of the Divine Presence. It is the light of this archetypal order of the Infinite that casts, firstly, the "shadows" of manifest existence that are natural phenomena that then, secondarily, themselves cast shadows within their own order of manifest reality.

The poet has, at this point, the symbolism of the shadows on the wall of the Platonic cave, as it were, deep in her poetic blood. This bloodline runs deeply and widely in her expression of the subtle interplay that perception and reality exchange. It colors the distinctive tone of her poetic diction, as it animates the structure of her imagination.

All evidence points to the fact that these poetic images are not "abstract" any more than they are simply emotional analogs. Were it not so then we would have to conclude that these are poems in which a flight of personal fancy has been allowed to build insubstantial mansions in the air. Not to acknowledge the operative presence of the Platonic symbolism as the implied ground on which the poet's imagination builds, must foreshorten our appreciation of what gives these poems their vital breath. It would be to miss the significance of the specificity of the poet's references to the natural order. For these are never objects that know only the laws of biological process, of birth and decay, measurable things to weigh and dissect. Tree, stone, star, shell, fish, rock, rain, wind, each is, in the light of the poet's perception—itself a spark of light struck from the Infinite—a world-image of wonder. As such they are powers that of necessity have a cause that is other than their effects; a source in the ineffable "beyond." These, the final lines of the early poem "Seed" tell us that it is so.

> External and innate dimensions hold
> The living forms, but not the force of life;
> From that interior and holy tree
> That in the heart of hearts outlives the world
> Spreads earthly shade into eternity.

In this last line, note how the poet's authenticity of vision allows her to reverse the direction from which the Platonic light flows—the inverted symbol being all the more effective for its imaginative daring.

The "Three Poems on Illusion" are central to the poet's achievement. They would be unthinkable without the effective resonances that accrue to an imaginative vision that registers the objects of nature as intimations of the soul's immersion in a world where the rigorous division of subject from object is refused by the experience of being "at one with nature." In the intuition of interpenetrating orders of reality lies the key to why nature can lift our perception beyond the merely human, to find its identity in the uncreated and undying as it is reflected in the transience of nature's protean lifecycle. "The Instrument," the second of the set of three poems, ends:

> And it may be that soul extends
> Organs of sense
> Tuned to waves here scarcely heard, or only
> Heard distantly in dreams,
> Worlds other otherwise than as stars,
> Asteroids and suns are distant, in natural space.
> The supersonic voices of angels reach us
> Even now, and we touch one another
> Sometimes, in love, with hands that are not hands,
> With immaterial substance, with a body
> Of interfusing thought, a living eye,
> Spirit that passes unhindered through walls of stone
> And walks upon those waves that we call ocean.

Toward the end of her long life the poet wrote many short poems—haiku-like in their verbal brevity, but having for all that expansive reverberations. She once told me that she thought these were her lasting contribution to the formal possibilities of English poetry. In many of these brief, condensed poems the interplay of the real and the illusory reaches a level of sophistication such that the poet's art is perfectly submerged in the artlessness that is the true mastery of her art. In the first of the "Short Poems" of 1994, the Archetypal Reality becomes totally translucent in order to affirm how its "nothingness" is nonetheless the measure by which the least instant of any one thing is granted its existence:

> Against the *nihil*
> One candle-flame, one blade of grass,
> One thought suffices
> To affirm all.

In the second of this series of eight poems, the poet in old age is forced to acknowledge that after all the possible attachments the soul may make with the objects of sense, there comes a bodily death such as will challenge and disabuse the soul of these false identifications.

> Time to unknow
> What has been known,
> Time to undo
> What has been done—
> What will remain?
> The naked soul
> To judgement come.

In yet another, the fifth, the poet's legacy to the reader is an offering of her life's imaginative work, a gift open only to those who have access to the one same identity we share, beyond possession, in the eternal order of the permanently Real.

> All I have known and been
> I bequeath to whoever
> Can decipher my poem.

If we are to avoid the error of thinking that the poet's use of natural imagery loses the identity of self to biological process, then we must grasp a further implication inherent in her deployment of these images. Here, it is all to their purpose that the poems convey to the reader, through emotional nuance based on sharply focused observation, something of the ineffable truth of the poet's inspiration, and how this relates to the technique of poetry making.

In response to a questionnaire on rhyme in *Agenda* in 1991, the poet made it clear that she thought matters of poetic technique in general are determined in advance of poetic utterance by the level of reality that informs the imagination—prose and free verse being, as she says, "appropriate to the natural mind, rhythm and rhyme to the formal genius of the soul ('For soul is form and does the body make'—Spenser) and to what the modern poets never mention, inspiration."

Given that the poet would certainly include herself among the poets of inspired imagination, at first sight this might seem somewhat at odds with the fact that in her own practice she seldom used traditional, formal verse structures. Her rejection of full rhymes, she confesses, revealingly, is "because the rhymes impose a kind of affirmative confidence proper to another experience, when life was full of certainties, religious . . . or the over-confidence in their own culture of Dryden and Pope." However, it becomes clear that for her the matter is more complex, for the question of form relates to the poet's level of consciousness. It is a question of that "inner music" that causes the soul to "dance" when a state of "enhanced consciousness" is attained, so that the form of the poem is determined by a pre-existing music or rhythm. This "vertical" conception is very different from the horizontal continuities of past practice in which shape is superimposed on word patterns in the light of an established precedent. Needless to say we are here as far away as it is possible to be from the assumptions that inform the freedoms of *vers libre* whose demotic manner proceeds from, in this poet's eyes, "the materialist ideologies of the modern West." Such freedoms assume, consciously or otherwise, that, as she says, "there is only one level of consciousness." All of which seems to imply that the poet thought of the necessary formalities of poetry making as discovering and revealing in the fusion of diction, image, and symbol, the true cadence inherent in the emotion of any given poem's subject matter.

The poet concludes, "The clearer the imaginative perception, the surer the form . . . the serious task of the poets . . . is to illuminate the world with glimpses of beauty and meaning as these are known to the soul. Sorrow and joy, and the sound-current of the universe, which is music and dance."

This is exactly what we find in that early, inimitable masterpiece "The World," with its simple, repeating vocabulary, spare, cyclical diction, and skillful evasion of a regular poetic form. The poem presents an unforgettable vision of the cosmic genesis's emergence from the measureless, eternal punctum—the birth point of the world from transcendent non-being.

> It burns in the void
> Nothing upholds it
> Still it travels.
>
> Travelling the void
> Upheld by burning
> Nothing is still.
>
> Burning it travels
> The void upholds it
> Still it is nothing.
>
> Nothing it travels
> A burning void
> Upheld by stillness.

Maintaining our hold upon the poet's continuities, and turning to the late "Wisdom of Words," we find the deeper breath and swell of the poem's longer lines flowing outward from that same punctum—which is here, additionally, the poet's "pen-point," tracing its way across the written page—to encompass the whole multitude of wonders that comprises the world as well as all that the "heart has known." Here is the latter half of the poem.

> From word to word I trace my way, seeking, divining
> Scarcely discernable messages, passing
> From life to life clarities, marvels, epiphanies
> All hearts, all souls have sought,
> Bring to my moment all those who once were, have dreamed,
> Have known and praised, have sung, have cried aloud.

> Cosmic music of water and wind and stars
> Flows on for ever, but this human realm
> Of meaning, none knows but we,
> These memories, told and retold, imparted
> From dream to dreamer by such as I,
> Whose only knowledge is what we have made to be.

Let these lines lead us back to one more of the poet's continuities—the place of the human heart, its voices, its pulses, its places, its loves; even, at times, as the seat of evil—in so far as these are instrumental in giving us knowledge of the rightful meaning of the substance of the cosmic fabric.

Through the medium of the soul's language that is human speech, the heart of love is revealed by the poet to be at one with all that lives and breathes as knowable nature. The heart is then the vital repository of all that is veiled from mere eyes of flesh. The task of the poet is to marry, by naming, each object to the essence of love that is its immortal birth. In the coming and going of the seasons, in the interval of bud to leaf-fall, the rise and fall of the tides, in the heart's systole and diastole, the one undying rhythm marks out the pulse of the Creation. Here is the theme radiantly expressed, albeit in the shadow of war, in the early poem, "Passion."

> The sky said to my soul, "You have what you desire.
>
> "Know now that you are born along with these
> Clouds, winds, and stars, and ever-moving seas
> And forest dwellers. This your nature is.
>
> "Lift up your heart again without fear,
> Sleep in the tomb, or breathe the living air,
> This world you with the flower and with the tiger share."
>
> Then I saw every visible substance turn
> Into immortal, every living cell new born
> Burned with the holy fire of passion.
>
> This world I saw as on her judgment day
> When the war ends, and the sky rolls away,
> And all is light, love and eternity.

Again and again in the poems human love is seen not only and simply as a reflection of the Divine Love, but as being, in that, subject to the joys, the rigors, the desolations, and the estrangements of the divisiveness (male/female) that the human heart is heir to. This, the soul's journey on earth, is most fully explored in the long sequence that is *On a Deserted Shore*. But this accomplishment, unsurpassed of its kind, is more than worthy of our full attention on another occasion, one that might give it the honor it deserves.

In the early, modest, "Woman to Lover," the eternal feminine that is the heart's resonating object of the lover, is identified as being wholly absorbed in the elements of the created world, as if to remind the lover of the extent of love's common source in the Creator's Love of his Creation. Much of the evocative power of this deceptively small lyric is in the way this subject-object relationship is transposed to the human couple and suggested only by silent implication. This true identification of Love's source is required by the very nature of human love which, if it is to bear its fullest meaning, must be understood in a context that relates to it beyond the passions of human sexuality. For the nature of love is ultimately cosmic. A man and a woman in love rehearse the reciprocal, generative rhythm of the Universe.

In "Woman to Lover" we find an intimation of the theme that, as we have seen, is the poet's presiding continuity: that a full understanding of human experience requires a larger vision of what connotes reality than that afforded by the world of fugitive, perishable mortality. In this poem in particular, the lover is invited to understand his love of a woman as part of the interweaving of the total cosmic projection, where it alone endures in an order of reality itself loved into being by the Divine Presence. Here is the poem.

> I am fire
> Stilled to water,
>
> A wave
> Lifting from the abyss.
>
> In my veins
> The moon-drawn tide rises

> Into a tree of flowers
> Scattered in sea-foam.
>
> I am air
> Caught in a net,
>
> The prophetic bird
> That sings in a reflected sky,
>
> I am a dream before nothingness,
> I am a crown of stars,
> I am the way to die.

Undoubtedly, in the later poems there is an accounting of the heart's enrichments and failings—the judgment again! This is especially so in the poems of *The Oracle in the Heart* (1980), where the theme of self-reckoning is the dominant mood. The record is unflinching, even at times harrowing, as it is written out in the poems and was lived out in the pages of life. In the self-accounting that is the occasion of "In My Seventieth Year," the poet sees herself as the medium of the Logos—"I myself a spoken word"—that one "majestic voice" that "raised me to life" and thereby set her upon the journey of her life. The poem speaks, then, not only of an empirical self that passively suffers and undergoes the experiences of a life lived, but also from the vantage point of that Self of all "selves," a presence

> Consubstantial with the earth,
> Contemporaneous with the stars,
> With the sun that lights the world,
> Morning and night of the one day
> In which I walk today, all days.

This poses the question of the authenticity of the identity of the self to whom the voice of poetic utterance belongs; the identity that, in its time, has been called upon to record the ongoing passage of life toward death? To what extent is the poet responsible for the "burden" of suffering caused by the self—seeing that the poem is cast in that light—by the interweaving "of good and evil, time and place"; all the sustaining opposites that are the generation of life as it is lived? The poem resolves its dilemmas by retracing the origins of the heart's loves.

Though not explicit in the poem we infer the contextual motif from earlier poems. The shadow serves in so far as it registers the light's presence. If what is known is that alone which is loved, then failure to love is an unknowing, for only in the light of love does anything realize its essential perfection. Failure to love is here a failure of knowledge, that ever-present category of the earthly condition—a condition whose burden we perpetuate rather more than we amend. The final responsibility for the failures of the heart must be weighed from within the context (with all the moral difficulties this may pose) in which the Author of the light is ultimately also the Author of the shadow. The heart of the individual we are created to be is part only of the great unfolding drama of the cosmic dream that is, as the poem has it, "earth's great cry of joy and woe"—that consummation of the cycle of the All-Possible that "must be/Before the concord can be full." As part only of the larger whole it is not given to the individual to weigh and judge the final outcome of the greater pattern of possibilities—always and ever the dilemma of moral judgment. Without evil and injustice, goodness and equity would lack occasion to be exercised and so would not exist. The poem ends,

> Shall we condemn what has been made,
> Who makes this world and calls it good,
> Amends and heals through endless time?
> All that I have done amiss
> All that I have failed to be,
> Since he creates he must forgive,
> Since he has made me he must love,
> For I am but his act and will,
> Who framed me both to give and bear
> The wounds and sorrows of the world.

In the final analysis only the saint, in perfect knowledge of the Real, possesses perfect love—*is* perfect love.

As the poet succinctly records in the brief "Soliloquies,"

> To make the imperfect perfect
> It is enough to love it.

And this by no means rules out "A saint's certainty respecting the unsure" in "Paradox."

In the way that it is love in all its modes that threads together the strands of the poet's experience in the earlier poems, so it is time that becomes the backdrop that unifies the world of human experience in many of the later poems. This gradual transmutation of imaginative context culminates in the poet's last substantial poem, "Millennial Hymn to the Lord Shiva." This is surely a latter-day genuflection in the direction of Yeats's "The Second Coming," in so far as it answers to the destructive powers that must emerge at the extinction of a civilization—this last now more certain to us than to Yeats. However, the Hymn, with its sometimes faltering rhythms and prosaic inventories, is not the poem where the theme of time is most profoundly embodied—even if it is the poem that most emphatically states the cosmic necessity for the intervention of time's end to be "the destroyer, / the liberator, the purifier" of the fruits of human conduct.

In the substantial, three-part "Hymn to Time" the multiple levels of reality that are manifest by the very nature of time are explored in the light of the poet's past personal life. Here, time's ever-flowing current is the engendering medium that conjures the seeming world of nature, as well as the domain of human imagining. As a seamless experience it is honored by the poet as being the repository of the "treasury" of memories—the making of a life recalled in wonder. But that same wonder reveals time, "whose now is unending," to be the instrument of beyond-time, around which the forces of creation and destruction revolve. This moment, never part of the action, is the absolver of all personal actions and their outcome, as each moment, mirrored in time, repeats the eternal patterns of love and pain brought to consciousness in the very fleetingness of the passing of their enactment.

At the center of this never-ending interweaving of the experiences of love, pain, time, memory, is the knower, the identity, the witness who never surrenders to the changes of time, and so knows all that once was and all that is to come—to whom no moment is lost.

> Now without end or beginning Time
> With your long necklace of skulls, who will add mine
> To your tally of lives, each rich in its infinite present,
> Nothing, take as you will all that was once ours
> As from moment to moment, day to day
> All that for ever is passes before us,
> Will ever not have been once and for ever.

Indeed, this identity of Self with the timeless moment is the sole guarantor of the reality of the experience in consciousness. Where else could the event be so inscribed but on those pages—"where life's a dream / of profound untellable mysteries"—if it were itself the subject of constant flux?

Something of the same theme spills over into "Fire," the following poem of the canon, where the interplay of the known and the unknown is captured in a meditation in praise of the nature of fire. Firstly, that of the "Beautiful, flickering, translucent flame" of the familiar hearth coals that return to the poet's present moment of contemplation the "carboniferous forests" of past millennia "where no one ever walked." In the act of burning in the grate the coals transform one worldly element into another. Next is fire as the embodiment of the world's living, principal substance, that in returning all to ash produces a "constant light" whose rays might "blaze / Into such a star" as would "comfort us with infinite forgiveness of our undoing."

Finally, there is fire as liberator from all that is the subject of impermanent reality. By its abiding measure alone, whatever is created of the sorrows and joys, the loves and losses that make and unmake human worlds, there is redemption by reabsorption into the Divine Principle—source and nature of all. The poems ends

> Fire, subtle undoer, loosener of bonds,
> Free, you are the freer
> Of all that is destructible, perishable, but we
> By flame cannot be burned, nor can you consume away
> The intangible thought I offer you in praise
> As you roar in glory through houses and worlds and universes
> Turning our dust to stars.

So we conclude. In examining the thematic continuities that form the central ground of Kathleen Raine's poetry, we find that a full appreciation calls for a recognition that the soul remains the proper organ of perception of the Real in all the multiplicity of its modes. Only in this, the "soul's native place," is the depth and complexity of human identity and knowledge found to have its fullest and most valid meaning. As the means of imaginative vision, the symbolic discourse of the soul is the essence of poetic expression. Against the diminishments of modernism Kathleen Raine has left us a body of poetry that affirms the perennial teaching, that true poetic vision is an imaginative re-creation of the inexhaustible ways in which the perception of reality is necessarily permeated by the Divine Presence, a Presence without which that reality simply would not be.

Acknowledgments
and Sources of Texts

THE EDITOR wishes to thank James Wetmore and John Riess for support of this project, and Jill Burrows for preparing the book's texts. My thanks, also, to Brian Keeble for helping track texts down and discussing the volume's contents.

Chapter 5, "Of Art and Skill," and chapter 11, "Archetype as Letterform: The 'Dream' of Edward Johnston," are reprinted here from *God and Work: Aspects of Art and Tradition,* published by World Wisdom (2009); and chapter 18, "Kathleen Raine: Poetic Imagination and the Vision of Reality," is reprinted from a chapbook of that title, published by the Temenos Academy (Temenos Academy Paper 28; 2008). My thanks to World Wisdom and to the Temenos Academy for permission to reprint these pieces; and to Stephen Williams at World Wisdom and Stephen Overy at Temenos for mediating my requests.

Thanks to Golgonooza Press (Ipswich, England) for permission to reprint a number of chapters in this book. The following chapters are reprinted from *Art: For Whom and for What?* published by Golgonooza (1998): chapter 1, "Introductory Remarks," as that book's introduction; chapter 4, "Art: For Whom and for What?"; chapter 6, "Man and Nature as Polarities of the Sacred"; chapter 7, "Work and the Sacred"; chapter 9, "Are the Crafts an Anachronism?"; chapter 12, "David Jones's View of Art"; chapter 14, "Michael Cardew: The Potter as Primordial Maker"; and chapter 15, "Samuel Palmer's Vision of Nature." ("Are the Crafts an Anachronism?" also appeared in *Ye Shall Know the Truth: Christianity and the Perennial Philosophy,* edited by Mateus Soares de Azevedo, foreword by William Stoddart, pp. 193–207 [World Wisdom, 2005]; and "Work and the Sacred" also appeared in *Every Branch in Me: Essays on the Meaning of Man,* edited by Barry McDonald, pp. 181–96 [World Wisdom, 2002]).

The following chapters are reprinted from *Conversing with Paradise*, also published by Golgonooza Press (2005): chapter 3, "A Time of Darkness"; and chapter 16, "Time's Glass Breaks: On the Poetry of Vernon Watkins" (with the title "Time's Glass Breaks").

Chapter 8, "Standing on Earth: Wendell Berry and the Two Economies," is reprinted from *Standing on Earth. Selected Essays of Wendell Berry,* edited by Brian Keeble (Golgonooza Press, 1991), for which it was the editor's introduction.

Chapter 10, "Eric Gill and a Holy Tradition of Working," originally appeared as the introduction to *A Holy Tradition of Working: An Anthology of the Writings of Eric Gill,* edited by Brian Keeble (Golgonooza Press, 1983).

Chapter 2, "Notes on *Art* and *Imagination,*" is reprinted from *Temenos* 6 (1985): 5–11, in which it was that issue's editorial.

Chapter 13, "Images of the Unknown: Looking at Cecil Collins," originally appeared in *Temenos* 11 (1990): 113–28.

Chapter 17, "Whose Is This Horrifying Face? Reading David Gascoyne's *Miserere,*" originally appeared in *Temenos Academy Review* 15 (2012): 153–65.

The punctuation and spelling in all pieces has been changed in accordance with the predominant U.S. style, and in a few cases very minor textual adjustments have been made to adapt content to the present context.

A Bibliography
of Brian Keeble's Publications

BOOKS

Art: For Whom and for What? (essays; Golgonooza Press, 1998).

Vernon Watkins: Inspiration as Poetry, Poetry as Inspiration (lecture-essay; Temenos Academy Papers 19, 2002).

Twenty-four Poems (Golgonooza Press, 2002).

Conversing with Paradise (essays; Golgonooza Press, 2005).

On the Nature and Significance of the Crafts: W. R. Lethaby, Edward Johnston, and Ananda K. Coomaraswamy, foreword by Keith Critchlow (lecture-essays; Temenos Academy Papers 22, 2005).

Shapes of Light (poems; Golgonooza Press, 2005).

Kathleen Raine: Poetic Imagination and the Vision of Reality (lecture-essay; Temenos Academy Papers 28, 2008).

In His Name and Other Poems (Golgonooza Press, 2008).

God and Work: Aspects of Art and Tradition, foreword by Wendell Berry (essays; World Wisdom, 2009).

Cecil Collins: The Artist as Writer and Image Maker (essays; Golgonooza Press, 2009).

From a Handful of Dust (poems; Golgonooza Press, 2011).

Far from the Dawn (poems; Golgonooza Press, 2014).

EDITED VOLUMES

The Inner Journey of the Poet, and Other Papers, by Kathleen Raine (Allen & Unwin, 1982).

A Holy Tradition of Working: An Anthology of the Writings of Eric Gill (Golgonooza Press, 1983).

What Is Civilisation? and Other Essays, by Ananda K. Coomaraswamy (Golgonooza Press, 1989).

Standing on Earth: Selected Essays of Wendell Berry (Golgonooza Press, 1991).

Meditations, Poems, Pages from a Sketch Book, by Cecil Collins (Golgonooza Press, 1997).

The Music of Silence: A Composer's Testament, by Sir John Tavener (Faber & Faber, 1999).

The Vision of the Fool and Other Writings, by Cecil Collins (Golgonooza Press, enlarged edition, 2002).

Temenos Academy Review 7: Kathleen Raine Memorial Issue (Temenos Academy, 2004).

Every Man an Artist: Readings in the Traditional Philosophy of Art, foreword by Seyyed Hossein Nasr (World Wisdom, 2005).

The Underlying Order and Other Essays, by Kathleen Raine (Temenos Academy Papers 30, 2008).

UNCOLLECTED PIECES

"Edwin Muir: Our Contemporary and Mentor." *Agenda* 12, no. 4 (1975): 79–86.

"Tradition, Intelligence, and the Artist." *Studies in Comparative Religion* 11, no. 4 (1977): 235–49.

"Perennial Values against Modern Decadence." *Studies in Comparative Religion* 13, nos. 1–2 (Winter–Spring 1979): 56–64.

Review of St.-John Perse, *Letters,* translated and edited by Arthur J. Knodel (1979). In *Temenos* 1 (1981): 257–61.

Review of Marc Drogin, *Medieval Calligraphy: Its History and Technique* (1980); Johannes Trithmius, *In Praise of Scribes (De Laude Scriptorium),* translated by Roland Ben Laudt (1974); Michael Gullick, editor, *Modern Scribes and Lettering Artists* (1980); Nicolete Gray, *The Painted Inscriptions of David Jones* (1981). In *Temenos* 2 (1982): 234–43.

Review of Martin Lings, *The Secret of Shakespeare* (1984). In *Temenos* 5 (1984): 288–92.

Review of René Guénon, *The Multiple States of Being,* translated by Joscelyn Godwin (1984); *Ananda Kentish Coomaraswamy: A Handbook,* compiled and published by S. Durai Raja (1979); and Walter Shewring, *Artist and Tradesman* (1984). In *Temenos* 6 (1985): 293–95.

Review of William Blissett, *The Long Conversation: A Memoir of David Jones* (1981); and *Inner Necessities: The Letters of David Jones to Desmond Chute,* edited and introduced by Thomas Dilworth (1984). In *Temenos* 7 (1986): 311–15.

Review of Kathleen Raine, *Yeats the Initiate: Essays on Certain Themes in the Writings of W. B. Yeats* (1986). In *Temenos* 8 (1987): 246–51.

Review of Edward Johnston, *Lessons in Formal Handwriting,* edited by Heather Child and Justin Howes (1986); *Contemporary Calligraphy: Modern Scribes and Lettering Artists II,* catalog, introduced by Peter Halliday (1986); and Nicolete Gray, *A History of Lettering* (1986). In *Temenos* 8 (1987): 251–57.

Review of *Edwin Muir: Selected Prose,* chosen, introduced, and with a memoir by George Mackay Brown (1987). In *Temenos* 9 (1988): 282–85.

Introduction to Walker Rose, *Good Neighbors* (Green Books, 1988).

Review of Wendell Berry, *Collected Poems, 1957–1982* (1985); *Sabbath* (1987); and *The Landscape of Harmony: Two Essays on Wildness and Community,* introduced by Michael Hamburger (1987). In *Temenos* 11 (1991): 263–67.

Review of Nicolete Gray, *The Paintings of David Jones* (1989). In *Temenos* 12 (1991): 220–26.

Review of Wendell Berry, *Life Is a Miracle: An Essay against Modern Superstition* (2000). In *Temenos Academy Review* 6 (2003): 196–99.

"An Interview with Kathleen Raine," dated December 10, 1977. In *Temenos Academy Review* 7 (2004): 27–58.

"Towards a Library of the Perennial Philosophy." In *Temenos Academy Review* 7 (2004): 242–46.

"Ananda K. Coomaraswamy: Scholar of the Spirit," *Sophia* 2, no. 1 (1996): 71–91; reprinted in *The Essential Sophia: The Journal of Traditional Studies,* edited by Seyyed Hossein Nasr and Katherine O'Brien, foreword by Huston Smith (World Wisdom, 2006).

Review of Frithjof Schuon, *Art from the Sacred to the Profane: East and West,* edited by Catherine Schuon, foreword by Keith Critchlow, and introduced by Barbara Perry (2007). In *Temenos Academy Review* 10 (2007): 271–72.

Review of Lord Northbourne, *Of the Land and the Spirit: The Essential Lord Northbourne on Ecology and Religion,* edited by Christopher James and Joseph A. Fitzgerald, foreword by Wendell Berry (2008). In *Temenos Academy Review* 12 (2009): 277–81.

Foreword to Titus Burckhardt, *Foundations of Oriental Art and Symbolism* (World Wisdom, 2009).

"Some Musical Settings of Poems by Kathleen Raine." In *Temenos Academy Review* 13 (2010): 223–24.

"The Dream Is All I Am: Reading *On a Deserted Shore.*" In *Temenos Academy Review* 14 (2011): 286–301.

"Who Speaks from the Dust? Kathleen Raine and the Vocation of Poetry." Paper delivered at the Temenos Academy conference "Ancient Springs: The Arts, the Imagination, and Our World," Oxford, September 14, 2013. Printed version forthcoming in *Sewanee Review.*

"The Making of a Canon—A Memoir." (A personal memoir about compiling the *Collected Poems* of Kathleen Raine.) Forthcoming in *Temenos Academy Review* 18 (2015).

Biographies

BRIAN KEEBLE was editor, designer, and publisher of Golgonooza Press in Ipswich, England, from 1974 to 2004; as well as one of the founders and editors of the journal *Temenos* (London, 1980–91). He is the author of *Art: For Whom and for What?* (1998), *Conversing with Paradise* (2003), *God and Work* (2009), and other essay collections; the editor of *Every Man an Artist: Readings in the Traditional Philosophy of Art* (2005) and other volumes; and the author of several collections of poetry, most recently *From a Handful of Dust* (2011) and *Far from the Dawn* (2014). Keeble is a Fellow of the Temenos Academy in London, and has served on its Council and Academic Board.

ANDREW FRISARDI, originally from Boston, has lived in the area of Orvieto, Italy, since 1999. His recent publications include *The Young Dante and the One Love* (Temenos Academy, 2013); *Death of a Dissembler* (poems, White Violet Press, 2014); and an edition of Dante's *Vita Nova*, which he translated, introduced, and annotated (Northwestern University Press, 2012). He is currently completing a new annotated translation of Dante's *Convivio*, for which he received a Fellowship from the John S. Guggenheim Foundation; and has another publication forthcoming from Temenos Academy in 2015, *The Quest for Knowledge in Dante's "Convivio."*